To Ruth I. Johns

with best regards,

Jonson

02.03. 2020

Whose Comfort?

Body, Sexuality and Identities
of Korean 'Comfort Women'
and Japanese Soldiers
during WWII

Photo taken by Kang Airan (artist and Professor of Art) at the funeral of former 'comfort woman', Pae Ch'unhŭi.

Whose Comfort?

Body, Sexuality and Identities
of Korean 'Comfort Women'
and Japanese Soldiers
during WWII

Yonson Ahn

Goethe University of Frankfurt, Germany

 **World Scientific**

NEW JERSEY • LONDON • SINGAPORE • BEIJING • SHANGHAI • HONG KONG • TAIPEI • CHENNAI • TOKYO

Published by

World Scientific Publishing Co. Pte. Ltd.

5 Toh Tuck Link, Singapore 596224

USA office: 27 Warren Street, Suite 401-402, Hackensack, NJ 07601

UK office: 57 Shelton Street, Covent Garden, London WC2H 9HE

Library of Congress Cataloging-in-Publication Data

Names: Ahn, Yonson, author.

Title: Whose comfort? : body, sexuality and identities of korean 'comfort women' and
    japanese soldiers during wwii / Yonson Ahn (Goethe University of Frankfurt, Germany).

Identifiers: LCCN 2019943872 | ISBN 9789811206344 (hardcover)

LC record available at https://lccn.loc.gov/2019943872

British Library Cataloguing-in-Publication Data

A catalogue record for this book is available from the British Library.

Cover illustration © Shonagh Rae.

For any available supplementary material, please visit
https://www.worldscientific.com/worldscibooks/10.1142/11444#t=suppl

Desk Editor: Sylvia Koh

Typeset by Stallion Press
Email: enquiries@stallionpress.com

Preface

The issue of 'comfort women' who were forced or pressurised into sexual servitude for the Japanese military during World War II has caused tensions especially in relations between Korea and Japan in the postwar period. Korean and Japanese media still highlight this unresolved issue to the public in their headlines. Unfortunately, sexual violence in armed conflicts still happens globally, but so many cases have not appropriately been dealt with and it looks like there is still a long way to go to achieve gender justice with this issue. As a gender scholar by training, my hope for this book is to contribute to the readers' understanding of both the long-standing issue of the military 'comfort women' and sexual violence against women.

This project started not only from an academic viewpoint but also from my commitment as an activist in the comfort women campaign since 1992. This book follows the trajectory of my 25-year journey to different places in the world, including South Korea, Japan, Britain, South Africa and Germany. It was an extraordinary experience for me to have personally met and listened to both the Korean survivors' unspeakable stories of trauma, pain, despair and violence and the Japanese veterans' unspoken stories, at the time of war and following their return. Sadly, over the course of this long project, almost all of the participants have already departed without seeing this issue resolved. Without their courage in breaking the 50-year-long silence and sharing their stories, this volume contextualising their traumatic experiences and emotions with a micro-level narrative account would not have been possible. Engaging with both narratives has helped me understand the complicated, paradoxical and delicate issues and the way in which the wartime violence and experiences are embodied in their identity and its persistent impacts on their postwar life.

Note:

In accordance with the East Asian custom, Korean and Japanese family names precede the given names in this text. Exceptions are authors who published in English and adopted English conventions for names.

This book's cover illustration is based on a bronze sculpture titled "P'yŏnghwaŭi sonyŏsang" (Peace Girl Statue 2011) by sculptors Kim Seokyung and Kim Eunsung (cover illustration © Shonagh Rae).

About the Author

**Yonson Ahn** is Professor and Chair of Korean Studies at the Goethe University of Frankfurt, Germany. She received her PhD degree in Women and Gender Studies at the University of Warwick in 2000. Her research interests include sexual violence in armed conflicts, the Korean diaspora and gender and migration with a focus on transnational nurse migration and transnational marriage migrants.

Acknowledgement

This volume is dedicated to the 'comfort women' victims/survivors, many of whom have passed away in loneliness and pain. My sincere gratitude goes to all the interviewees who shared their life histories with me. To all those who have supported, inspired, nurtured and accompanied me in uncountable ways in my journey during this project, I owe you more than can be expressed in words. Very warm thanks go to my family who have been always on my side whenever I needed your support.

Contents

Summary

This volume draws on my extraordinary personal encounters and relationships with former Korean 'comfort women' and Japanese veterans, and focuses on their narratives and emotions as expressed during numerous interviews — incredible and often unbearable stories of trauma, pain, despair and violence in everyday life at the time of war and following their return.

The focal points of this work are located in contextualising the re/shaping of body, sexuality and subjectivity of these two key groups as a 'comfort woman' and a 'warrior' through the comfort station system within the prevailing context of masculine, colonial power during World War II.

In these practices, hegemonic military masculinity was imposed on the Japanese military men, while the idea of 'fallen' womanhood pervaded the lives of the Korean 'comfort women', a status which is defined with paradoxes and complexities. Both groups' complex reactions towards the practices they endured include conformity, negotiation and resistance. This includes the question of the women's multiple positionalities as both victims and actors facing persistent sexual, physical and emotional exploitation in their interactions with Japanese military personnel during WWII. The intricate connections between Japanese colonialism, Korean nationalism and pre-existing concepts of Confucian womanhood in constructing the 'comfort women's' bodies and subjectivity during and after the war are also explored.

The final chapter of this volume deals with the eventual rupturing of the victims'/survivors' silence, memories and commemoration, and emergence of solidarity within the broader context of wartime sexual violence and global movements for gender justice.

This work represents an attempt to untangle the web of complicated, paradoxical and delicate issues that surround Japan's military 'comfort women' system from the perspective of embodied experience, employing the narratives of both 'comfort women' and Japanese military men, to paint a picture of this complex topic in the context of colonial masculine power, the body and sexuality.

Chapter 1

The Military 'Comfort Women': An Introduction

It is welcoming news that the 2018 Nobel Peace Prize has been awarded to both Nadia Murad, a survivor of rape by members of the Islamic State (IS) militia in Iraq and an activist, and Denis Mukwege, a Congolese gynaecologist who has treated countless victims of sexual violence committed by armed forces, for their efforts in combatting sexual violence in armed conflict. As brutal sexual violence still takes place in various regions experiencing armed conflict, the 2018 Nobel Peace Prize has drawn more international attention to issues of sexual violence in armed conflict situations as representing violations against humanity. The last century saw the denial of, and subsequent coming to terms with, the histories of Korean victims/survivors of systematic sexual violence. These so-called 'comfort women' were pressed into service of the Japanese Empire's military during World War II in Asia (1931–1945).[1] Korea was a colony of Japan from 1919 to 1945, and the 'comfort women' issue represents an overlooked, pressing and unresolved colonial legacy.

Historically, both the body and sexuality have served as sites of problematic nationalist and military power struggles. In the 'comfort women' context, the body and sexuality were used to shape patriarchy, ethnic hierarchy and colonial power. This volume investigates broad themes such as the politics of sexuality, the intersection of gender, colonialism, militarism and war, along with the juxtaposition of femininity and masculinity as tools of colonialism. Specific questions addressed include how and why the bodies and sexualities of Korean 'comfort women' and Japanese military men have been mobilised by masculine, colonial powers to implement nationalist agendas. In particular, the entanglement between individual and collective implications of sexual enslavement is examined. As lived experience and embodied identity are essential for illuminating not only the structural, but also the microcosmic, emotional dimensions of the 'comfort women' system, this study examines personal narratives of both Korean victims/survivors and Japanese veterans. The accounts of the women are juxtaposed with those of the men to highlight complex and traumatic encounters between the two groups. This volume's introductory chapter defines the nature of the 'comfort women' system, and provides historical background.

Perhaps the most extraordinary aspect of the military 'comfort women' system is the self-imposed silence that surrounded the topic for half a century after the war. That this significant piece of World War II (afterwards WWII) history escaped the scrutiny and consciousness of the Allies as well as the attention of the post-war war crimes tribunals, is particularly striking given the massive, institutional scale of the 'comfort women' project. The direct and indirect role of the Japanese military in overseeing, and in some cases administering and implementing the system, along with the fact that millions of Japanese soldiers participated in the 'comfort women' system should have been case enough for the issue to have taken centre stage in the negotiation of treaties and reparations. The Allies were well aware of the magnitude of the 'comfort women' system in Asia and numerous US military documents from 1944 refer to 'Japanese Army Brothels' and 'Korean comfort girls'.[2] However, unlike cases of abuse and maltreatment of Western prisoners of war by the Japanese military forces, the issue of military 'comfort women' only briefly and belatedly became a subject of a war crimes tribunal during the Batavia Trial in 1948, when the cases of 35 Dutch women forced into sexual servitude for Japanese soldiers during the Japanese occupation of the Dutch East Indies were heard, and the perpetrators found guilty and sentenced to imprisonment (Dolgopol and Paranjape, 1994: 12). Yet neither the Batavia Trial nor the Tokyo War Crimes Trials (International Military Tribunal for the Far

East, 1946–1948) raised the issue of Asian 'comfort women' for either investigation or trial. The fact that both WWII tribunals failed to address these gross violations of human rights demonstrates a negligence that raises questions of race and gender in the war criminal justice system.

My late grandmother, who lived through the devastation of both WWII and the Korean War (1950–1953), talked extensively about daily life in her town at that time. She recalled rumours that young girls were being taken somewhere to the war front during WWII, a war she still remembered as *Taedonga chŏnjaeng* in Korean (*Dai Tôa Sensô* in Japanese), the 'Greater East Asia War'—a name indicative of the Japanese Empire's expansionist ambitions in Asia at that time. Her stories occupied my thoughts and piqued my curiosity as to what might have happened to these women both during and after the war. Beyond being a strictly academic pursuit, this project represents the outcome of my own personal engagement with the 'comfort women' advocacy movement since 1992.

It was during the summer of 1992 that I first met Mun P'ilgi (1925–2008), a military 'comfort woman' survivor whose energy could be felt even before she entered the small basement room where she lived in the outskirts of Seoul. She had just returned from her work sweeping a nearby park. Softly-spoken and reserved in manner, she agreed to share with me the story of her silenced past. Since then I have met a number of ageing victims/survivors who were eking out a living through manual labour as park attendants, or in restaurants and food stalls. In many cases, these elderly women had lived in poverty during the early 1990s when there was no support provided for them by the South Korean government. Some of them hesitated to let me visit their homes, probably considering their dwellings too squalid for hosting guests.

Four years later, during the summer of 1996, I met a handful of elderly Japanese veterans in the Tokyo area to listen to their stories of the war, and particularly those concerning the 'comfort women'. My encounters with these two groups, Korean 'comfort women' victims/survivors and Japanese veterans, were challenging and charged with deep emotion, and it often took a significant amount of time to digest their narratives. It has been a long time since my first encounters with both groups. Sadly, almost all of my respondents have already passed away. Though the women shared with me their painful pasts, they never received justice, and went to their graves bearing the emotional scars and social stigma associated with their wartime experiences. The majority of the women, who did not wish to identify themselves as former 'comfort women', have passed away in silence, taking their unspeakable ordeal quietly with them. Their funerals have been disheartening, but have also provided the impetus to further engage this issue. With each passing year, there are fewer survivors who can recount their stories. Amongst the victims/survivors, very few are still living. As of 26 September 2018, of the 240 individuals who came forward to register as former 'comfort women' in South Korea, only 27 women are still alive.[3] A North Korean authority reports that out of 52 victims/survivors who gave public testimonies in North Korea, all have passed away as of November 2018.[4] Hence, there is a real urgency to record and pay attention to their narratives and lived experiences during and after the war, before it is too late to capture a history that should never be repeated.

The Korean victims/survivors' stories rank alongside other horror stories of war, ranging from the well-documented ethnic cleansing in Kosovo and Bosnia[5] to more recent accounts of resurgence of sexual violence in armed conflicts in Africa. This study comes at a time when questions of sexual violence in armed conflicts and war are increasingly raised as public issues of international concern; when memories and representations of the colonial past are essential to charting the future of nations, and when memory politics actively define contemporary political agendas.

The 'Comfort Women': An Unresolved Issue

Since the experiences of victims/survivors of Japan's WWII system of sexual slavery began receiving international attention in the 1990s, there has been extensive discussion on the usage of the appellation with which they are commonly referred to: 'comfort women'. The women are euphemistically referred to in Korean as *chonggun wianbu*. In Japanese they are referred to by a similar term: *jûgun ianfu*, literally translated as 'comfort women' who followed the military. In this terminological debate, a majority of mainstream liberal scholars and advocators contest these terms, indicating that the use of the term 'following' the military implies a voluntary action, like that of a war reporter or army nurse (Takaki, 1992: 3). Japanese neo-nationalists are against the term *jûgun* (following the military) for a different reason: Fujioka (1996: 36) argues that *jûgun* is a reference to *gunzoku*: civilians with official status in the military. The concern expressed here is that the term *jûgun* implicates the Japanese military as having been involved in the comfort facilities; a claim they strongly refute. As a group, Japanese neo-nationalists seek to distance the state and the military from the 'comfort women' system by insisting that the women had no official status in the military. However, the euphemistic use of the term *ianfu* ('comfort women'), has been conveniently ignored by these same neo-nationalists (Ahn, 2008a: 33–34).

At the First Asian Women's Solidarity Forum on Japanese Military Sexual Slavery held in Seoul, Korea in 1992, an alternative term *kangje chonggun wianbu*, (forced 'comfort women' who followed the military), was suggested to draw attention to the element of coercion involved in the programme. However, this term is inherently contradictory in its use of both the words 'forced' and 'followed'. In UN reports on the issue of 'comfort women' by Radhika Coomaraswamy (UN Commission on Human Rights, 1996a, 1996b), a Special Rapporteur on violence against women and its causes and consequences, and Gay J. McDougall, a Special Rapporteur to the UN Sub-Commission on the Prevention of Discrimination and Protection on Minorities, the 'comfort women' system was recognised as 'a clear case of sex slavery' (UN Sub-Commission on the Promotion and Protection of Human Rights, 1998: 3–4). Coomaraswamy maintains that the phrase 'comfort women' does not in the slightest reflect the sufferings and multiple sexual and physical abuses the women suffered throughout the war. Thus, she considers the phrase 'military sexual slaves' to be a much more accurate and appropriate term. On the basis of the extent of coercion, confinement and the deeply engrained isolation of daily life at the comfort station, some previous studies on the 'comfort women' have represented the comfort station system as systematic 'rape by the state' (Suzuki, 1993: 25), 'sexual slavery exclusively for the military' (Kawata, 1995: 5) or 'gang-rape' (Yoshimi, 1995a: 231).

Given the women's circumstances whereby they were denied autonomy, endured forced confinement and were coerced into sexual servitude, it is clear that the term 'comfort women' fails to adequately describe the experiences and views of the victims, but rather reflects the viewpoint of the perpetrators for whom 'comfort' was to be provided. Nevertheless, it may be worth maintaining phrases like military 'comfort women' or 'comfort stations' as these were the contemporary terms used during the war. They serve to demonstrate both the established purpose of the comfort facilities and to preserve the linguistic history of Japanese colonialism. Furthermore, the most widely-used terms in government documents, media and advocacy groups in South Korea, Japan and the wider international community have been 'military comfort women' or 'forced military comfort women'. Consequently, I have retained this terminology in the current volume, but have attempted wherever possible to reveal the euphemistic and deceitful implications of the terms, and to disclose the colonisers' purpose for the 'comfort women' programme.

Media attention brought the unresolved 'comfort women' issue into the public eye in South Korea and Japan, and raised awareness across the international community and within the UN. In 2007, the European Parliament along with the national assemblies of the US, the Netherlands and Canada adopted and released resolutions on 'comfort women' calling for the Japanese government to formally acknowledge, apologise and accept responsibility for its coercion of young women into sexual slavery during the war. The European Parliament resolution also calls for state-supported education for current and future generations on the true nature of these war crimes.[6] Almost 10 years later, in December 2015, Japan's conservative Abe administration and South Korea's conservative Park administration reached a historic deal defined as 'final and irreversible'. The Japanese government accepted responsibility for establishing and upholding the system, and offered an official apology to the victims, allocating 10 billion yen to establish a Korean-run *Hwahae ch'iyu chaedan* (Foundation for Reconciliation and Healing) to provide support for the victims/survivors.[7] In return, Japan asked that a monument representing 'comfort women' called *P'yŏnghwaŭi Sonyŏsang* (Peace Girl Statue) be removed from its current position in front of the Japanese Embassy in Seoul and demanded that South Korea refrain from making criticisms of Japan to international audiences.[8]

However, this stipulation triggered further disputes, with 'comfort women' victims/survivors and advocacy groups such as *Han'guk chŏngsindae munje taech'aek hyŏbŭihoe* (the Korean Council for the Women Drafted for Military Sexual Slavery), which is the leading Korean advocacy group focused on redressing the 'comfort women' issue, protesting the new agreement's failure to address Japan's legal responsibility for the system, arguing that it 'excluded the victims, and it does not reflect their demands and the international human rights principles'.[9] Criticisms included the view that Japan's monetary offer represented an aid project, rather than official reparation for the victims, as the Japanese government has rejected state payments to individual survivors on the grounds that war reparations were finalised with the Treaty on Basic Relations between Japan and the Republic of Korea (*Hanil kibonjoyak*) to normalise diplomatic relations in 1965.[10] The dispute over the 2015 agreement has unfolded on both an international and domestic level, as a series of ongoing protests in Korea and global protest tours in Europe and North America by survivors and advocacy groups have sought to retract the deal and raise public awareness. South Korea's current, liberal Moon administration has attempted to revisit this issue, and announced its decision to dissolve the Foundation for Reconciliation and Healing funded by Japan according to the 2015 agreement on 21 November 2018; a move which Japan's foreign minister Taro Kôno considers 'unacceptable'.[11] Japan's response to the engagement of the Moon administration with various unresolved colonial legacy issues such as the 'comfort women' and victims of forced labour during WWII has sown the seeds for a trade dispute between Korea and Japan. The Abe administration's imposition of restrictions on exports to South Korea of materials used to make semiconductors and smartphone displays in July 2019 has further escalated tensions in Japan–Korea bilateral relations. This action prompted swift retaliation from South Korean consumers, who began to boycott Japanese products in July 2019.[12] To a casual observer, this may appear to be just one of many trade and tariff disputes that are currently dominating the international news agenda. However, those with more knowledge of post-colonial Korea–Japan relations will be aware that the roots of the conflict go much deeper. The role of the 'comfort women' in this context is evidenced by the re-politicisation of the issue during Japan's conservative Abe administration, indicating that it remains a major source of tension between the two nations as questions of responsibility for the colonial past and the debate around historical memory have become politically prominent in the modern era.

While there exists a long history of tension and dispute not only between Japan and its neighbours throughout East Asia, but also within Korea itself and Japan, over Japan's wartime past (including the issue of 'comfort women' and forced labourers), the current scale of controversy in South Korea is relatively new. The history of the 'comfort women' system is a contested issue not only in the political sphere, but within academia as well. These debates have led to tensions between different groups and recently a legal action has been brought in South Korea. In 2014, a handful of victims/survivors and their supporters, including academics and activists, filed a defamation lawsuit against Park Yu-ha, South Korean professor of Japanese literature, for her highly controversial book, *Chegugŭi wianbu* (*Comfort Women of the Empire*, 2013). South Korean and Zainichi Korean scholars like Chŏng Yŏnghwan (2016) and Son Chongŏp *et al.* (2016) have raised concerns that Park's works serve to feed Japanese neo-nationalists' memory of the 'comfort women' system. In particular, both of Park's books dealing with the topic of 'comfort women' (2005, 2013) have been criticised for expressing biased, pro-Japanese views, and in particular for challenging the coercive nature of the recruitment process of Korean women for sexual slavery, describing the victims as 'prostitutes' and 'collaborators with the Japanese military', almost romanticising their experiences. The lawsuit alleged 'false', 'exaggerated' or 'distorted' content; a case which, among other issues, raised questions about freedom of scholarship.[13] The Seoul Eastern District Court found the author not guilty in January 2017, but the Seoul's Court of Appeals reversed this acquittal on 27 October 2017, finding Park guilty of defamation. Park then appealed the verdict and brought her case to the Supreme Court of South Korea.[14] Park (2018) recently published another book in which she makes counter-arguments against criticisms of her work. These ongoing controversies in court and in academia make clear the delicate and contested nature of the issue, not only as a point of contention between Korea and Japan but also within each of the countries.

Establishing Military Comfort Stations

The following three sections give a brief overview of the historical background of the 'comfort women' system. The earliest military comfort stations appear to have been largely private enterprises in Manchuria, consistent with the Japanese army's advance into China at the beginning of the 1930s during WWII in Asia (1931–1945). These dates are confirmed by the account of a victim/survivor, Chʼoe Chŏngnye, who reported that she was taken to China in 1932 (Han'guk chŏngsindae, 1997: 11). Concurrently, Japanese Military archives indicate that the Japanese Navy set up the first state-sanctioned military comfort station in Shanghai in 1932. Extensive deployment to set up exclusive military facilities for 'the comfort of the troops', however, only began to occur between December 1937 and January 1938, following the Nanking Massacre (Yoshimi, 1995a: 22). The Rape of Nanking motivated the military to establish highly regulated 'Hygiene Facilities'[15] where the Japanese forces would have access to institutionalised sexual servitude. These facilities were purportedly intended to curb the unrestrained rape of local women throughout the areas where forces were stationed. Especially after August 1942, when the Japanese military invaded and occupied vast swathes of China, the Ministry of War began to take responsibility for systematising its policies regarding comfort facilities in Japan's Asian and Pacific Island territories. According to a 1944 report by the United States Office of War Information, 'the comfort girls were found wherever it was necessary for the Japanese Army to fight'.[16]

Women from nations such as Korea, Japan, Taiwan, China, the Philippines, Indonesia, Vietnam, Burma and the Netherlands, among other nations, were forced, pressured or lured into sexual servitude for the Japanese military during the war mainly via contractors or agencies working for the army. Some women were even drafted by force. As the Japanese government destroyed many of its official documents at the end of the war, it is difficult to determine an accurate, official total for the number of 'comfort women' throughout the war, but estimates range from 84,000 (Senda, 1992a: 177) to 200,000 (Kim, 1976: 79), with Korean women from Japan's colony at that time comprising a majority of the total number of 'comfort women' (Yoshimi, 1995b: 95). Disputing these figures, Japanese right-wing revisionist, Hata Ikuhiko, estimates the total number to have been no more than 20,000 (Hata, 1993).

Comfort facilities primarily served military and industrial workers, troops stationed in or near war zones and workers in mining towns, construction sites, or industrial areas producing goods for the war (Yun, 1991: 7–13). The management of comfort facilities ranged from those directly managed by the military to standard civilian brothels (Yoshimi, 1995b: 89). This volume focuses on military comfort stations, which comprised the vast majority of the system's stations. Many comfort stations managed by the military were later handed over to private contractors under the direct supervision of the military (Senda, 1992b in Chai, 1993: 69). Testimonies and military documents reveal that it was the Japanese military authorities themselves who supervised and administered the stations, and organised regular inspections of the women's health, sanitation and security (Chung, 1993: 23 in Yang, 1997: 58). Military authorities were also responsible for arranging the overseas transportation of recruited women to facilities in areas where Japanese forces were stationed.

Recruitment and Transportation

This section identifies the ways in which the women were recruited and transported to the comfort stations. Under Japanese colonial rule (1910–1945), especially in the 1930s, the impoverishment of Koreans, especially those living in rural areas, grew severe. Unemployed women in poor families increasingly left their home villages to head for a city and find work. These women became easy targets for direct recruitment by agents, with many lured into the prostitution sector indirectly via trafficking. State-regulated prostitution introduced by the colonial government to Korea drove many more women, including young girls from impoverished peasant families, into the sex industry. The majority of 'comfort women' victims/survivors whose testimonies have been released report being taken to comfort stations at a young age, often in their teens. A historian, Song (1997), links state-regulated prostitution and the comfort station system, pointing out that the widespread experience gained in the recruiting or trafficking of women through the operation of the state-managed prostitution system and the efficiency of the networks established in the process enabled the subsequent mobilisation of Korean girls in great numbers as 'comfort women'.[17]

The recruitment of Korean women was carried out in several ways. One was conscription in the name of *Yŏjajŏngsindae* (the Women's Volunteer Labour Corps).[18] The conscription this body authorised was mainly enforced towards the end of WWII and involved massive mobilisation of Koreans through educational institutions and councils. In the case of Kim Ŭnjin and Kang Tŏkkyŏng (1929–1997), even though they were first recruited in the name of the Women's Volunteer Labour Corps through their schools, they were later sent to comfort stations (Han'guk chŏngsindae, 1997: 239; Kang Tŏkkyŏng, personal interview, 1992). Similarly, a number of girls among the Corps were apparently taken to military comfort stations instead of doing standard physical labour. Some Japanese schoolteachers in Korea were involved in recruitment for the Women's Volunteer Labour Corps. A former Japanese teacher at Pangsan Elementary School in Seoul, Ikeda Masae, reported being instructed to recruit 'healthy girls from poor families' (Jûgun ianfu hyakutôban, 1992: 65). She admitted publicly that she had recruited six girls from such families from her class while she was working in colonial Korea.[19] It has been reported that school principals who succeeded in sending a large number of girls to the war front were rewarded with promotion.[20] Hwang Kŭmju (1922–2013), interviewed in 1995, said that in Hamhŭng (currently in North Korea), where she was living at the time, girls were drafted from each family to work in ammunition factories. Her account indicates that there might have been a per province quota for recruitment in Korea.

Secondly, recruitment of the girls through employment agencies or traffickers was a widespread practice. Towards the end of the war, a series of advertisements appeared in Korean newspapers, such as Kyŏngsŏng Ilbo on 16 July 1944 and Maeil Shinmun on 27 October 1944. In the latter, healthy women between 18 and 30 were urgently sought to serve as 'comfort women' for a military unit comfort facility. This advertisement shows that young women were specifically targeted. In many cases they were lured with the prospect of well-paid jobs, better access to education, plenty of food and a new, better life abroad. For girls from poverty-stricken families, these deceptive inducements looked attractive. One victim/survivor, Sin Kyŏngnan (1921–2005) confirmed this view: 'I was attracted by the promise that I would get an education and become a nurse after that' (Han'guk chŏngsindae, 2001b: 29). Similarly, many women were lured to be taken on as cleaners, cooks, waitresses, secretaries, entertainers, or nurses for the Japanese forces, as para-military personnel, or voluntary corps (Jûgun ianfu hyakutôban, 1992: 90).

As Sarah Soh (2008), an anthropologist, astutely points out, the young girls' aspiration for a better life and desire to escape from their patriarchal family systems led them to become vulnerable to the attractions of such offers. While economic need must have been a core motivation for those taking up these positions, other factors such as personal aspiration, ambition and the quest for education were also involved, as girls were often denied access to schooling. Alternatively, the advertisements may have simply been perceived as offering an opportunity for a better life; representing an escape from the traditional, more restricted roles of women in rural society and culture. Mun P'ilgi (1925–2008), who agreed to go to Manchuria in 1925, was attracted by the proposal from an elderly villager to have a chance to study—something which her father had not allowed her to do:

> As it was a deep resentment for me not to be allowed to go to school, I wanted to have a chance to get educated without my parents knowing about it, and to live a better

> life. If I were to marry a rural man, my future would be
> the same as it was: without hope of improvement. I had
> ambition and I really wanted to study. If I had been a son, I
> would have been allowed to be educated to as high a level
> as I desired (Han'guk chŏngsindae, 1993: 109).

This aspect of young girls' aspiration and hope to escape from patriarchal gender discrimination has not received much attention in analysis of the recruitment process, while more emphasis has been put on forced procurement or economic hardship as a motivation to leave.

In cases of trafficking, it was carried out by private agencies, employers or even their families without the girls' knowledge of what was happening to them, as was the case with Chin Kyŏngp'aeng and Pak Yŏni (Han'guk chŏngsindae, 1997: 20). Some were even sold to brothel keepers by their fathers or husbands (Han'guk chŏngsindae, 1999: 97). This reveals the status of a daughter in a family as expendable.

There were basically two avenues by which the women were recruited; one was through military or local authorities, the other was through trafficking markets (Kang, C., 1997: 219). Both routes seem to have been controlled and supervised by agents of the Japanese imperial state. While recruitment was carried out by civil agencies including Koreans in many cases, it was the Japanese Imperial Army who screened and selected the participating agencies. Police and military police cooperated to take Korean girls (Jûgun ianfu hyakutôban, 1992: 91) to the war front to 'serve' the Japanese soldiers. Some recruiters worked to take girls and women to the war front in active cooperation with, or with the tacit support of, the military police and the state police. Many of the women recall the presence and involvement of the military police or the state police when they were taken away. No Subok (1921–2011), taken to Singapore in 1942, also confirmed the presence of a Japanese policeman, and remembered him saying to her that she had been chosen to be sent abroad as a representative of the Emperor (Asian Women's Resource Centre, 1996: 9). It must also be noted that for reasons ranging from intimidation to personal gain, some Koreans cooperated with the Japanese authorities and assisted with the recruiting of women. Local private agencies in Korea are reported to have cooperated with the military and local police in carrying out the initial recruitment and subsequent transport of the girls (Yoshimi, 1992: 32, 99–106).

Different sources give accounts of the means by which the girls were escorted[21] involving the use of military equipment and accommodation, for example by train,[22] naval ship,[23] or military truck.[24] It should be pointed out that the utilisation of military transportation required official sanctioning, as civilians were not allowed to board naval ships without a military permit. All civilians needed an official pass to leave the country and travel abroad (Chung, 1997: 228). The military authorities and the state of Japan were therefore involved in the process of recruitment and transportation of the 'comfort women' during the war. This involvement has not been acknowledged by the current conservative Abe administration in Japan. The current Prime Minister, Abe Shinzô, and right-wing groups in Japan continue to contest the Kôno statement, made by Chief Cabinet Secretary Kôno Yôhei on 4 August 1993, in which the direct or indirect involvement of the Japanese military in the establishment and management of the comfort stations was recognised.[25] However, it would have been very difficult to recruit such a large number of women and girls throughout colonial Korea without systematically orchestrating the operation of recruitment by the colonial authorities and without the assistance of local Korean collaborators or agents. In summary, various methods were employed to recruit 'comfort women' from Korea; ranging from being lured or sold, to being coerced, rounded up or mobilised as a labour force. By whichever means the women and girls were recruited initially, they were not informed in advance that they were to be subjected to any form of sexual coercion in the process.

Family Background

As noted above, during the Japanese colonial period (1910–1945), colonised, mostly poor women were more vulnerable to force, or to deceptive financial inducement, because they had less power and less protection from their families. Some of the military 'comfort women' came from single parent families, especially single mother families, as in Kim Tŏkchin's case. She left home to reduce the burden on her mother to feed her other children, and to earn some money, but ended up at a comfort station (Han'guk chŏngsindae, 1993: 41–42). An abusive family environment could have been another factor in the decision to leave home. Some women's fathers were often ill, alcoholics, or gamblers such as the fathers of Chŏn Kŭmhwa (1924–1994, personal interview, 1993) and Oh Omok (1921–1999) (Han'guk chŏngsindae, 1993: 65). These fathers did not, or could not, provide for their families who consequently remained economically destitute. Another vulnerable group were orphan girls who had even less social protection and power (Han'guk chŏngsindae, 1993: 50).

Another interesting observation among 'comfort women' whose testimonies have been released is that many of them were the eldest daughters in their families. As such, they may have felt a sense of responsibility or obligation to support their families at the cost of their own well-being (Han'guk chŏngsindae, 1993: 134). Daughters, especially the eldest ones, tended to be considered as profitable resources for the family or as assets that could generate supplementary income for impoverished families. A few daughters were even persuaded by their own families to sacrifice themselves to save their fathers and brothers from being conscripted into the Japanese army or sent to work in the coal mines or other areas of forced labour in Manchuria and Kyushu, Japan (Chai, 1993: 70). As Hyunah Yang (1997: 65) argues, the Korean patriarchal family did not always represent a shelter which protected women from economic and social hardships.

Daughters of the poor often worked as live-in maids for other families to reduce the economic burdens on their own families. Some of the girls were working as maids at the time they were taken away to a comfort station. Hwang Kŭmju (1922–2013) recounts:

> In Hamhŭng, Japanese officers went around telling each family to send at least one daughter to the army ammunition factory. Three daughters of my foster parents [my employer] were studying in school or college. My employer's wife was worried. I therefore volunteered to go in place of those girls. I felt obliged to repay the kindness shown by my employer to me. I therefore suggested that I be allowed to go, in order

to earn more money and improve my economic situation
(Dolgopol and Paranjape, 1994: 93).

Girls training at *kisaeng* (female entertainers) schools constituted another target group for recruitment, because they lay beyond the 'protection' a patriarchal Confucian family system may have provided. *Kisaeng* schools provided training for girls to become entertainers who sang, danced and served men at banquets. Most *kisaeng* also came from socio-economically marginalised families like Kim Haksun (1924–1997) (personal interview, 1992) and Hong Aejin (Han'guk chŏngsindae, 1995: 44).

Although impoverished women and girls were particularly vulnerable, there were exceptions. It would be wrong to assume that all the women who were pressed into 'service' were poor. While the majority of 'comfort women' were taken from economically disadvantaged groups, the rich were not always exempt. There are occasional examples of women who were from wealthy families like Yi Sangok (1922–2004) (Han'guk chŏngsindae, 1993: 183) and Kim Sanghŭi (Dolgopol and Paranjape, 1994: 99), but these cases seem to be an exception to the norm. Some were taken for political reasons. Daughters from families who were involved in the Korean independence movement were another target group, for example Chŏng Soŭn and Yun Sunman, (Ajia taihen, 1997; Dolgopol and Paranjape, 1994: 78). However, daughters of lower-class families in colonial Korean society seem to have constituted the primary targets for the recruitment programme. Therefore, aspects of both class and gender as well as colonial dominance were involved in the recruitment of military 'comfort women'.

Chapter Outlines

This book has been over 25 years in the making and by sharing survivors' unspeakable stories with readers seeks to share and reclaim the traces of an almost obliterated past which escaped the attention of the WWII war tribunals. In this volume, I have set out to delineate the ways in which this past was forgotten, remembered and reconstructed drawing on personal narratives of both Japanese veterans and Korean 'comfort women' victims/survivors with whom I interviewed and second-hand interview sources published in this field. Chapter 1 provides historical background to the comfort station programme. Chapter 2 draws on my extraordinary personal encounters and relationships with former Korean 'comfort women' and Japanese veterans, and focuses on their narratives and emotions as expressed during numerous interviews; incredible and often unbearable stories of trauma, pain, despair and violence in everyday life at the time of war and following their return.

In order to explore and contextualise the pasts of the 'comfort women' and Japanese military men, Chapters 3 and 4 analyse narratives of both groups. The subject-positionings enforced on the bodies of these two groups in terms of femininity, masculinity and national identity reconstructed through the comfort station system and masculine, colonial power are the focus of these chapters. Another theme is both groups' complex reactions ranging from conformity, negotiation and resistance in the face of the reshaping of gender and national identities during the war and, in the case of the 'comfort women', its aftermath. Chapter 5 deals with the eventual rupturing of the victims/survivors' silence, memories and commemoration, and emergence of solidarity within the broader context of wartime sexual violence and global movements for gender justice.

Lastly, this work endeavours to transcend the problematic dualism reflected in term pairings such as victim/perpetrator, victim/actor, coloniser/colonised and virtuous/fallen women in the 'comfort women' debate by engaging with the entanglement of these binary categories. To achieve this objective, the dichotomous relationship between colonialism and gender is deconstructed in an effort to untangle the web of complicated, paradoxical and delicate issues that surround the military 'comfort women' system. In striving to adequately represent the texture of the ideologies and practices which patriarchy, colonialism, nationalism and militarism impose on both male and female bodies, I bring together these four categories, (gender, colonialism, nationalism and militarism) not as extraneous 'additions' to this study, but as integral components in understanding the construction of the body and sexuality. The issue will be investigated from the perspective of embodied experience, employing the narratives of both 'comfort women' and Japanese military men, to paint a picture of this complex topic in the context of colonial masculine power, the body and sexuality.

Notes

1   This volume covers the wartime periods in Asia from the early 1930s till 1945, often called the Asia-Pacific War.

2   Inter-Ministerial Group on the 'Comfort Women' Issue, Republic of Korea, Military 'Comfort Women' Under Japanese Colonial Rule, Interim Report, July 1992, Seoul, Korea in Chung, 1994, 182.

3   *JTBC Nyusŭrum*, 26 September 2018, http://news.jtbc.joins.com/article/article.aspx?news_id=NB11701600.

4   ' "Konggae chŭngŏn" puk wianbu p'ihaeja 52myŏng sesang ttŏna', *KBS News*, 11 November 2018, https://news.naver.com/main/read.nhn?mode=LSD&mid=sec&oid=056&aid=0010641104&sid1=001.

5   For the Bosnian case, see Pettman, 1996: 190–191; Zarkov, 1997.

6   'European Parliament resolution on Comfort Women', http://www.europarl.europa.eu/sides/getDoc.do?type=MOTION&reference=P6-RC-2007-0525&language=EN; http://sv124.wadax.ne.jp/~wam-peace-org/en/wp-content/uploads/2013/05/foreign_res_text.pdf.

7   'Announcement by Foreign Ministers of Japan and the Republic of Korea at the Joint Press Occasion', 28 December 2015, http://www.mofa.go.jp/a_o/na/kr/page4e_000364.html.

8   'South Korea, Japan reach agreement on "comfort women" ', *CNN*, 29 December 2015, https://edition.cnn.com/2015/12/28/asia/south-korea-japan-comfort-women/index.html.

9   The Korean Council for the Women Drafted for Military Sexual Slavery by Japan, Report submitted to Committee on the elimination of discrimination against women (CEDAW), 2016, https://tbinternet.ohchr.org/Treaties/CEDAW/Shared%20Documents/JPN/INT_CEDAW_NGO_JPN_22816_E.docx.

10 The 1965 treaty includes $800 million paid by Japanese government for the colonial rule directed to the Korean government in the forms of loans and grants to finance the ambitious economic development project during the Park Chung-hee regime (1962–1979), so that individual victims' rights to claim reparation has been obscured.

11 'Anger in Japan as South Korea dissolves "comfort women" foundation', *The Guardian*, 12 November 2018, https://www.theguardian.com/world/2018/nov/21/anger-in-japan-as-south-korea-dissolves-comfort-women-foundation?CMP.

12 'South Korean consumers boycott Japanese products', *The Hankyoreh*, 9 July 2019, http://english.hani.co.kr/arti/english_edition/e_business/901133.html); 'Ilbon pulmae undong hyogwa nat'anago itta', Hankook ilbo, accessed on 22 July 2019, https://www.hankookilbo.com/News/Read/201907221646340919.

13 Ch'oe, Sanghun, 'Professor ordered to pay 9[sic.] who said "comfort women" book defamed them', *New York Times*, 13 January 2016, https://www.nytimes.com/2016/01/14/world/asia/south-korea-park-yu-ha-verdict.html.

14 Professor cleared of defaming 'comfort women', *Korea Herald*, 25 January 2017, http://www.koreaherald.com/view.php?ud=20170125000962&ACE_SEARCH=1;

Appeals court convicts professor of defaming wartime sexual slavery victims, *Korea Herald*, 27 October 2017, http://www.koreaherald.com/view. php?ud=20171027000434&ACE_ SEARCH=1.

[15] Konsei dai 14 ryodan shireibu (14th Mixed Brigade Headquarters). 'Eisei gyômu jumpô,' report from the end of March 1933, Kokuritsu kôbunsho kan (Japanese National Archives) in Yoshimi, 1995b: 47.

[16] Inter-Ministerial Group on the 'comfort women' Issue, Republic of Korea, Military 'comfort women' under Japanese colonial rule, Interim report, July 1992, Seoul, Korea in Chung, 1994: 182. So far, evidence of comfort stations has been confirmed in China, Hong Kong, the Philippines, Malaysia, Singapore, Borneo, Indonesia, Thailand, Burma, New Guinea, Okinawa, Korea, Vietnam and numerous southern Pacific islands (see Yoshimi *et al.*, eds., 1995: 4–5).

[17] For example, the operators' expertise in licensed prostitution was brought unchanged into the military system (Song, 1997: 203).

[18] The National Mobilisation Law (*kokka sôdôin hô*), passed by the Diet in Japan in March 1938, authorised emergency measures providing among other things for the direction of labour and materials, the regulation of wages and prices, government operation of certain industries, even a compulsory savings scheme and a system of national registration (Beasley, 1963: 253).

[19] *Hankyoreh shinmun*, 14 January 1992.

[20] *Donga ilbo*, 14 January 1992; *Chosŏn ilbo*, 15 January 1992 in Choi, 1992: 99.

[21] Mun P'ilgi and Yun Turi were escorted to Manchuria by the Japanese forces (personal interview in 1992).

[22] Hwang Kŭmju was taken to Jilin in China by a military train (Personal interview in 1995).

[23] Mun Okchu, Yi Sunok, Yi Tŭngnam were taken to Rangoon, to Singapore and to Sumatra, respectively, by naval ships (Han'guk chŏngsindae, 1993: 156, 175, 204).

[24] Mun Okchu was transported by military trucks in Rangoon and in Thailand (Han'guk chŏngsindae, 1993: 158, 97, 156, 175, 204, 160).

[25] Ministry of Foreign Affairs of Japan, 'Statement by the Chief Cabinet Secretary Yohei Kôno on the result of the study on the issue of "comfort women"', 4 August 1993, https://www.mofa.go.jp/policy/women/fund/state9308.html.

Chapter 2

Speaking the Unspeakable: Overwhelming Encounters

The Search for Respondents

I was fortunate enough to personally meet some of the last living survivors and key participants in the 'comfort women' system, and to be able to conduct in-depth interviews with them in South Korea or Japan between 1992 and 1996. In South Korea, I met and talked with 10 Korean victims/survivors, a daughter of one of the survivors along with activists, scholars, a handful of journalists and a lone, post-war era Japanese diplomat. Last but not least, in 1996, I travelled to Japan where I met Japanese activists and WWII veterans, whose wartime roles had ranged from foot soldier, to high-ranking officer, to military doctor; men who might have had direct contact with 'comfort women'.

By the time I began my research, locating victims/survivors in Korea was no great feat, since many had already come forward to identify themselves as former 'comfort women' and registered with advocate groups and/or the Korean government. A couple of those with whom I made contact were reluctant to speak out of concern for what backlash their families might suffer or anxiety over what they might remember about a past they were trying to forget.

Considering the sensitivity of the issue, all the women were interviewed individually in the private space of their own homes. It is worth noting that the living places in which these interviews took place were frequently run down and dilapidated, often in a small hovel, a basement room or other cramped space lacking adequate facilities. It was a stark reminder that the state had in some way abandoned them— a context evocative of the bleakness of the 'comfort women's' personal narratives. By 1996, when I met some of my respondents again, they had moved into small but modern flats provided by the South Korean government. Since 1993, victims/survivors have been supported with state-subsidised amenities such as housing, healthcare and social benefits.

Owing to the fact that almost the entire Japanese population served in some capacity in WWII, there were many more veterans than 'comfort women' survivors. However, locating Japanese veterans was not an easy job. I established contact through my advocate group networks in Japan, or through my circle of Japanese friends. Initially, I approached those who had previously written books about their wartime experiences or tried to make contact with those who had shared what they witnessed or experienced during the war via hotlines provided by Japanese activists collecting information on 'comfort women'. Eighteen agreed to talk with me in the summer of 1996 and were curious as to who I was, why I had come to Japan, and what I was doing. Some of them were wary of my motives and wondered how I would use their stories.

Among my male respondents, some held defensive views about Japan's colonial war history, but one group was particularly critical of this same history. This group was composed of members of the Association of Returnees from China (*Chûgoku kikansha renrakukai*). At a press conference at the House of Parliament in Tokyo, June 1996, I came across a couple of veterans who had been retained in China as prisoners of war after WWII and were put into 'rehabilitation' programmes run by the Chinese Communist Party, through which they were made to recognise the aggressiveness and brutality of the war that Japan had waged (Ahn, 2018: 13). Upon their return to Japan, the group was actively involved in anti-war campaigns and was even willing to give public testimonies concerning Japan's wrongdoings.

These men offered a collective message built on a strong sense of peer identity stemming from their 'rehabilitated' status and shared experience as former prisoners of war in China. Rather than speaking as individuals, they gave a united message of reflection and delivered testimonies collectively. They often started their story with the subject pronoun 'we'. There were pros and cons of interviewing a group in such a collective setting. Accounts of one member often stimulated the recollection of another, so a greater variety of detail emerged. However, sometimes people talked at the same time which proved problematic when privacy was needed to address the most sensitive and personal topics.

Clearly, gaining the ability to engage with and listen to Japanese war veterans who may have been involved in systemic sexual abuse was also a challenging undertaking for me personally. However, it was an unavoidable process as I wanted to discover, and attempt to understand, what realities the men had faced in the war, beyond the official version presented in documents and historical timelines. Their lived experiences both during and after the war included their wartime deeds, any suffering they had experienced as a result, and sensitive issues surrounding sexuality. What prompted them to behave in certain ways? How does trauma change human perceptions of survival? What rationales lay behind their current views and wartime memories? Gaining a comprehensive understanding of the issue meant that hearing their point of view was just as important as hearing the narratives of the victims/survivors themselves. Thus, listening to narrative elaborations of the past from both key groups was pivotal and provided rich insights into the microcosmic world of the 'comfort women' system. The generosity of these individuals in reopening old wounds and contributing to a broader process of truth and reconciliation cannot be understated.

Personal narratives from in-depth interviews that I conducted with Japanese veterans and Korean victims/survivors have been used to reconstruct traumatic encounters between the two groups. Details of the interviewees are itemised in the Appendix to this volume. During the course of this undertaking, I have also had access to a significant body of interview data compiled and published by researchers and campaigners, most of which had been generated by the organisation *Han'guk chŏngsindae yŏn'guhoe* (The Korean Researchers for Women Drafted for Military Sexual Slavery by Japan), of which I was a member.

Listening to the Unspeakable

Writing this book has been one of the most challenging tasks I have ever undertaken, and has required both great faith in the importance of the nuanced messages communicated by these long-silenced voices and the ability to empathise with interviewees' emotional troubles. Encounters with Korean comfort women stretched over several lengthy, intense sessions, as the women recalled and unveiled their pasts in their own ways. In most cases, each woman was interviewed two to three times, with each session lasting often half a day. Their narrative elaborations jumped back and forth from wartime memory to the present, following unique temporal and spatial flows. These are traumatic, emotionally charged and often highly sensitive tales of wartime ordeals. It was in moments of sheer emotional rawness that the floodgates were opened. The sense of intense emotional involvement, which occurred at the time of the encounters with the former 'comfort women', was often overwhelming.

Encounters with the Japanese war veterans were fraught with different issues. I was distinctly conscious of the limited time I had at my disposal to compile their narratives. In the majority of cases, only the one interview opportunity was available. I could not return to speak to them repeatedly as I had been able to do with the 'comfort women' survivors. One single moment of balancing clarity, respect, understanding, unease and empathy; one single moment to get it right. Enquiries into such a sensitive topic had to be strategic, therefore before visiting them I spent time thinking over how to bring up the sensitive topic of the 'comfort women' in the course of the conversation. Four of my respondents had published books about their wartime experiences, giving a context that would help me navigate through a variety of backgrounds with ease. If I was informed on the locale in which they had served, and what had happened there during the war, a much deeper level of conversation could be achieved. Reading their books before the interview allowed me to zero in on important issues and dispense with trivial background discussion.

I made efforts to facilitate the veterans' remembrances and recount their experiences of army life during the war. In talking with the Japanese war veterans, precautions were taken because of the sensitive nature of sexual topics, which are rarely discussed in either Japan or Korea. Furthermore, it should be acknowledged that brief meetings allowed little time to build rapport with participants.

The atmosphere of the interview and degree of empathy achieved with the Japanese veterans largely depended on their attitudes towards the issues with which I was concerned. For example, when the participants and I shared a similar view on war, gender and/or colonialism, I felt less unease while I was listening to them. However, there was very little gender sensitivity shown even amongst the 'rehabilitated' group of the Japanese war veterans with whom I shared views concerning Japan's colonial rule and its involvement in the war.

When interviewing a former high-ranking officer in the Imperial Japanese Army stationed in Indonesia during the war, his wife was in attendance and her wariness was obvious. From the beginning of the dialogue, it was evident that he wished to defend the conduct and the honour of the Japanese military during the war. During the course of the conversation she even attempted to stop him from talking several times: by interjecting, 'Are you sure? If you are not really sure, isn't it better not to say anything about that?' After about one hour, she gently reminded us what time it was. Her husband, on the other hand, wanted to continue talking because he was in the midst of enthusiastically recounting Japan's contributions to the post-war development of Korea and Indonesia. In the end, I found myself feeling uncomfortable with her for a different reason. She did not appear to have much sympathy for the 'comfort women' or for the sexual violence that they had endured and it is more than likely that she did not consider them as victims. Some questions only occurred to me afterwards: Did her national identification override identification along the lines of gender? Did her loyalties as a wife, and the interests she shared with her husband lie behind a reaction of denial and a refusal to acknowledge the full extent of the damage inflicted on the victims/survivors?

On the contrary, the 'rehabilitated' group of veterans were quite open-minded, and willing to discuss what happened during WWII to 'the girls' at comfort facilities, and what they or their 'buddies' did to 'the girls'. Some brought up the issue with little hesitation while I was still trying to find an indirect manner of leading up to the topic. Once they decided to talk, stories (including their encounters with the 'comfort women') were told with little reluctance or hesitation on their part. This represented a quite different atmosphere to that prevailing during my interviews with the victims/survivors with whom I needed to wait patiently to build up sufficient rapport before they began to speak of their wartime experiences. What could account for these differences? What made the war veterans less diffident in talking about their or others' visits to comfort stations? I found little evidence that the Japanese veterans felt any pain in discussing the subject. The men had faced virtually no social stigma as a result of their wartime sexual behaviour and, rather than speaking of their own account, the men usually told stories about others' violent behaviours and generalisable features of the poor treatment of the 'comfort women'. It was simply a matter of describing the common experience of all soldiers, albeit a subject that most had rarely discussed, either among themselves or with family members, in the more than half a century that had passed since the war (except for the 'rehabilitated' group). In my encounters with the veterans I attempted to understand not only what they had done during the war, but also their own standpoint on the context in which they had done it.

The two groups, the veterans and the victims/survivors, frequently employed different words to portray their experiences and situations at comfort stations. Whilst telling their own stories, my 'comfort women' respondents often struggled to find adequate language to describe the nature of the sexual exploitation and violence they had been subjected to or to articulate their emotions. The physical and emotional pain the women endured resists verbal objectification. For this reason, the women often spoke obliquely. At times, the meaning of their nuanced speech could be often understood only by the context. A phrase that recurs in their accounts is: 'How could I describe it all?' or 'It is beyond words'. Having been mute for so long has contributed to the difficulty of communicating their suffering and anger in words. The absence of adequate language to articulate traumatic exposures has been noted by Elaine Scarry (1985), whose persuasive work on torture suggests that pain destroys certain capacities of language.

I have found the voices and language of the 'comfort women' to be estranged entities, separate from the bodies on which they feel recurring and embodied physical and emotional pain. The women have limited language with which to describe the atrocities. Masculinist phraseology primarily reflects the male experience and point of view, with the language of sexual acts presented as androcentric. The meaning of 'having sex' is to have intercourse, it does not matter if it is with or without the women's consent. The primary imagery of sexual intercourse is 'to penetrate'. Within this frame of male experience and androcentric language, it is hard for women to find words to express their experience of sexuality and to construct a coherent narrative around this part of the past.

Their accounts reveal their inner torment, and their sense of leading an invisible, marginalised existence, due to their experiences of remaining unvoiced for such a long period of modern Korean history. The women's narratives are primarily about their anger and the prolonged pain they endured during the time of the war and afterwards, the pain of having been subjected to repeated sexual violence inflicted on their bodies and the societal stigma they felt afterwards as a result. When expressing their emotions, all of the women deplored the fact that their youth was irretrievable. In speaking the unspeakable, repressed memories of the physical and emotional pain they went through were transformed into narratives interwoven with a broad range of emotions and interspersed with frequent silent pauses.

As the words and terms the victims/survivors used during the war were in Japanese, such as military rankings and names of food, the women's accounts were frequently characterised by 'linguistic hybridity'; a term I have used for their incorporation of Japanese words into Korean discourse. Many of them were still able to sing some wartime military songs with the original Japanese lyrics.

A further disparity between the accounts of Japanese veterans and the 'comfort women' can be discerned in the observation that the men narrated their encounters often within the framework of a romantic relationship. Furthermore, some stressed positive aspects of the system, while at the same time insisting that it constituted nothing more or nothing less than common prostitution. With regard to the Japanese veterans who visited the comfort stations during the war, it is worth noting that those who treated the women with violence and contempt were perhaps less likely to share their stories with others, whilst surviving 'comfort women' were more likely to express personal narratives about their suffering from sexual violence, rather than focus on their personal relationships with the military men. As there were prolonged silences while they were narrating sensitive topics from their pasts, I would argue that such periods of silence stand as much in need of interpretation as their actual words. Paradoxically, silence may be eloquent. It is also important to pay attention to those stories that are more difficult to be told, and to exactly what lay behind the women's silence in their recounting.

The narrative elaborations of both groups shaped and reshaped not only the events of the war they experienced but also their subjectivity. The language they used to depict their experience offers insight into the construction of this aspect. Giving testimonial narratives demonstrates the ways in which 'each woman understands and reflects her experience in her own words' (Anderson and Dana, 1991: 23 in Kimura, 2016: 143). Through presenting the women's experience through their own words, albeit they are restricted by the inherent limitations of masculine phraseology, their subjectivity can be recovered and reclaimed from their silence, as they become subjects of their own stories. Speaking and sharing personal narratives of the past is a way of reconstructing or restructuring subjectivity.[1] Throughout the investigative process, it is also important to observe a wide and complex range of subject-positioning for the women victims/survivors and the veterans, which is illustrated in the following two chapters.

For the 'rehabilitated' group among the former Japanese military personnel, narrating testimonies can be interpreted as a form of confession, a way of coming to terms with the war. They were able to distance themselves from their own wartime activities due to their experience of 'rehabilitation' in China after the war. As Michel Foucault discusses, confessional testimonies are a means of 'uncovering the truth of the self', and can thus be seen as a 'practice of freedom' in and through the reinvention of the ethical self (Foucault, 1991: 3–20 in Mills, 1995: 100). Narrative elaborations of wartime memory appear to define their status as 'rehabilitated' and thereby serve to reconstruct their subjectivity through distancing themselves from their wartime activities.

For some veterans, unlike the 'rehabilitated group', talking to me was primarily an outlet for recollecting what they perceived to be, although undeniably painful, their essentially brave and honourable wartime pasts as members of the Imperial Japanese Army. They might have seen the interviews as a way to convince me of the validity of their point of view on the war. They often strove to control and lead the interview into a form of 'tutorial' session which would enable me to be better educated about Japan's wartime actions.

Ken Plummer discusses the phenomenon of story-altering by the interviewee according to what the interviewer expects to hear and defines this process as 'joint actions' (Plummer, 1995: 20). However, the interview setting with Japanese veterans did not constitute these kinds of 'joint actions'. The majority of Japanese veterans I talked with actively expressed their own personal thoughts on the war and some set out to legitimise the wartime endeavours of the Japanese forces. It seems that for these men, particularly the apologist veterans, narrating was a means of 'self-assertion' (Schütze, 1987: 39 in Grenz, 2005: 2096), and facilitated justifying individual and collective behaviour as members of the Imperial Japanese Army or Navy, which disclosed a certain moral ambivalence towards the sexual enslavement of the women.

My Positionality

In the course of encounters with both groups to talk about their traumatic past, reflective thoughts on my own position surfaced in my consciousness. Until recently, most ethnographic research in post-colonial societies has been undertaken by researchers from former colonial societies. As such, the dynamics of my interviews and research processes clearly differed from this genre of ethnography. As Pat Caplan points out, '[ethnographers] are painfully aware of their own privileged position on the grounds of race, class, education or whatever' (Caplan, 1993: 24). My encounters with the Japanese war veterans were, in some sense, the reverse. I was a researcher from a former colony of Japan. Categories of nationality, gender and age placed me in a less privileged position in terms of Japanese social hierarchies. I might have had educational advantages, but these were not particularly apparent during the interviews. The participants were men who had sought to contribute to building a Japanese Empire. In many respects, the power relations assumed in the above discussions of ethnographic research were not applicable. It is noteworthy that some of my respondents assumed an authoritative stance during interviews asking in great detail about what information I was seeking from them, and what exactly I was planning to do with their narratives. In some cases I was required to send them my curriculum vitae in advance. I gladly provided all the information they requested, not only because I wanted them to agree to an interview but also because this enabled interactive relations and a flow of information and questions in both directions: between the individual narrators and the listener/researcher.

When the veterans talked about sensitive issues surrounding male sexuality and experiences at comfort stations, I had mixed feelings. While I welcomed the access this openness gave me to their, or others', experiences at the comfort facilities during the war, their willingness to speak, as well as the terms in which they framed their stories, contained unsettlingly confident affirmations of masculine right, power and authority—both in relation to sexual access to the 'comfort women', and in relation to their perceived male authority over me.

I frequently felt an irresistible temptation to argue with them when they actively expounded defensive or patronising ideas on war and male sexuality. In order to maintain the flow of communication, however, I felt obliged to listen placidly to what was being said without interrupting and to display polite and appropriately neutral facial expressions, often throughout the entire encounter, without revealing my true inner feelings. Given the depth of my involvement with the 'comfort women' victims/survivors, there were some difficulties in maintaining emotional distance when listening to the men. This emotional dissonance I experienced could be managed by adopting a counselling approach to interactions with the men, that of being non-judgmental. Even though an element of potential tension could be sensed between some of the veterans and myself, I tried to keep myself in a non-judgemental stance and remain 'detached', by not displaying discomfort or interrupting them. This was in the interests of creating a smooth interview process through allowing conversation to flow. These interviews with some of the Japanese veterans brought up the issue of 'emotional labour' (Hochschild, 1983), as I became aware of the necessity to manage my own feelings and encountered emotional dissonance between 'felt' emotion and 'displayed' emotion. This dynamic may also be understood from the point of view of cultural practices that position women as listeners to expressed masculine needs (Grenz, 2005: 2091). Consequently, the role of listener/researcher could be said to have involved a strategic compromise in the interest of achieving my research goals.

Throughout this project, some efforts to maintain a degree of emotional detachment or 'neutrality' were necessary for me in order to avoid becoming too overwhelmed; either through excessive identification with the suffering of the 'comfort women' victims/survivors, or through resentment at the defensive and patronising ttitude of some of the Japanese war veterans. Overall, this was quite a challenging task, especially because my relationship with the female respondents had developed into a more complex connection than a simple binary one of researcher/interviewer and researched/interviewees.

My experience as a woman who had previously counselled victims of sexual violence has given me a heightened awareness of associated issues. This awareness led me to sympathise profoundly with the women's ongoing trauma, and helped me understand the narrators' emotional and psychological background. Personal counselling skills acquired through working with rape victims were employed to manage the encounters and allow the interviews to represent a safe space to provide both reassurance and an outlet for long–repressed emotions for the women. The opportunity to talk about the past could offer these victims/survivors a sense of catharsis or empowerment by giving them a voice and a chance to release some of their pain. In a sense, thinking about this positive aspect appeared to mitigate my feelings of impotence and anxiety over my inability to end their incessant pain.

On the other hand, interviews could also force the women to relive the vulnerability, precarity and lack of dignity or control that they experienced in the comfort stations. As they spoke, they did indeed appear to relive the moments of violence inflicted upon their bodies and their minds. They agreed to meet me to talk about their wartime experiences upon my request, but I had to consider the extent to which they might become distressed through recalling their trauma. They could be retraumatised by remembering and talking about traumatic, and/or inexpressible topics. Therefore, narrating trauma could potentially be both cathartic and distressing.

My interactions with the 'comfort women' victims/survivors in Korea also differed from the typical researcher–participant relationship found in most ethnographic work. It was 'same culture' ethnography viewed from the perspective of a third party. My respondents and I shared a gender and ethnic background while jointly engaging with accounts of their unspeakable trauma. A shared gender and ethnic background with the victims/survivors has helped with these in-depth interviews. Shared experiences through my positionality as a woman who had grown up in patriarchal Korean society enabled me to have an insider view in understanding their experiences. At the same time, residing outside Korea for over two decades provided me with a stance from which I could view the narrators' experiences from a third party perspective. The spatiality and temporality of my position were encoded in my role as an interlocutor questioning the narrators and presenting their narratives in my research.

Differences and similarities in the personal backgrounds of narrator and researcher are worth exploring. Rather than assuming transcendence of the boundaries between the respondents (the Japanese veterans and Korean survivors) and myself, I attempted to identify, acknowledge and explore both the differences and similarities between us and how these were encoded throughout our encounters. However great my compassion, vast differences remain between the knowledge gained via listening or reading, and that gained from direct embodied experience. The acute awareness and acceptance of affinity and distinction between us may have helped me handle the cross-gender and cross-border encounters, and curtailed any misplaced attempts to put myself in their place.

Having worked on the 'comfort women' issue inevitably led me to the question: why was I so engaged with this topic? Born as a child of post-colonial South Korea, what could I share with both the Japanese war veterans and the Korean victims/survivors and how could I relate to these tales from an era which predated my birth? Their narratives of traumatic enclosure in an environment of absolute hierarchical military system resonated with my 30 years spent in Korea under a military authoritarian regime (1961–1993). The legacy of the Korean War (1950–1953) lives on in the tensions apparent in inter-Korea relations, and creates a pervasive awareness of war and the threat of war or war-mongering on the divided Korean Peninsula. The Korean War left a deep imprint on the majority of Koreans. In addition to between two and four million casualties, the war divided 10 million family members between North and South and gave rise to a permanent sense of emergency and imminent war, if sometimes exaggerated during the former Korean military regime. Like most South Koreans, I was brought up on stories of experiences of the war from diverse sources; my family, novels, films and anti-communist political propaganda projected by former authoritarian governments, who had a vested interest in legitimising their military regime by keeping alive the fear of war between North and South Korea. This post-war cultural climate has been one in which consciousness of war as a reality or a threat is profound. Having grown up in martial-law Korea with a recurring sense of imminent war, listening to the stories of former Japanese soldiers led me to discover the root of my own strong objection to militarism. This part of my identity was formed from an upbringing under a militaristic regime and my position as a woman in a male-dominated society. These circumstances ensured that I was no stranger to narratives concerning war trauma and helped me to share and understand the frustration and oppression both the women and the war veterans experienced during the war, albeit in different ways. I acknowledge a sense of both closeness to and distance from war.

In writing this book, one of the most challenging tasks for me has been coming to terms with the inexplicable and incessant pain endured by so many individuals both during and after the war, while seeking to faithfully convey the nuances of unspoken, choked voices and the emotional outbursts of both the women and the veterans in textual form. Difficulties emerged in listening to descriptions of their enduring pain and how they responded to reliving their trauma. Recurring questions confronting me included: 'How do I present and contextualise the enduring pain of others?', 'Do respondents stand to become objects by being used as 'data' for my research purposes?' and 'Am I a consumer, and/or co-producer of their story of war?' I am keenly aware of issues of authority and power hierarchy between researchers and researched. Once narratives were collected through interviews, the data was left in my hands to be processed and represented. The process of presenting and disseminating the research results through analysis of their narratives is 'ultimately that of the researchers.... registered in a researcher's voice' (Stacey, 1991: 114). I have attempted to define my role as an academic, to evoke and reveal this traumatic but forgotten history of WWII through writing this volume.

Expected and unexpected emotions such as empathy, compassion and unease came up through the course of my encounters with both groups who had endured war and trauma. Learning that the 'comfort women' sometimes experienced complex feelings towards the soldiers surprised me. On those occasions when I met Japanese veterans, I was even more surprised to find I had a degree of sympathy for them while listening to and witnessing the ongoing traumas which some of the men were still dealing with. With some of them I could also relate to their present hardships of poverty, isolation and deteriorating health in their old age. Experiencing this reality through my personal encounters with the war veterans helped me understand the spectrum of grey areas that exists between a seemingly straightforward binary of villain and victim, and that one individual could be viewed as both, depending on the perspective of the onlooker. I left Japan with mixed feelings towards the Japanese former military men after I had reflected on my talks with them.

Note

[1] Maki Kimura astutely illuminates the importance of the 'comfort women's' testimonies as the site of subject formation in her book, *Unfolding the 'Comfort Women' Debates: Modernity, Violence and Women's Voices*. London: Palgrave Macmillan, 2016.

Chapter 3

The Making of a Warrior

T he current chapter explores the construction and implementation of the prototype of military masculinity of men enlisted in the Japanese Army which was achieved through formal and informal training procedures during WWII.[1] The objective is to show how sexuality, gender and national identity were used in the construction of colonial military masculinity in the process of remaking soldiers through everyday resocialisation practices of members of the armed forces. A key question in this chapter relates to the way in which military masculinity was created and reinforced in the combatants' own minds and bodies through the concept of the 'defiled' femininity of 'inferior' women involved in the operation of the 'comfort women' system. Primary references cite literature on the provenance of Japanese military masculinity and the soldiers' own narratives, including encounters between the two groups.

In Service of the Empire

Before discussing the construction of military masculinity and considering the central role of the 'comfort women' system in the military's colonial project, this chapter begins with an explanation of Japanese colonialism and its realisation in the military system. The core national identity of Japanese military men at the time can be defined in terms of colonial domination. A state ideology of a 'master' or 'superior' race championed Japanese moral and biological superiority. The state wartime propaganda emphasised a sense of pride in one's own country as well as a sense of superiority over other peoples in Asia. Wartime propaganda drew an exclusive boundary of superior Japaneseness drawn by distancing the Japanese from other peoples. The Japanese citizenry were exposed to, and surrounded by, such propaganda from childhood via the education system, mass media, local community organisations and military training. This indoctrination thus served to establish a Japanese national identity based on racial uniqueness and dominance. This essentialist construction of racial superiority operated in conjunction with the dominant/subordinate power relations between Japan and the rest of Asia.

The differences between the Japanese and other peoples were deemed to be immutable, biological and intrinsic with emphasis on differentiation between the superior and the inferior. The ideology of Japanese exclusiveness was predicated on a sense of belonging and fraternity. Rooted in the ideology of ethnic superiority, tropes of both the great nation (*taikoku*) and Japan as the uncontested leader of Asia (*toyo no meishu*) emerged. This theme was explicitly articulated in countless written forms:

> We, the Yamamoto race, are presently spilling our 'blood' to realize our mission in world history of establishing a Greater East Asia Co-Prosperity Sphere. In order to liberate the billion people of Asia, and also to maintain our position of leadership over the Greater East Asia Co-Prosperity Sphere forever, we must plant the 'blood' of the Yamamoto race in this 'soil' (Dower, 1986: 227 in Kim, 1997: 89).

This vision was projected in Japan's ambition in directing the building of the Greater East Asia Co-Prosperity Sphere (*dai tôa kyôeiken*), thereby providing an ideological justification for colonial expansion. The trope of the Japanese as the 'leading race' thus provided both a rationale for their mission to 'civilise' the rest of Asia, and an excuse to legitimise the Japanese annexation of Korea. Relationships between Japan and other Asian nations in the Greater East Asia Co-Prosperity Sphere, which was an economic and military geopolitical bloc under Japanese hegemony (Duus, 1976: 229), were euphemistically figured in familial fashion as that of 'elder brother and younger brother' or that of 'parent and child'. For example, a colonel from the War Ministry in 1942 represented the Japanese as 'the guiding race' in the context of regional familial relations: 'Because Japan was best equipped to guide the backward societies of the southern region, the relationship between Japanese and local peoples must be that of elder brother and younger brother'.[2]

The Japanese imperial vision apparent from government propaganda was that the nation played the role of liberator of the Asian people from Western imperialists. The rhetoric employed included phrases such as 'purely for Asian self-defence, Asian brotherhood and Asian liberation from "white oppression"' (Mark, 1999: 141 in McGregor, 2016: 10). However, the proclaimed 'prosperity' was not to be shared, it was meant exclusively for the benefit of Japan. There are substantial numbers of Japanese veterans who still believe that the war was fought for justice and to achieve the liberation of other Asian countries from Western imperialism (Senkyûhyakunanajûni, 1992: 307–308). This belief was revealed in expressions of 'imperialist nostalgia', as evidenced by Miyamoto Shizuo, a former high-level officer who served in Indonesia: 'We [Japan and Korea] used to get on well and cooperate together. We used to be one. We considered Koreans as Japanese. Japan has done a great deal of work for Korean people' (personal interview, 1996).

This concept of racial superiority had various aspects. Firstly, xenophobia was a defining feature highlighting the exclusive boundary which marked the Japanese out as a 'superior race'. One of my male respondents, Yuasa Ken, a military physician who served in Shanxi, China during the war, indicated how a deep xenophobia had been ingrained in him from his early days: 'The sense of disdain for other Asians including Koreans, and the ideology of the Japanese Emperor system (*tennôsei*) were poured into me from my childhood through education' (Yuasa, personal interview, 1996) (Ahn, 2010: 216). The communal, patriotic sentiments of state propaganda expressed disdain for other Asians, while emphasising the need for loyalty to the Emperor and the imperial nation. An example can be found in the terms used to refer to Koreans. Expressions such as '*Hantojin*'[3] and '*Chôsenjin*'[4] themselves have derogatory connotations and evoke contemptuous images of the subjugated, while simultaneously implying the relative respectability of the Japanese as a 'leading race'.

Xenophobic sentiment was provoked and encouraged in everyday life in the army. Examples include the insulting remarks about and the disparaging treatment of Korean 'comfort women', along with the callous brutality meted out to local people in the territories Japan occupied. Patronising views were expressed by a veteran: the military were looking after 'the starving girls' from Korea with 'well-paid and well-fed jobs'. 'If they were in Korea, they would hardly have had any food to eat. But they ate white rice[5] and nice food there [at comfort stations]' (Senkyûhyakunanajûni, 1992: 272).

Xenophobic ideas facilitated a sense of Japanese superiority and of 'the contamination' of Korean blood. Not only the 'comfort women' themselves, but also any babies born at comfort stations who had been fathered by the Japanese servicemen were deemed 'to be polluted' with inferior blood. These children were regarded as a 'disgrace' to the Japanese Imperial Army. In this way, the Japanese men's national identity was affirmed in relation to the denigration of Koreanness. A sense of superiority was reinforced by creating negative images of the 'comfort women' by means of racial and sexual domination—topics explored in more depth in the following chapter. The comfort station project consequently represents a material expression of this superiority trope.

Secondly, Japanese wartime identity was imbued with a specific sense of patriotism. The rhetoric of Japanese 'ultra-nationalism' in wartime called on affective relations, bonding, familial loyalty and self-sacrificing behaviour for the sake of the Empire. The needs or interests of the community had a higher priority in politics than those of the individual.

> The traditionalist ideas of social harmony, of duty and self-sacrifice, of loyalty to the Emperor and obedience to parents, and of the special character of the Japanese *kokutai* [national polity] were thoroughly embedded in the minds of most Japanese (Duus, 1976: 207).

Patriotism and moral education were instilled in the army's soldiers through everyday practices. Rituals such as the recitation of the Imperial

Precept to Soldiers and Sailors (*Gunjin Chokuyu*) took place at the start of each day, in which a heavy emphasis was placed on loyalty to the Emperor (*tennô*), and submission to one's superiors (Nishino, 1992: 145–146). This text specified five primary virtues of the military: loyalty, propriety, valour, fidelity and simplicity. Among these five virtues, loyalty ranked first: 'Fulfil your essential duty of loyalty, bearing in mind that duty is weightier than a mountain, while death is lighter than a feather' (De Bary *et al.*, 1958: 198–200 in Tsurumi, 1970: 122–123). This text expresses one-directional, bottom-up loyalty and reflects the obligation placed on recipients of benevolence or '*on*'.[6]

Patriotic identity was closely associated with an absolute loyalty to the Emperor, especially during the national emergency of war. The Emperor, 'semi-divine father to the national community' (Weiner, 1995: 449), was defined as the symbol of national unity and became the ideological centrepiece of the imperial state (Gluck, 1985: 73). This definition served to sustain Japanese identity and to weaken potential internal resistance against the Emperor, by portraying the imperial state as a source of common pride in terms of its participation in the 'great work of modern civilization' (Jansen, 1984), and the superiority of the Japanese race's unique spiritual properties (*yamato damashi'i*). The Japanese Emperor system (*tennôsei*) was therefore deeply involved in the construction of Japanese identity, and in the inspiring of loyalty. The theme of loyalty was spread through moral education in the army, which acted as an ideological device aimed at producing subjects ready to die for the sake of the Emperor or the nation. This deep loyalty was a key element in the version of Japanese male identity imposed on the servicemen: a national masculine ethos. In this context, brutal war crimes were supposedly committed for the sake of the nation, and were hailed as evidence of bravery in the name of patriotism.

Japanese national identity was fortified through 'spiritual education' and a strong sense that the nation was under threat. This intensive 'spiritual education' was intended to compensate for the poorly-developed infrastructure of the Japanese military. When compared with the western powers, the Japanese military lacked adequate infrastructure for war preparations. Peter Duus (1976) describes how this unreadiness for war was demonstrated by Japan's lack of a strong industrial base, and the absence of industrial or technological resources needed to support its war efforts:

> Japanese industry lacked the productive capacities to support their far-flung forces in a war of attrition. Japan was economically outstripped to begin with, and steadily lost ground thereafter. Her military technology began to lag behind as the Americans developed and refined new tools of war (Duus, 1976: 230).

In order to compensate for this lack of physical resources, the Japanese war effort relied heavily on human resources. The above-mentioned 'spiritual education' played a role as government war propaganda emphasised the unique qualities of the Japanese people, who were portrayed as having the mental superiority necessary to withstand the hardships of war (Matsumura, 2004: 808, 816). The revised Infantry Drill Book (*Hohei Soten*) specifically exhorted soldiers to overcome 'material forces' by means of 'spiritual forces' (Fujiwara, 1961: 111). 'Spiritual education' was an essential resource for war preparations in these circumstances. The Infantry Drill Book states that:

> On any battlefield we should steel ourselves to win glorious victory despite military forces and weapons inferior to the enemy's. Since we must be prepared for such a situation, it is self-evident that more spiritual education is necessary (Fujiwara, 1961: 111–114).

Therefore, intensive levels of what was termed as 'spiritual education' were integral to resocialisation in the military. Self-sacrifice and honour were such highly-valued attributes in this context that many military men committed suicide following Japan's defeat. The feudal samurai ethic of dying honourably for the sake of one's lord in Japanese history was revived in the act of killing oneself rather than being 'disgraced' for being captured by the enemy. This idea was culturally present and the army and state capitalised on its presence. Such honour suicide for the sake of the Emperor could wipe out the shame of defeat. In WWII, the Japanese army took the suicide mission that had historically been expected of leading officers and extended it to all enlisted men and then civilians by means of state propaganda. One Japanese veteran recalled the moment of a group suicide: 'After shouting three times "Hurrah", loud and continuous sounds of firing rifles, "Bang, bang, bang", or the sound of an explosion of a bomb were heard' (Nishino, 1992: 74 in Ahn, 2010: 220). Suicides were rituals of honour enacted at the time of Japan's surrender. The prevailing masculine, military code of honour demanded either victory or death: as the Field Service Code of 15 January 1941 states, 'If alive, do not suffer the disgrace of becoming a prisoner; in death, do not leave behind a name soiled by misdeeds'.[7]

The suicidal *Kamikaze* (Divine Wind) pilots and the *Kaiten* (Turning of the Heaven) human torpedoes might represent the final outcome of the spiritual education of soldiers in the military. Suicidal attacks were an official strategy of the Imperial Japanese military. Escorted to their targets by fighters, *Kamikaze* pilots were instructed to dive bomb-laden aircraft directly into enemy ships (Cook and Cook, 1992: 265). Self-sacrifice for the sake of the nation was highly praised and enshrined as 'the highest calling for any Japanese subject' or described as 'honourable service' (Humphreys, 1995: 49). Soldiers were told that 'They would become gods of the fatherland and would be worshipped in the Yasukuni shrine in Tokyo. To be made a Yasukuni god is a special honour bestowed only on national heroes' (Tsurumi, 1970: 125 in Ahn, 2010: 223). Hence, incentives were utilised in the process of indoctrination into state ideology. The paradoxical nature of the servicemen positioning towards the state propaganda is discussed later in this chapter in Paradoxes and Complexities.

Finally, both state ideology and war propaganda were highly gendered. Japanese men were supposed to fulfil a military duty, and women were expected to fulfil a maternal duty to create a supply of future soldiers under the slogan: 'Bear children and multiply' (*ume yo fuyase yo*).[8] Accordingly, women were supposed to serve the nation biologically, through the reproductive function of their bodies. Deniz Kandiyoti argues that it is 'the purely instrumental agenda of nationalist policies' (Kandiyoti, 1993: 376) to mobilise women's bodies during national emergencies. The myth of the common destiny or unity of the Japanese was stressed to strongly urge female responsibility for physical, cultural and social reproduction on behalf of the imperial nation. Hayakawa Noriko, a Japanese women's historian, highlights the construction of Japanese women as 'mothers of the nation':

> The mother's role which supports and conveys the Japanese Imperial tradition was fanatically stressed as an ideology integrating women and men into the war effort in the period of 1937 to 1945 (Hayakawa, 1996: 114).

To some extent, rather than only being passive victims of patriarchal state power, those Japanese women who conformed to this ideology created conditions that enabled the colonial state to function. Many of them were actively involved in perpetrating colonialism, through teaching, nursing and writing.[9] As Strobel and Mills point out, in the context of the historical process of British expansion, the colonising women could benefit from the economic and political subjugation of indigenous peoples and shared many of the accompanying attitudes of racism, paternalism, ethnocentrism and national chauvinism (Strobel, 1991: xiii; Mills, 1994: 39). Therefore, Japanese women's position could be said to simultaneously constitute 'centre' and 'periphery' within the colonial project.

In summary, the national identity inculcated in the Japanese soldiers in service of the Empire was characterised by muscular patriotism, self-sacrifice, loyalty to the Emperor, xenophobia and collectivism against a background of gendered roles for the nation. In particular, the Emperor system played a crucial role in fortifying Japanese national identity along with a prevailing masculine nationalism. The hegemonic national identity of the Japanese men was defined through 'othering' the colonised, and reinforced by state propaganda commenting on the relationship between the coloniser and the colonised. The Japanese construction of Korean identity in negative terms served, in contrast, to define Japanese identity in more positive terms as superior.

Military Masculinity

In the wake of feminism, 'the men's movement' and 'men's studies' have increased interest in the study of masculinity. The shift within feminism from an emphasis on 'women's studies' to 'gender studies' has helped to encourage this development (Seidler, 1989, 1992, 1997; Weeks, 1985; Morgan, 1992). Much of gender studies work has focused on the construction of dominant class or race masculinities. This focus was destined, sooner or later, to bring about analyses of the relationship between these dominant masculinities and the Western imperialist project (Chapmann and Rutherford, 1988; McClintock, 1995). The body of literature dealing with masculinity and either imperialism or colonialism has converged with works such as that of Mrinalini Sinha (1995) on the 'emasculation' of the dominated, or colonised male 'other' in the context of Bengali men's experiences under British colonial rule in the late 19th century.

In many cultures, war has provided the furnace in which the dominant forms of masculinity are forged and reinforced, and some interesting work has been done on military masculinity (Dawson, 1994; Mosse, 1985). The relationship between masculinity, violence and militarism is one of the main themes discussed in the literature on gender and war (Cockburn, 2004; Segal, 1990). In particular, an inherent link between masculinity and violence has been contested in recent works by Segal (1990, 2008), Moser and Clark (2001), Tosh (2004) and Zarkov (2007) (Ahn, 2018: 4). Furthermore, even though a close connection between masculinity and militarism exists, Cynthia Enloe argues that masculinity is not inherently militaristic:

> If masculinity as a social construct was identical to militarism, no state would risk its legitimacy with harsh conscription laws, and military institutions would not require extended 'basic training'. If masculinity were inherently militaristic, each would be redundant (Enloe, 1987: 531–532).

Lynne Segal also contests an inherent masculine tendency towards warfare by stating that war does not occur because men are eager to fight. Neither Enloe nor Segal views masculinity and militarism as isomorphic, meaning that their works represent opportunities to examine the relationship between masculine identity and militarism in the context of wartime Japan.

Janna Thompson employs Sigmund Freud's (1920) positing of a destructive instinct to explain why men who are otherwise rational willingly obey leaders and go to war without question, and why they participate in the group activity of war (Thompson, 1991: 68–72). If the instinct exists, it must be present in all men, yet not all men are equally willing to engage in warfare, to kill or be killed. Indeed military aggression arguably requires carefully controlled and systematic training and indoctrination via propaganda (Segal, 1987: 162–203 in Steedman, 1988: 271). Therefore, it must be considered that socio-political and educational conditions also shape the relationship between manhood and militarism.

In Japan there exists a historically close connection between masculinity and militarism, which Thomas Cleary calls 'samurai machismo' (Cleary, 1992: 55). Before 1868, the samurai tradition was confined to men of the ruling class and only became accessible to the male population at large following the West's forced opening of Japan (Tsurumi, 1970). The tradition of the samurai system in which military values and needs were emphasised was culturally embedded in the indoctrination received by combatants and therefore formed the bedrock of Japanese military masculinity.

Defining characteristics of military masculinity in wartime Japan encompassed bravery, aggression, virile sexuality, collectivity, honour and sacrifice as crystallised in the samurai spirit of a determined will to die for the nation. Military service in the Imperial Japanese Army and Navy facilitated participation in, and indoctrination into, this specific form of manhood. The masculine identities of Japanese combatants were forged under the pressures of war and colonial expansion, within an overwhelmingly male-dominated institution, resulting in a hegemonic masculinity.

Scholars who work on masculinity, like Connell (1987, 2005), Demetriou (2001) and Tosh (2004), suggest that hegemonic masculinity is culturally shared, and argue that accepted gender performances are constructed in relation to various subordinate masculinities as well as in relation to women. Consequently, men's dominance and authority are maintained not only over women but also over subordinate masculinities. The Japanese combatants' hegemonic military masculinity during the war (when Korea was still a colony of Japan) was constructed in relation to both the colonised, including Korean men and 'comfort women', and military subordinates within their own ranks.

In the context of examining the hegemonic masculinity of Japanese military men, it is worth reviewing concepts of Korean masculinity. You-me Park (1995) has described the Japanese image of Korean men as 'emasculated and infantilised': in turn, the image of a subjugated colony was feminine. The Korean state was feminised because of its subordinate position in relationship to the masculine and dominant Japanese imperial state. Moreover, the assumption that women were the property of both men and nation led Korean men to be regarded not as 'real' men or as insufficiently masculine because of their inability to protect their women. In this context, the hegemonic colonial masculinity of Japanese men is constructed in relation to both the subordinated masculinity of the colonised Korean men and the 'inferior and promiscuous' positioning of the 'comfort women'. In this way, Japanese colonialism is associated with male virility, simultaneously producing and reproducing colonial masculine power.

There are ample narratives from the soldiers themselves, acknowledging that to be a soldier meant to be a 'real' man. This idea may be illustrated by the case of the son of a village shopkeeper, an apprentice in an auto repair shop before the war, who was sent to Manchuria during the war for military service and who evaluated his experiences thus:

> Usually people say that army life is hard to bear. But I think it did me good. In the army, we were beaten and we suffered from the discipline. But looking back I can see that *the army made a man out of me.* In the army I experienced the inside story of human life. Industry alone is not enough, neither is shrewdness. You should combine both in order to succeed in life. That is what I have learned from the army experience (Tsurumi, 1970: 129).

His account confirms the commonly held belief of the time that manhood could best be achieved through military service. Kazuko Tsurumi (1970) recognises the multiplicity of reactions of the military men to army discipline in her study of social change and the individual before and after WWII. She illustrates that student-soldiers who were conscripted when they were studying at university complained about the army life. Others, from peasant backgrounds, found conditions relatively easy in comparison to the hardship of making a living from the land. However, while the effects of army discipline may have varied depending on the class origins of the recruits, they converged towards the production of hegemonic masculinity, a dominant model of manhood.

As previously noted, Japan's lack of material preparedness led the war effort to rely heavily on human resources. Strict rules of discipline and tough combat training during the war were important for enhancing the fighting spirit characteristic of military masculinity. In inspiring this fighting spirit, the military leaders deeply impressed upon the soldiers both aggressiveness and absolute obedience (Ahn, 2010: 219). The combination of intense training and harsh treatment created an association between soldiering and violence, hence, instilling an aggressive spirit among the soldiers.

Another feature of military masculinity produced through military resocialisation is collectivity. Collective suicide at the end of the war, especially among officers, was widely reported (Dolgopol and Paranjape, 1994: 89; Cook and Cook, 1992: 289). The men shared a sense of collective identity and common destiny with their peers and the nation in facing defeat. If to excel in war represented the epitome of masculine honour, defeat was consequently interpreted as a loss of both core values: masculinity and honour.

Military masculinity in wartime is a combination of pre-existing ideas of masculinity drawn from the samurai code and psychological fighting spirit reinforced by military training to compensate for delayed provision of the physical infrastructure required for war. A core trait of military masculinity constructed during the war was becoming a 'real warrior' like a samurai. In the following section I argue that military versions of masculinity propagated in military rhetoric are contradictory, in that they simultaneously enact masculinisation and feminisation. Jean Elshtain (1987), Kazuko Tsurumi (1970) and Carolyn Steedman (1988) either hint at, or explicitly discuss, feminisation or infantilisation in the military. Steedman (1988) argues that the working class British soldier in the second half of the 19th century, like his counterpart in civilian life, the policeman on the beat, was engaged in practices which generated a paradoxical feminisation of the uniformed working class in these most stereotypically masculine occupations. However, none of these authors adequately engages with the paradox of simultaneous masculinisation and feminisation and its reconciliation in a military context. This work will attempt to develop these contrasting but interdependent concepts in exploring how processes of resocialisation in the Japanese military gave rise to a type of military masculinity reflecting aspects of both.

Military Resocialisation: Masculinisation and Feminisation

The first stage of resocialisation among the armed forces was to establish rigid hierarchical relations through various institutional regulations. A former student-officer confirmed this in his diary: 'In the army, there is an absolute line between enlisted men and officers' (Matsunaga and Matsunaga, 1968: 176 in Ohnuki-Tierney, 2006: 158). Within the army, superiors were proxies for the Emperor under the axiom 'commands from your superiors are commands from the Emperor' (Kim, 2001: 614). The military's hierarchical order was modelled, in part, on the parent–child relationship of the *ie* (Japanese family) system and reflected conventional familial ideology: in the military barracks, the company commander was specially designated to act as a surrogate father, a sub-officer as a surrogate mother, and new conscripts as their children (Ahn, 2010: 216).[10] Punishment and control of men in uniform was much like the disciplining of young children by stern fathers.

A further ideological function of the family-state system[11] was to provide an ethos of service for the nation. The idea of the family-state system placed special emphasis on the family as the foundation of the state and as the basic unit of the ruling order of the state. The nation was imagined as a family within which filial piety was equated with loyalty to the Emperor, who represented the exalted father of all Japanese subjects in the family-state, *kazoku kokka*[12] (Uno, 1993: 297). The extensive use of violence by superiors was justified on the pretext that it was an expression of the parents' 'benevolent feelings', *on jo*, and would benefit the children (Iizuka, 1950: 43–45 in Tsurumi, 1970: 98; Ahn, 2010: 216–217).

Subsequently, the ideologies of hierarchy and familialism enhanced expressions of submissive and sacrificial behaviours on the part of the soldiers, and are hence linked to a process of feminisation in the context of army resocialisation. The suppression of personal interests with the overriding goal of obeying hierarchical orders from the military organisation runs parallel to the expectations for female family members, who could be expected to make sacrifices for their male counterpart/s within a patriarchal family structure. Infantilisation of military men in the military's configuration of the family was achieved through the men's positioning as metaphorical children lacking autonomy in relation to their stern fathers, who took on the masculine roles of heads of the pseudo-family. Tsurumi describes how 'the absence of privacy and the subjection to humiliation, terror and anxiety also helped to evoke childhood roles of dependence and obedience' (Tsurumi, 1970: 124 in Ahn, 2010: 220). Consequently, through the trope of hierarchy and familistic ideology, the obedient and self-sacrificing 'feminine' features of military masculinity were consolidated.

Hierarchical differences between superiors and subordinates in the military were obscured or made more acceptable where this pseudo-familistic ideology characterised by voluntary filial piety was applied to the military hierarchy. Iizuka (1950) argues that fusion of the two ideas, hierarchy and familialism, led enlisted men to internalise obedience to such an extent that the individuals would feel that they were acting on their own volition while in fact they acted under compulsion.

Within this system, violence was a disciplinary tool instrumental in training and resocialising combatants and establishing military masculinity. Under the austere tyranny of intense military training, recruited soldiers were subjected to arbitrary beatings in the so-called *jigoku* (hell) style of military training, coercion and punishment, and physical punishment or public humiliation of soldiers for even minor infractions was widespread. A veteran recalled this daily routine:

If your reactions were slow or the maintenance of your rifle poor, or if one of the 'vets' was simply in a bad mood, you would be punched or slapped. There was never a day I didn't get hit. I often counted how many times it happened in one day (Oguma, 2018: 10).

Rather than being an intrinsic and pre-existing component of masculinity, structural and embodied violence was intentionally implemented in the intensive process of intensive military resocialisation (Ahn, 2018: 4). One side effect of this disproportionate violence was that the men could, in turn, become more violent or brutal to those lower in the military hierarchy or to their enemies. This trickle-down effect manifested in acts such as the killing of Chinese prisoners of war, plunder, rape or arson. Having to undergo such brutal treatment within the army barracks aroused anger and resentment in the enlisted men. From the individual soldier's viewpoint, he could only retrieve and demonstrate his power through venting this anger by displaying cruelty towards his enemies or subordinates. One Japanese veteran described army resocialisation as a process designed to strip away one's humanity, so that the soldiers would become 'devils' in human form (Nishino, 1992: 63).

Japanese soldiers were thus able to act simultaneously as agents and as objects of power relations with respect to the 'comfort women' and the process of army resocialisation. The pseudo-familial hierarchies lent themselves to certain ways of understanding and structuring the comfort station system as well. Women occupy subordinate positions within patriarchal families, as daughters and wives. The model of the stern father disciplining wives and daughters 'for their own good', and feeling able to bully and maltreat them if he so chooses, is very evident in the accounts of the oppressive power wielded over the 'comfort women'.

To produce goal-oriented soldiers who held a collective identity as warriors, a totalitarian disciplinary regime was instituted, in which individuality, privacy and humanity were denied (Ahn, 2010: 217, 220). The soldiers' private lives were regulated in various ways by the military authorities. Private conversations were often listened to and reported on, soldiers' diaries, notes and any other personal writings scrutinised, and their received and sent letters strictly censored (Oguma, 2018: 12; Tsurumi, 1970: 96–97, 123). The actions and lives of military personnel, and rank and file soldiers in particular, were strictly controlled and regulated. Yuasa, a former military physician, explained the soldiers' lack of autonomy:

> Soldiers never had any rights or chances to decide things by their own will, or to refuse obedience during the war. It was very much like living in a prison…. This is all while the officers indulged in enjoyment with the 'comfort women'. There was no freedom given to the soldiers. They were always supervised and watched (Yuasa, personal interview, 1996).

Ultimately, military resocialisation taught the Japanese soldiers to subordinate their own needs, desires and comfort, even their lives, to the interests of the nation. A veteran, Yokota, reports that the search for a place to die for his country, thereby fulfilling a *Bushido* ideal, was his 'fervent desire and long-cherished dream' (Cook and Cook, 1992: 309). Sacrifice was an ideal which lay at the very foundation of the Japanese military ethos, as underlined by Akira Fujiwara:

> The army was set up with peasants who were in semi-serfdom, and were put through severe training and punishment. In this procedure, the human rights and lives of the soldiers were totally ignored. This is a particular characteristic of the Imperial Japanese Army. Therefore, the wars Japan waged were based on the sacrifices of its soldiers (Fujiwara, 1977: 73–74).

Yet, despite the rhetoric of familialism and filial piety and the trainings soldiers underwent to engrain ideas of loyalty, during interrogations following Japan's defeat, rank and file Japanese prisoners of war displayed an unusual level of contempt for their officers who, they thought, ought to have acted *more* like fathers in caring for their men.[13] One veteran cynically commented on the corruption of the officers in the forces: 'Officers could not have managed to carry on the war without the women. Even in an air-raid shelter, they were keeping hold of the women for themselves' (Jûgun ianfu hyakutôban, 1992: 144). There appear to be multiple reasons behind the rank and file soldiers' lack of respect for their seniors in contrast to how the relationship was ideally supposed to operate.

While noting that this military form of machismo certainly included stereotypical masculine features such as aggression, destruction and sexualisation, it is worth noting that these features coexisted alongside stereotypical features which are more commonly associated with femininity.[14] I argue that the military version of masculinity is deeply contradictory, in that masculinisation and feminisation are enacted simultaneously. These contradictory characteristics are very closely dependent on each other. Harsh military training was designed to facilitate two contrasting aspects of military masculinity; to make soldiers tough and brave, on the one hand, and to instil subservience and self-sacrifice on the other. The resocialisation of the recruits in the military under a regime of harsh training, surveillance, arbitrary discipline, strict supervision and violence was designed to achieve militarised masculinity by reinforcing bravery, aggression, collectivity, honour and sacrifice in them through conjoint processes of masculinisation and feminisation.

Offering 'Hygienic' Sex: Regulating Comfort Stations

In the military, resocialisation processes involved strict control of the combatants' lives, including control over their sexuality. Two crucial axes of control, violence and sexuality, which represented two halves of a 'stick and carrot' approach, were set in opposition in order to utilise the men more effectively in performance of their wartime duties. To offset the exhaustion and brutality of military service, the men were offered sex as a reward via the 'comfort women' system. It was important that this 'service' should be hygienic. This section explores issues of control relating to the sexuality, systemic hygienic supervision and the way in which access was managed through military regulations primarily designed to promote safe sex.

Soldiers' narratives disclose that the provision of access to 'comfort women' was a top priority for the military authorities. When the Japanese Army advanced or relocated, some of the officers' primary concerns were the transportation of the 'girl army'.[15] After finding a room, whatever conditions the space was in, they were immediately forced to 'serve' soldiers (Goyama, personal interview, 1996). For some camps in China where there was no comfort station, 'comfort women' were regularly sent by truck 'to serve' soldiers in the field (Itô, pseudonym, personal interview, 1996). The women were taken to mobile comfort stations, sometimes set up in tents, where they were made to 'serve' soldiers stationed in remote areas (Dolgopol and Paranjape, 1994: 113; Kawata, 1987: 90; Jûgun ianfu hyakutôban, 1992: 124; Han'guk chŏngsindae, 1997: 57). Even during bomb raids, the women were obliged to continue 'serving' the soldiers whether in caves (Han'guk chŏngsindae, 1993: 143) or fox holes (Dolgopol and Paranjape, 1994: 80).

An officer who served in Nha-tran, Vietnam during the war describes seeing this grotesque scene outside a military comfort station:

> It was a comfort station often talked about. The non-too-simple reality of it was that, rather than being stimulated, I felt I had been exposed to some grotesque world. Standing in line in broad daylight, doing it right under the nose of the people waiting for their turn, and the vivid image of men coming out one after another with their pants still half open. This ritual proceeded in conveyor-belt fashion in an atmosphere of a particular sort of tension, and rather than raising my spirits, made me, who knew nothing of the forbidden fruit of the tree of knowledge, flinch (Nanbara, 1983, 202 in Yoshimi, 1995b: 140).

Having sex was considered a form of recreation or a welcome distraction from battlefront duties. On or near the battlefields, there was simply no other place to go and nothing else to do for 'leisure'. The troops were not granted regular leave (Yoshimi, 1995b: 73). A veteran, Miki, reported that almost every soldier visited the 'comfort' facility when he was off duty (personal interview, 1996). Another veteran, Yoshioka Tadao, recounted killing as an everyday routine for the soldiers: 'On a battle field at least, men become like beasts, because they keep killing each other everyday. There is nothing but *killing, eating and sex*' (personal interview, 1996).

Military authorities drew up and distributed regulations for the use and running of comfort stations to the soldiers and station managers. In some areas, there were even military officers in charge of selecting agents to recruit new girls, and granting permission to open, supervise or run military brothels or comfort stations. For example, when Ichikawa Ichiro arrived to take up his post in the military police in Manchuria, he was told by his commander that he was to be in charge of a comfort house (Dolgopol and Paranjape, 1994: 124). Regulations covered time allowed with the women, rates and prices, mandatory condom use, keeping military secrets and bans on drinking and fighting (Yoshimi, 1992: 229, 262). Regulations for the military brothel managers involved issues of sanitation, working hours and working conditions for the 'comfort women'. When enlisted men wanted to go to a comfort station, they needed to buy a ticket from the corps headquarters (Jûgun ianfu hyakutôban, 1992: 64).

The officers' tickets for the comfort stations had higher prices than those of the rank and file (Mun P'ilgi, personal interview, 1992). According to the rule in the December 1944 Appendix on discipline in the Serviceman's Club Regulations, set out by Okinawan unit Yama #3475, officers were to pay a three yen service charge, while non-commissioned officers and paramilitary personnel were to pay a two and a half yen fee, and soldiers only two yen (Kawata, 1987: 80). These prices were determined by the length of time the men were allowed to stay at the comfort station and the origin of the woman who 'serviced' them. Japanese women were the most expensive, while native local women from Southeast Asia or the Pacific Islands were the least expensive (Miyamoto, personal interview, 1996). Military brothels disguised as comfort facilities, beyond being a means exerting sexual control over army personnel, also represented a profitable sideline for those in charge.

Hierarchical relationships within the military as discussed above were sustained in the comfort stations through official regulations.

Narratives from Japanese veterans indicate that officers had privileged access to the 'comfort women' (Han'guk chŏngsindae, 1997: 56) and could select women by age, appearance or nationality, with virginity being especially prized, while the foot soldiers had limited access and were obliged to 'share' the 'comfort women'. Separate time limits and allocations were granted in the comfort stations to common soldiers and officers. Mun Okchu recounted:

> From around 9.00 a.m., straight after breakfast, we started to serve soldiers. Sometime soldiers lined up from early morning. The rank and file stopped coming at around 4.00 p.m., and then officers would visit until 10.00 at night. After that, some officers came and stayed overnight (Han'guk chŏngsindae, 1993: 158).

The institutional regularisation of access to the women marks social and hierarchical differences among the Japanese combatants. Class issues and social background played out in this hierarchy as the military doctors and officers were usually better-educated than the rank and file.

A sense of rivalry and possessiveness towards the women was sometimes apparent in narratives. There were cases of men competing for access to their favourite women and these conflicts between the men sometimes resulted in death. Yuasa, a former military doctor, reported a death that occurred as a result of fighting with another soldier over the same woman, noting that the incident was officially reported to the military authorities as a death in battle (personal interview, 1996). Military hierarchies also played a role in the way such tensions were settled. Sexual access was determined by power in the hierarchy, and this served to reproduce distance and superiority. Through these formal and informal practices in the comfort stations, hierarchical relationships were enacted and consolidated.

A variety of other regulations in using comfort facilities were implemented by the military authorities. The number of visits made to the same woman by a single soldier was reported to the authorities that monitored and regulated the frequency of visits (Dolgopol and

Paranjape, 1994: 125 in Ahn, 2010: 220). A veteran, Ichikawa Ichiro, reported the control of access to a 'comfort woman':

> Every morning the Korean couple [responsible for managing the military brothel] provided to the military police a list of users for each woman and the military police would look to see if one particular soldier was visiting the same woman too often (Dolgopol and Paranjape, 1994: 125).

The authorities also feared that soldiers might share military secrets such as the movement of troops with the women. There was also the fear that personal attachment to these women would dilute the men's loyalty to the military, resulting in desertion in extreme cases if a man were to run away with a woman (Ahn, 2010: 220).

Condoms and other prophylactics such as 'Secret Star Cream' disinfecting lubricant were made readily available to the Japanese servicemen as contraceptive and protective measures for promoting safe sex at the onset of war in 1939. *Sakku,* condoms, were distributed to soldiers in order to minimise the spread of sexually transmitted diseases. The domestic consumption of crude rubber was restricted in order to reserve material for the continued production of condoms for the armed forces. Nakano Takashi, a former officer, recalled that checking to ensure that the soldiers possessed condoms before allowing them to leave the barracks to visit a comfort facility was one of his weekly tasks (personal interview, 1996).

Despite regulations requiring condom use, Kim Tŏkchin, a 'comfort woman' victim/survivor, reported:

> Quite a few would rush straight to get down to business without condoms, saying that it wouldn't be a big deal if they caught diseases since they were likely to die on the battlefield at any moment anyway (Han'guk chŏngsindae, 1993: 51).

Other reasons the men may have given for refusing to use condoms included hopes that infection with a venereal disease would gain them passage back to Japan as invalids or, for the strangest reason of all, because they believed themselves to be in love with a 'comfort woman' (Jûgun ianfu hyakutôban, 1992: 105). According to a report by First Lieutenant and Kônodai Army Hospital psychiatrist, Torao Hayao, there was a higher instance of venereal disease among commissioned officers and high-ranking officers in particular, than among enlisted soldiers, since these officers were likely to frequent several different comfort stations and to do so more often than common soldiers (Yoshimi, 1992: 215). Apparently the officers could 'use' a variety of 'comfort women', of Korean, Japanese or local origin, either on a short or long-term basis.

Because sexually transmitted diseases were widespread, the army authorities were tasked with protective measures and conducting hygienic supervision of both the 'comfort women' and the military personnel through regular medical check-ups. If the men were found to have caught a venereal disease, they were not only given treatment, but they and their commanding officer might even be punished, as contracting venereal diseases was regarded as a great disgrace for a member of the armed forces (Jûgun ianfu hyakutôban, 1992: 57; Nishino, 1992: 96, 104).

Yuasa, a former military doctor, told of his duty to conduct routine examinations of the women as well as compulsory attendance at regular headquarter meetings to decide price and time limits for 'service' at comfort stations (personal interview, 1996). The results of health checks of the women's bodies were released to the combatants in order to provide information on those with whom the soldiers could have safe sex. A veteran, Suzuki Yoshio, recalls that he was told that 'these and those could be played with' or 'these and those should not be mingled with, as they had diseases' (personal interview, 1996). In this way, the women were regulated as a part of the forces like 'civilians attached to the military' (Iwasaki, personal interview, 1996). This systemic hygienic supervision can be understood as an undertaking primarily for the benefit of the military forces to prevent the loss of military efficiency by ill health due to infection by venereal diseases (Dolgopol and Paranjape, 1994: 125).

The high number of infectious sexually transmitted diseases like gonorrhoea, syphilis or lymph granuloma inguinal present among the Japanese armed forces during the war was a matter of great concern to the military authorities and a question of military honour. Hospitalisation and recovery periods for sexually transmitted diseases were lengthy. Furthermore, if the men returned home before being completely cured, they risked spreading diseases domestically in Japan (Yoshimi, 1995b: 68–69). According to the section entitled 'Prevention of Social Diseases' in the North China Area Army's 'Procedures for the Hygiene Education of Key Officers' (1940), 'social diseases [venereal diseases] damage the body, destroy the family and ruin the country' (Yoshimi, 1992: 235). As illustrated by the use of the term 'social disease' in this military document and others issued during the war, the spread of venereal disease was seen not only as an individual issue, but also as a social issue linked to broader population policy. Maintaining a healthy and 'uncontaminated' body was considered important to sustaining the social status of the nation.

Hence, the sexuality and bodies of both 'comfort women' and military men were highly regulated through medical practices designed to ensure 'hygienic' sex. To some extent, the politics of military sex were camouflaged as merely the politics of soldiers' health (Ahn, 2010: 221). State interventions into sexuality, sexual relations and health were enacted in the name of 'hygiene management'. The establishment of comfort stations was structured to provide sexual services for Japanese forces at controlled 'hygiene facilities'.[16]

'Sex as Gasoline for a Car': Proving Virility

The warrior figure was the epitome of the Japanese Empire's particular breed of military masculinity, and his role was reaffirmed by his sexual prowess. Sexuality can be a significant part of hegemonic masculinity as it is a means of asserting virility. Cynthia Enloe, who has conducted pioneering research on militarism and gender, states that 'to be real men, soldiers had to satisfy their sexual appetites' (Enloe, 1988: 22). The comfort station was a space specifically designated for this purpose.

The comfort station system was widely used by almost all military personnel. There are ample veteran accounts and even a few wartime photos which portray soldiers waiting impatiently for 'their turn' outside a comfort station. The military men had various motives for visiting the comfort stations. Firstly, veterans' narratives make reference to the idea of a biological motivation, with visits taken for the men to fulfil their sexual needs: 'I frequented comfort stations because of sexual drives. Thus, I *had to* go there' (Ogawara Goichi, personal interview, 1996). This assumption was reiterated in most of the men's accounts, and even appeared in those of the progressive 'rehabilitated' group of veterans. A 'comfort woman' confirmed this by reporting that the men looked 'starved' and crazy at the sight of women (Kim-Gibson, 1997: 260). Male sexuality was represented as a basic biological function, and men were presumed to have innate sexual needs.

Yuasa expressed this idea via the metaphor of fuelling an engine: 'sexual pleasure was to the soldiers as gasoline was to a car' (personal interview, 1996) (Ahn, 2010: 226). Another respondent, Yoshioka Tadao, confirmed how crucial the 'comfort women' were in the control of the soldiers by military authorities: 'In fact, the most important people in the forces were the women. Soldiers all went crazy or behaved like animals. To make them manageable and keep them going, the "female staff" were required' (personal interview, 1996).

A desire for a sexual experience, especially in the face of the prospect of death in battle, was another reason frequently cited as to why the men made visits to 'comfort women'. This male desire for sex stems from the belief that manhood can be achieved through sexual experience. For men, sexuality is deemed a way of affirming and validating their male identity, and desire for such affirmation was seen as especially potent when the men's lives were on the line:

> Including me, there was a rampant feeling that it is really a shame not to have any chance to have sex with a woman before being killed, if one was born as a man. If not, one could not be a real man (Wada, personal interview, 1996).

The men seemed to have understood the comfort system as a form of prostitution. Substantial numbers of the men still assert today that the 'comfort women' programme was one of straightforward prostitution. This explanation is often used as an excuse by the men who visited the comfort stations to obtain sexual 'service'. One Japanese veteran, Dokoda Masanori, reaffirmed the view that the comfort stations were nothing more than brothels on battlefields, exactly like ordinary brothels (personal interview, 1996). Another veteran confirmed: 'It was a business. The women's attitude was "please purchase and have me". It was as though they tried to solicit as many men as possible' (Senkyûhyakunanajûni, 1992: 272). Veterans, especially in the right-wing revisionist camp, strongly asserted that it was legal and the women were paid (Senkyûhyakunanajûni, 1992: 318).[17] A flourishing culture of state-regulated prostitution already existed in pre-war Japan, and the soldiers' familiarity with this system allowed them to interpret the comfort station system as an extension of the one on the home front:

> I also thought the women came over to China to make money. So, we felt no sense of guilt at using their services. We felt exactly the same as we did when we sometimes bought a prostitute on a red light street in Japan (Hara, pseudonym, personal interview, 1996).

The existence of a legalised prostitution system in Japan's pre-war sexual culture informed the establishment of the 'comfort women' system and the military men's perceptions of the 'comfort women'. In fact, the Japanese imperial regime had a long history of using women's bodies for the sake of colonial projects, notably the *karayuki-san* (literally 'China-bound persons'), who were Japanese women sold into debt bondage to brothel keepers throughout Southeast Asia and China, mostly between 1905 and 1930 (Hane, 1982: 218–222). These women were sent abroad to sexually entertain Japanese men stationed overseas for military and trade activities, and the practice was an integral tool of colonial expansionism (Suzuki, 1993: 221–222). These 'cultural prescriptions' legitimised sexualised 'services' for the soldiers' 'comfort' through state-established facilities. The atmosphere and setting of the comfort stations was meant to make the men feel at home (Senkyûhyakunanajûni, 1992: 271). For example, in several areas, the 'comfort women' had to wear kimonos and welcome the military men with the Japanese greeting, '*Irasshaimase*', which means 'welcome' or 'come in'.

In contrast, another group of my respondents claimed to have been reluctant to visit the 'comfort women' for several reasons. Some men admitted to a sense of shame at having sex without affection: 'I did not go to a comfort station as I was brought up to think that kind of sex [at a comfort station] is dirty and obscene. I was educated that sex without affection is shameful' (Yoshioka Tadao, personal interview, 1996). Another man, an officer, affirmed his reluctance to allow his biological urges to overcome his humanity: 'I was conscripted when I was in the second year in the University of Tokyo as a student soldier. As I am an educated person, isn't it sensible that I should be able to control desire?' (Nakano, personal interview, 1996).

Perceiving 'comfort women' to be 'filthy' or 'dirty' also may have deterred some of the men from having sex with them. Iwasaki remembered that he felt the women in the comfort stations were like animals, dogs and cats, with whom it would be deeply shameful to have sex (personal interview, 1996). However, his explanation of abstinence is not rooted in consideration for the women's humanity, but clearly displays misogyny.

Others claimed that their full devotion to the fight for the nation repressed all thoughts of sex. Yuasa described his experience during the first four or five months of his service, during which he believed that he was involved in a war fought in the interests of justice to liberate the Chinese from Western imperialists such as Britain and the USA. He claimed that he had no desire to visit a comfort station as he was armed by the highest spirit to fight for justice (Yuasa, personal interview, 1996). His abstinence and belief in his mission in support of the Empire held strong at the beginning of the war. Yet, he admitted that as time went on his initial beliefs faltered and eventually he also utilised the 'comfort women' system.

Men were actively encouraged to visit the comfort stations by both the military culture surrounding male sexuality, as well as by senior officers in the military barracks. Seniors took their subordinates, especially young virgin soldiers, to the comfort station, and urged them to 'lose' their virginity before death, since they were liable to die on the battlefield at any moment (Jûgun ianfu hyakutôban, 1992: 69). The seniors even went so far as to check on them from outside. Nakano, a former student-officer, reported that his commander stayed near the room he was in [at a comfort station] and often checked whether he was 'doing OK' with the girl (personal interview, 1996).

Another practice was the ritual of having sex at comfort stations in groups led by officers or senior-ranking soldiers. A victim/survivor reported that some soldiers were marched into her room singing a military song (Han'guk chŏngsindae, 1995: 70). This was a ritual in which every group member was supposed to participate. Consequently, the men faced peer pressure to prove their virility. Satô, one of my respondents, recalled experiencing such group pressure:

> If I did not go the station even after I became a non-commissioned officer I would have been left out and the rumour circulated that I did not enjoy being with a girl. I did not want to be excluded by others in the troop so I went for a girl (Satô, pseudonym, personal interview, 1996) (Ahn, 2010: 216).

A psychiatrist at the Kônodai Army Hospital confirmed that those who did not go to comfort stations were ostracised and regarded as 'abnormal'.[18] Staying in line with one's peer group through performing sexual actions was deemed 'normal'. The practice seems to have been considered an essential aspect of army life and vital to the expression of military masculinity expected of the men. In fact, the internal, masculine cohesion of the military group was necessary to foster a sense of loyalty to the army and was therefore promoted through these shared sexual experiences at the comfort stations. As a member of the Imperial Japanese Army male bonding was achieved through shared domination of the weak. Having sex with 'comfort women' was therefore sometimes a *pressure* exerted on the men so as to not be ostracised by their peer group, and most often seen as the men's *right*, regardless of whether they had some objective sexual need or personal, emotional feelings. Therefore, the peer pressure from comrades and seniors to conform to the prevailing standards of masculine behaviour was one component of establishing male bonding and reinforcing a collective group assertion of masculinity through sexuality, implicit in the comfort station system.

Military life generates contradictory pressures and needs. Another example is the juxtaposition of male bonding within an absolutely hierarchical army power structure. Masculinity or fraternity could be affirmed through shared experiences of dominating, heterosexual sex at the comfort stations. A heightened sense of group belonging may have helped to mitigate tensions generated through the strictly hierarchical and segregated relationships of the military. As an added benefit, a sense of kinship among the men helped to promote totalitarian and collective masculine identity which fostered the in-group solidarity required to collaborate in carrying out the war project. Michel Foucault convincingly points out that while unity among group members through sex is fictitious, it is perceived as having powerful meaning. He describes how the shared notion of sex 'made it possible to group together, in an artificial unity, anatomical elements, biological functions, conducts, sensations and pleasure, and it enabled one to make use of this fictitious unity as a causal principle, an omnipresent meaning, a secret to be discovered everywhere: sex was thus able to function as a unique signifier and as a universal signified' (Foucault, 2007: 154).

Foucault's point resonates with the nature of Japanese military men's male bonding in which sex signifies a performed collectivity and artificial unity, while group coherence is concurrently signified by male bonds of camaraderie. At the core of this construction of sex as an activity accessible to group members, there was the 'comfort women' system. This cohesion in performance among the men helped to construct a collective military masculinity through which a group of men were tied together as members of a common army, while hierarchical order separated them from each other into clearly defined ranks. These contradictory horizontal and vertical axes met at the point of the comfort stations. The 'comfort women' system could be said to provide a significant mechanism for holding this contradictory reality together. In this sense, the significance of the comfort system was its utilisation to simultaneously reinforce both military masculinity and military hierarchy.

'Sex Like the Need to Eat': Legitimisation

Behind urges to validate and prove sexuality lies the trope of uncontrollable male sexuality which was used to rationalise the sexual practices of the military men at the comfort stations. This sexual need was described as the same as 'the need to eat, or to excrete' in a document issued by the 11th Division of the Signal Corps (Yoshimi, 1995a: 222). The formidable patriarchal myth of irrepressible male sexual desire and the supposed necessity for women to be available for the provision of sexual services were ideas widely circulated in the military. Nakano Takashi, a former officer, asserted that 'if there are troops, a facility like a *piiya* (a brothel) is needed. Otherwise, local women will be raped' (personal interview, 1996). In fact, acts of rape committed by Japanese soldiers against local populations in those areas where the Imperial Japanese Army had advanced and had been stationed were rampant. One of the veterans with whom I spoke confirmed this:

> Once fighting started we could take Chinese girls at our pleasure, so I heard we could do freely on battlefields what we were not allowed to do, or restricted in doing, in Japan (Wada, personal interview, 1996).

John Costello, who has conducted research on sex and war, asserts that war makes a very significant contribution to the sexual liberation of both men and women, giving as an example the relaxation of sexual suppression caused by the urgency and excitement of wartime. He identifies 'sex as one of the few freely available wartime pleasures' (Costello, 1985: 9–20). But his idea of 'freely available' sex begs critical questions: for whom is it freely available? Above all, how should sex and rape be defined? He appears to romanticise sexuality in wartime by ignoring the power relations that structure it, and does not adequately address potentially violent aspects of wartime sexuality.

High rates of sexual violence perpetrated against local women by the Japanese military were a concern for the military authorities. The 'comfort women' system was implemented in part to prevent the rape of locals, acts that would inflame anti-Japanese sentiment. One of my respondents,

Miyamoto, a former high-level officer, asserted and appreciated this role of the 'comfort women' programme:

> The programme ['comfort women' system] was really wonderful in terms of two aspects; one is to keep the soldiers from committing rape and so being imprisoned, the other was to avoid provoking anti-Japanese sentiments from the local people because of the attempted rape of local women by the Japanese soldiers. If there were no 'comfort women', many soldiers would have been put into prisons, and the local people would have resisted the Japanese military government... The women were among the most important in the Japanese forces. And owing to them, military governing of the local population could go on smoothly. So, I would like to thank the women very much (Miyamoto, personal interview, 1996) (Ahn, 2010: 226).

However, various military reports during the war, including a report from a general in Wuhan, China, disclosed the fact that rape continued to occur even though 'comfort women' accompanied the forces (Yoshimi, 1992: 95). A veteran reported that when the forces went out in turns to plunder two or three times a month in China, condoms were distributed in advance (Jûgun ianfu hyakutôban, 1992: 142). In this case, rape was conveniently tolerated in order to heighten the soldiers' appetite for war and boost morale by making them think of themselves as indomitable men.

The same assumption of irrepressible male sexuality is found in the reasons commonly given for the establishment of comfort stations. A top-secret 1939 report, 'Unique phenomena on battlefields and measures to cope with these problems', by the aforementioned psychiatrist at the Kônodai Army Hospital also drew upon this myth:

> The army authorities established comfort stations in central China because they assumed that it was impossible to suppress the sexual urges of the soldiers. The main purposes in setting up comfort facilities was to relieve soldiers of daily stresses by giving them a sense of sexual satisfaction, and

to prevent rapes which would damage the reputation of the Imperial Army (Yoshimi, 1992: 228).

There exists an enduring commonality across cultures and time periods in which prostitution is defended as a method for protecting 'innocent' women from rape. The 'comfort women' programme, however, itself constituted an enactment of the very sexual violence it was allegedly trying to prevent. Although presented as a deterrent to the rape of local women in newly-occupied Japanese territories (such as China, Indonesia, the Philippines etc.), the 'comfort women' programme represented in effect the systematic rape of already-colonised Korean women under the jurisdiction of the military authorities. In other words, the argument that the comfort system provided protection against sexual violence conveniently ignored the fact that the programme itself represented a form of sexual coercion against the women whose bodies were provisioned for its existence.

A fatal problem with the essentialist understanding of male sexuality as something uncontrollable so as to legitimise the 'comfort women' system is that it reduces a social phenomenon to a biological one, making the men's actions appear to be inevitable and unavoidable. This understanding of a nature thought to be beyond human control has often been used to rationalise sexual violence and prostitution and has frequently been employed to keep women in subordinate or victimised positions. As Wendy Hollway convincingly argues, the acceptance of an irrepressible nature of male sexuality confers power to men which, in a circular way, motivates them to take up the position of sexual conqueror (Hollway, 1984: 251). Moral and legal restraints on sex and even rape are readily suspended in wartime, since under extreme stress such behaviour is deemed to be 'only natural'. This trope of uncontrollable male sexuality and the practices of military male sexuality reinforce each other, constituting a cohesive 'discursive practice' as was clearly the case within the Imperial Japanese Army during the war.

Based on biological determinism, the universality of the existence of military brothels is emphasised in the Japanese neo-nationalists' statements on the 'comfort women' system. They claim that military brothels are normal facets of military life in wartime and there was nothing especially cruel or unusual about the case of the Japanese military (Fujioka, 1996; Hosaka, 1996: 65; Kusaka, 1996; Hata, 1996a). An outspoken neo-nationalist, Hosaka Masayasu (1996: 66–67), contends that the Japanese soldiers of WWII were human beings who needed sexual outlets like any other military personnel, and also assumes an inevitable connection between the military and sex. Some have even gone so far as to rationalise rape in times of war. Another neo-nationalist author, Hata Ikuhiko (1996b), asserts that rape is bound to follow war, due to young soldiers' 'natural' needs for sexual outlets.

In defending the validity of the universal existence of military brothels, Japanese right-wing authors employ two tropes; that of an 'uncontrollable' male sexual desire and the role of women in fulfilling this 'need'. Right-wing authors, such as cartoonist Kobayashi Yoshinori, whose cartoons are widely read, acknowledge the existence of 'comfort women' for the Japanese military forces while expressing appreciation for the 'comfort' they gave Japanese soldiers (Kobayashi, 1998: 38). His assertion is essentially that the rape of women or their use in prostitution is 'natural' in war—an idea which legitimises using women in this way for colonial or national projects.

In contrast with Japanese nationalist narratives of legitimisation, Korean nationalists emphasise the Imperial Japanese Army's extreme cruelty. Rather than representing just another instance of the widespread phenomenon of military brothels located near military bases, the 'comfort women' system is considered unique in world history: 'The "comfort women" system, which was a contemporary form of sexual slavery, is a proof of the uniquely inhumane and cruel nature of the Imperial Japanese Army' (Kang, 1997: 36). However, the claim of the uniqueness of the 'comfort women' project as created by the Imperial Japanese Army needs to be supported with comparative evidence—what is it that makes the Japanese case unique in comparison with other military systems of sexual servitude? How does institutionalised prostitution for the British army in India (1858–1947) or for the Nazis in Third Reich Germany (1933–1945), and mass rape camps in Bosnia-Herzegovina (1992–1995) differ from the 'comfort women' system?

Assumptions of irrepressible male sexuality aside, the harsh circumstances of war were used to legitimise almost any sexual act on the part of a combatant. A majority of veterans with whom I spoke justified the existence of military brothels like the comfort stations by simply saying 'it was wartime'. Their remarks over-emphasised the exceptional nature of war, which has been used as a method for exempting individuals from responsibility or blame for sexual violence perpetrated against women. 'Before going to the war, we were good husbands, good fathers, good brothers. So why did we change so much in the war? The Forces were a prison' (Nishino, 1992 in Hicks, 1995: 53). Such narratives imply that war entailed insensitivity, and that force and violence against the women were forgivable offences.

In these narratives, sexual exploitation or even sexual violence was often rationalised by blaming the system rather than attaching any responsibility to individual soldiers. Yuasa argued that the soldiers never had any rights or opportunities to exercise their own will, or to refuse obedience during the war. The men were presented as victims of war who bore no responsibility for the things they were ordered to do.

> The Japanese government insists that comfort stations were set up in order to keep their soldiers from raping local peoples in the occupied areas. However, this explanation is to throw the responsibility or blame onto the soldiers (Yuasa, personal interview, 1996).

This social explanation of the harsh circumstances of war was put forward not only by the wartime military authorities and post-war Japanese right-wingers but also by most of the veterans I interviewed, including the progressive 'rehabilitated' group. This demonstrates a significant commonality pervading both biological and social assumptions regarding male sexuality and war.

One former officer, Miyamoto, even put forward the women's safety as an excuse for the involvement of the forces in the comfort station system: 'The forces protected the women's safety from street gangs, or from bribery by the local police' (personal interview, 1996). The systematic involvement of the military was further deemed necessary for protecting the women from exploitation at the hands of proprietors of military brothels or comfort stations, maltreatment from soldiers, or sexually transmitted diseases. Another justification put forward for recurrent sexual coercion in the comfort stations was that it had been carried out in the name of serving the nation, or the Emperor. When Yun Sunman, a 'comfort woman' victim/survivor, asked the Japanese why they were assaulting Korean girls, the soldiers responded by saying that they were working for the Emperor (Dolgopol and Paranjape, 1994: 79).

The 'comfort women' system was a site in which sexual violence was sanctioned, and the men were offered right of access to women's bodies as a tangible reward for their service—undertaken in conditions where there were limited tangible rewards and little opportunity for relaxation. Providing the soldiers' access to 'comfort women' was a priority of the military elite, because their power over the servicemen, disciplinary procedures and general management depended in part on the ability to act as a provider of sex as a reward. The establishment of comfort stations marks not so much an end to Japanese soldiers' rape of the local population, as it is a shift from unplanned, uncontrolled sexual assaults to institutionalised and sanctioned sexual violence.

Military Metaphors and Misogyny

Military metaphors abounded in descriptions of the encounters between the men and the 'comfort women'. The usage of military metaphor in sexuality is striking. Sex for men was imagined as an act of assault and conquest. The penis was an instrument of attack, like a gun. Before going out to visit a comfort facility, the soldiers were warned by officers, as Yoshioka (a former officer) instructed his subordinates:

> Wear a helmet when making an assault! Clean the muzzle after firing a rifle! Wearing a helmet means using a condom, and cleaning the muzzle means disinfecting one's private parts after you do your business (Yoshioka, personal interview, 1996) (Ahn, 2010: 215).

In this instruction to the soldiers, virile sexuality is a metaphor for military valour. Sexual intercourse as military assault is a metaphor further revealed in the name used for condoms: they were called *Totsugeki ichiban* which means 'Attack, Number One' (Nishino, 1992: 85, 88). Coarse or sexual military vernacular was commonly used to amplify misogynistic masculine identities, reinforcing the objectification of women in the process (Carroll and Hall, 1993: 20). An example of such linguistic practice was the use of the metaphor of 'tasting' women (Jûgun ianfu, 1992: 69), within which women were represented as 'tasty objects' to be consumed. These kinds of demeaning sexual metaphors which circulated in the army devalued women and celebrated aggressive, misogynistic masculinity (Ahn, 2010: 215).

Such expressions reveal the military's view of masculinity and sex, which was realised through lived military experiences. Beyond appearing in language, such violence often spilled over into the comfort stations. The men sometimes threatened the women with swords, bayonets and other weapons of war to get the service they wanted. Japanese military men's virility was often presented in the form of violence. While the sexualisation of violence and violent sexuality were not unique to the Japanese military, it was essential to its construction of military masculinity, and the men employed violence to obtain the 'service' they wanted from the 'comfort women'. Violence was widely employed as a necessary 'currency' among the men, not only in transactions with the women but also, as observed earlier, in behaviour towards their subordinates and the local population. The 'comfort women' endured not only forced sex, but sex routinely accompanied by violence. Grotesque and brutal acts ranging from lynching to whipping, cutting off body parts, cigarette burns, stabbing or shooting have been reported by former 'comfort women' and prisoners of war (Han'guk chŏngsindae, 1997: 62; Dolgopol and Paranjape, 1994: 89–90). Extraordinary examples of unthinkable behaviour come up in narratives, such as the consumption of human flesh or brains on either the grounds of lack of food, or in the mythical belief that this practice cured syphilis (Nishino, 1992: 73; Dolgopol and Paranjape, 1994: 130). Excessive levels of corporeal and vernacular violence at the comfort facilities were routine, remorseless, and normalised.

Masculine identity was affirmed by sadistic treatment, by subjecting women to pain. Others' pain might even be 'enjoyable' to the perpetrator. Chŏng Haksu, a victim/survivor, reported such a case:

> In Harbin, the men gang raped a Chinese woman and tortured her, and we were forced to watch it. In the end they threw a bucket of petrol and burned her. The men *enjoyed* the woman's pain. After that, we could not dare to resist (Han'guk chŏngsindae, 1995: 160).

Here, acting to deliberately inflict physical pain on the woman can be understood as a source of the men's amusement and a demonstration of their power. Violence and power were implicit in sexual practices at comfort stations. Inflicting pain through perpetrating violence onto the women gave the combatants a sense of exercising power as men. This was an act of oppression exercised by the relatively powerful against the relatively powerless.

Except for exercising male power and dominance, a further question to be explored is whether this kind of sexual violence carries any underlying sexual meaning for the men. Diane Scully points out that rape affords a sense of exercising both power and sexual pleasure (Scully, 1993: 234; MacKinnon, 1987). By contrast, in their work on the mass rape in Bosnia-Herzegovina, Folnegovic-Smalc and Seifert argue that rape, especially gang rape, is a manifestation of power, rage and dominance over a woman, and serves no sexual purpose (Folnegovic-Smalc, 1994: 175; Seifert, 1994: 55). The sexual nature of rape is repudiated in their work. However, in the 'comfort women' context, as far as it provides an outlet for sexual frustration as well as for the vulnerability of Japanese soldiers, it contains both aspects of misogynistic sexuality and colonial masculine power. Within this particular military framework of masculinity, sex is associated with violence against and contempt for women; even rape can be classed as sex and sex as rape.

However, a distinction can be drawn between the interpersonal and sanctioned violence of the battlefield and violent forms of sex, although it is possible to argue that they are connected and that the one may lead to the other. Not all Japanese soldiers who had engaged in acts of violence on the battlefield were cruel in their interpersonal and sexual relations with the 'comfort women'. It cannot be assumed that it is 'natural' or inevitable that violence in the battlefield would lead to violence against the 'comfort women'. It is possible to speculate that there was an element of deliberation in the design of a system of military resocialisation that linked these two dimensions of violence and sexuality.

If masculinity in its military form during this period entailed the view of (hetero) sex as a right to which soldiers as 'real men' were entitled, then a corollary of this view was that women were merely sexual objects for their gratification. Access to women was theirs by virtue of, and as evidence of, their status as 'real men' and members of the Japanese Army (Ahn, 2010: 215). In this context, masculine sexuality (which is a core component of military masculinity) is closely linked to a way of enacting male dominance while controlling and degrading women who were viewed as sexual objects. Sexualised military masculinity is therefore associated with misogyny and repudiates the feminine. This form of masculinity is anchored in the creation and perpetuation of female otherness.

The necessity that many soldiers felt to exert power through sexuality often provoked additional violence:

> Once there was a soldier who was in such a hurry to come that he ejaculated even before he had entered me. He was very angry, and he grabbed my hand and forced me to fondle his genitals. But it was no use, because he could not become erect again. Another soldier was waiting for his turn outside the room and started banging on the wall. The man had no choice but to leave, but before going out, he hit my breast and pulled my hair... Whenever the soldiers did not feel satisfied, they vented their anger on me (Henson, 1996: 65).

Such behaviour can be interpreted as not just the expression of violence against those lower in the hierarchy, but as an attempt to reinstate masculine identity through sexual activity, often in violent form. The derogatory term, *Chôsenpii* (a vulgar Japanese term for the 'vagina' of a Korean woman), marks a total devaluation of the women, who were reduced to representation by a sexual organ, and instrumentalised for sex. The implication of this term is that a woman's body carries both an ethnic/racial identity as Korean and a sexualised gender identity as a sex object. This misogynistic term reveals that the Korean 'comfort women' were viewed as the literal female embodiment of colonised Koreanness.

The Search for Comfort

Combatants faced physical and psychological hardships during the war, and considered access to the 'comfort women' as a type of reward for their struggles. In addition to the biological explanation of irrepressible male sexuality, the men listed social or psychological factors that led them to visit the comfort stations, including feelings of vulnerability, frustration, fear or anxiety. The former military doctor, Yuasa, observed: 'They [the soldiers] must have felt no hope as they were in danger on the front lines of a battlefield, and were quite often blamed and beaten by their seniors' (personal interview, 1996). Another veteran confirmed that 'sex at a comfort station could enable one to forget imminent death' (Jûgun ianfu hyakutôban, 1992: 69). Staring into the face of impending death must have been one of the men's most vulnerable moments. It is reported that the soldiers were particularly desperate in seeking emotional outlets through contact with the women towards the end of the war, when death appeared to be the inevitable outcome (Dolgopol and Paranjape, 1994: 128 in Ahn, 2018: 10).

Some sought spaces to avoid this vulnerability through brutal behaviour, or spaces to express vulnerability via emotional support derived from human contact. Soldiers thus displayed two contradictory attitudes towards the women when facing death: one more violent and the other more generous (Han'guk chŏnsindae, 1993: 53, 1997: 46–47). In extreme cases, there were also some soldiers who forced 'comfort women' to commit suicide alongside them. Song Sindo (1922–2017) was stabbed in the side of the chest by a desperate soldier who tried to force her to accompany him in committing suicide (Kawata, 1993: 119 in Yoshimi, 1995b: 151).

Contrary to the image portrayed by hegemonic military masculinity, the actual emotional states of the military men could be fragile. John Tosh (2004) and Lynne Segal (2008: 30–33) have discussed the psychological burdens war places on men, such as trauma and vulnerability, as well as the physical burdens of injury and death (Ahn, 2018: 10). In fact, former 'comfort women' observed that when facing the prospect of death in battle, rather than expressing eagerness to die for the imperial nation, the men displayed vulnerability: 'They were so scared to go to fight that they wept and cried when they were with the women' (Han'guk chŏngsindae, 1993: 46, 75). On the battlefields, the men were basically combat ammunition. Though they could gain a sense of power from killing enemies and terrorising villagers where they advanced or occupied, they were at all times susceptible to injury and death.

Under these circumstances, the 'comfort women' were effectively vessels for the release of soldiers' stress before and after combat. The men in uniform even expressed a sense of euphoria relating to the women when the battles were over: 'The times when we would be holding down our penises as we ran [to the comfort station] were when we had just come back from a long battle jumping for joy and we headed immediately over there....' (Yoshimi, 1995b: 74). Following battle, the men wished to be freed from the stress of having walked the line between life and death.[19] Yuasa confirmed that the soldiers 'felt liberated and got a sort of catharsis at comfort stations' (Yuasa, personal interview, 1996).

The servicemen reported that through interactions with the 'comfort women', they felt their humanity restored and a sense of normalcy attained in the midst of war, stating: 'It was not only sex, but also the chance to share many things... chatting about one's life before the war and one's family' (Hayakawa, personal interview, 1996) (Ahn, 2018: 10). As John Costello reports, wartime research has revealed that 'battle fatigue', or 'combat stress', is a major contributor in cases of mental breakdown (Costello, 1985: 135).[20] Therefore, the women were expected to provide not only sexual, but emotional, services as well. Women were taken to be both sexual objects and maternal figures whose purpose was to attend to the men's psychological well-being (Ahn, 2010: 225).

Many military men often sought a mother figure when faced with death, and soldiers including *Kamikaze* pilots of the *Tokkôtai*, Special Attack Forces, wrote extensively about their mothers in their diaries. A 'comfort woman' survivor recounted:

> When they [wounded soldiers] were dying, not one soldier said 'Tenno Heika Banzai!' (Long live his majesty, the Emperor!). They would look at pictures of their mothers or their wives, and say, weeping, 'Mother, I may die. If I die, let us meet again at Yasukuni Shrine'.[21]

The trope of 'maternal need' presents an image of the men as suffering children in need of motherly 'comforting'. In his diary, *Kamikaze* pilot Hayahi Ichizô wrote about his mother, disclosing his agony about the thought of separating from her permanently at death, and his search for comfort in the hands of a caring mother:

> I will die with dignity as a soldier... Nevertheless, Mother, I am sad. When you are sad, please cry. I too will cry; let us cry together to our hearts' content.... *I still want to be spoiled by you...* I wish I could see you once more. *I want to be held in your arms and sleep...* (Ohnuki-Tierney, 2006: 173).

Given the prevalence of such sentiments among the military men, and the ways in which they were reported to have interacted with the 'comfort women', it was no accident that the term 'comfort' was applied to them.

The comfort stations provided a safe environment where men could not only affirm their masculine subjectivities as aggressive, violent and sexualised warriors, but also display their vulnerability. During a public conference on 13 May 2013, Toru Hashimoto, the mayor of Osaka, described the 'comfort women' system in such terms, arguing that:

> When soldiers are risking their lives by running through storms of bullets, and you want to give these emotionally charged soldiers a rest somewhere, it's clear that you need a comfort women system.[22]

The women were used to provide a space for the expression of both masculine aggressiveness and feminine submissiveness inculcated in the military men. First of all, the soldiers could retrieve a feeling of masculine power lost within the context of forced obedience and submissiveness towards their military superiors, through which their masculinity may have been damaged. From the perspective of Japanese military men, the environment at the comfort stations was different from that of the battlefields. The soldiers were not in danger or under threat of death in the comfort stations. In this intimate space, they could control the women and re-establish their sense of agency as brave warriors. The 'comfort women' provided a safety valve for the effects of the extreme regimentation to which the soldiers were subjected (Ahn, 2010: 227).

The women were not only one-dimensional sexual objects, but also functioned as a welcome target on which to safely project the recruits' own frustrations or rage. The soldiers retrieved a specifically masculine subjectivity in their relations with the 'comfort women' through sexual objectification and dominance of the women. Therefore, the paradox of simultaneous masculinisation and feminisation in the military could be reconciled at the comfort stations.

Within the punitive, hierarchical military system, the women could serve simultaneously as inferiors, onto whom oppression could be safely transferred, and as sources of 'comfort' (Ahn, 2010: 224–225). This mirrors the way in which young children direct feelings of both frustration and dependency towards their mother. The violence, frustration and combat stress suffered by the soldiers were redirected and/or released onto the 'comfort women', who had to play a subordinate, and at the same time a 'comforting', role at the very bottom of the hierarchical, gendered military system.

The trope of woman as a sexual object for 'uncontrollable' male sexual need, as noted before, can be seen to have existed alongside the trope of woman as provider of 'maternal care'. The whole practice of the comfort system draws on two tropes: the trope of uncontrollable male sexual need, and the trope of women's 'natural' maternal instincts utilised to attend to the men's needs for 'maternal comforts' under the stress of war. Both of these needs were invoked in the rationalisation of the 'comfort women' system. These rationalisations feed into the paradoxical juxtapositioning of masculinisation and feminisation in the resocialisation of soldiers for military life, and the way that this is articulated within the sexual division of labour of the Japanese family system, as well as with the hierarchies of rank, age and class. A hierarchy of brutal discipline placed the men in three male familial roles: as stern and powerful 'fathers' of children; as sexual 'possessors' of wives/women's bodies, and as 'young children' in relation to caring mother-figures. All of these aspects of the familial model were involved in the construction of military masculinity. The trope of women's maternal instincts became most effective as social forces when they were embedded in everyday practices in the military. Hence the concept of 'discursive practices' as practices establishing militarist masculinity, but also enacting certain ideas and making them seem more true. In this way, the 'comfort women' system could be said to have promoted the war through a complex articulation with patriarchal family positionings.

Paradoxes and Complexities

The practices employed to create loyal subjects of the imperial nation, and the creation of hegemonic masculinity did not follow consistent trajectories, but were defined by paradoxes and complexities. This section details the inherent complexities of these patterns. Firstly, fluctuations in the identities of the soldiers within Japan's totalitarian regime can be witnessed in the complex ways in which they reacted to everyday army life: compliance, consent, inaction and resistance.

The soldiers played an important role as members of the Imperial Japanese Army or Navy which was at the 'core' of supporting the regime in waging total war for colonial expansionism (Ahn, 2010: 227). Tsurumi points out that 'no peasant-soldier raised any doubt about why he had to die for the Emperor, any more than he questioned why he had to work to support his parents, wife and children. Both duties were simply taken for granted' (Tsurumi, 1970: 133). One consequence of intensive military resocialisation was the production of self-sacrificing, obedient and loyal 'warriors'. The imperial expansionist project relied on the internalisation of compulsion to such an extent that socialised individuals would feel that they were acting of their own accord.

Many soldiers, in a sense, complied and collaborated with the totalitarian regime, believing that their role as the 'core' of the regime entitled them to benefits, tangible or intangible rewards or power (Ahn, 2010: 228). *Kamikaze* pilot, Hayashi Ichizô, displayed his duty of patriotism in his final letter (1945) to his mother from Wonsan Air Base, Korea:

> Mother, I am a man. All men born in Japan are destined to die fighting for the country. You have done a splendid job raising me to become an honourable man [rippana otoko].... I will do a splendid job sinking an enemy aircraft carrier. Do brag about me (Ohnuki-Tierney, 2006: 173).

His attitude when facing imminent death in a suicidal bombing demonstrates unwavering support for the totalitarian regime.

However, such sentiments may have weakened towards the end of the war. Some military men began to show scepticism about the purpose of the war and the meaning of their deaths. As the war dragged on, the number of deserters from the army rose. Such actions could potentially have had serious repercussions, including military trials for treason. Very few soldiers risked direct resistance, and negative feelings were usually expressed through the neglect of official duties or seeking temporary relief from stress in the form of alcohol, opium and/or sex. Matsunaga Tatsuki, *Kamikaze* pilot in China during the war, wrote in his wartime diary:

> Let me jot down the truth about life on the base in north China. Daily life at our post consists of drinking and talking about our longing for home—every day. Officers spend all night visiting prostitutes and playing mahjong. Enlisted men seek momentary pleasure, while counting the days [before they are] released from the army... (Matsunaga and Matsunaga, 1968: 166–167 in Ohnuki-Tierney, 2006: 156).

Ohnuki-Tierney's (2006) analysis of *Kamikaze* diaries and written correspondences demonstrates that some student soldiers wrote heartbreaking private texts in which they expressed their anguish and fear, reluctance to die and yearning for their families. Despite the state propaganda used to indoctrinate the Emperor's subjects and intensive military resocialisation, apparently not all men in uniform were fully persuaded that death for the state was a worthy cause.

Nevertheless, Japanese men, whatever their status, were expected to be ready to die for their nation with a samurai spirit. Yoshioka, a former officer, confirmed this: 'Whoever he was, if he was a Japanese man, he had to die for his country during the war. When I was conscripted, I was prepared myself to die. No other path to choose, if he was a Japanese' (personal interview, 1996) (Ahn, 2010: 228–229). They might have found themselves in a battlefield scenario where the only option open to them was either death or suicide. For some soldiers, the delusion that death for the state was of the utmost importance was self-inflicted, as *Kamikaze* pilot, Matsunaga observed:

> But come the day of battle, they [the soldiers] meet their death instantly. Then suddenly all become Japanese 'deities'… With such ease they believe that they are brave soldiers to protect their country. They pride themselves in believing 'No ancestral land without us.' It is just cheap sentimentalism…. By comforting themselves in this way, they are spared from regretting the waste of their youth (Matsunaga and Matsunaga, 1968: 169–170 in Ohnuki-Tierney, 2006: 157).

Whether by way of self-delusion or coercion, for the soldiers there might have been no other choice than participating in the war and finding a way to come to terms with the sacrifice of one's life at the front, particularly towards the end of the war. Fujiwara argues that the patriotic identity of the soldiers was forcibly imposed. He writes that 'the army was based on orders, force and coercion, by which the soldiers had to submit and became slaves, instead of voluntary involvement in the defence of their nation' (Fujiwara, 1977: 28). Fujiwara's hypothesis is supported by some testimonies of Japanese veterans such as Yuasa:

> So-called brutal war crimes were rewarded as bravery in the name of patriotism. The brutal behaviour of Japanese troops including myself was committed because of deceit and force by the state power of the Japanese Emperor System (tennôsei) (Yuasa, personal interview, 1996).

In this sense, Japanese military men were to some extent invisible victims who were mobilised, controlled and victimised under a totalitarian regime through violence and propaganda. On men's positionality in war, some works such as those of Connell and Tylee, posit that the men may have also been victims. Connell proposes that 'men have been the main actors of war as well as the primary victims' (Connell, 1992: 176), while Tylee notes that both men and women are depersonalised in militaristic societal contexts (Tylee, 1988: 205–209). These views seem to focus on a single aspect of men's experiences in war. As 'men', and even 'soldiers' do not constitute a monolithic category, the costs and the outcome of the war are bound to be unevenly distributed, to a large extent along the lines of class and an individual's position in the military hierarchy. Hence, it might be conceded that Japanese military men could have been assailants and beneficiaries as well as victims. Considering this situation, there were both similarities and differences in experience between the rank and file soldiers and the 'comfort women'. The forced submission and humiliation of soldiers by their superiors invites comparison with the experience of the 'comfort women' in their relations with soldiers. There seem to be some similarities in the manner in which military authorities and the imperial state set out to control and regulate both the women and the soldiers. However, such an acknowledgement should not overshadow the fact that though the men may have been victimised, they also stood to receive tangible or intangible benefits and rewards, especially in the case of victory.

Conceptualisations of the warriors as being just as much victims as the women they victimised risk obscuring the men's tendency to victimise others when acting out destructive forms of masculinity.

Becoming a violent and brave warrior eventually leads men to danger or injury, and in some cases results in even death or long-lasting mental disorders. This is a self-destructive aspect of military masculinity and it is also destructive towards others, like the 'comfort women', whose bodies were violated. However, the impact of war was qualitatively and intensely different in terms of how the particular ways of colonial and gendered domination affected the lives of the 'comfort women'. One of the most striking differences is that the soldiers, unlike the women, did not face life-long social stigmatisation following the war.

The solidiers' multi-layered postion of agency, coercion and consent remains open for further discussion. As Jie-Hyun Lim (2010) points out, among those who do consent, consent itself is a multi-layered experience ranging from forced participation, coerced consent, passive conformity, self-mobilisation and internalised coercion to voluntary consensus. The boundary between coercion and consent is blurred here. There must be a two-sided process involving the shifting balance between coercion and consent to self-sacrifice in the men's subjectivity. Japanese soldiers might have been forced to fight on the battlefield and/or to prepare themselves to endure hardships and self-sacrifice on behalf of the imperial nation, even to the point of laying down their lives 'willingly'. Fujiwara's (1977) argument of forcibly imposed patriotic identity begs the question of whether the soldiers managed to retain and exercise their own agency or if they were only socially determined to perform the role of patriots. For some, in particular for the *Kamikaze*, pilots of the *Tokkôtai* forces, their active involvement in the so-called 'Holy War' for Japan's imperial expansion emerged from rational calculations carried out to present their deaths as honourable: 'We were ready to die anyway, so to choose to die as a suicidal attacker was a genuine expression of our youthful pride to make our death most meaningful' (Ueyama, 1964: 2–3 in Tsurumi, 1970: 136). Yuki Tanaka (2005) convincingly argues that the *Kamikaze* fought out of a combination of loyalty to their country and family, solidarity with fellow pilots, and a fear of appearing irresponsible or cowardly in front of the nation. He explains that the defence of one's mother in one's hometown was the most basic—almost instinctive—reason used in rationalising a cadet's death as a *Kamikaze* pilot (Ahn, 2010: 230). One might have initially believed the rationale given for the warfare, but later have experienced disillusionment with the propaganda surrounding the imperial war. The complexity of soldiers' shifting range of experiences as assailants, beneficiaries and/or those who conformed to the totalitarian regime, as well as being victims of the total war system, needs to be considered. Thus, monolithic, non-contradictory and unitary concepts of gender and national subjectivity cannot accommodate the complexity of self-subject positioning that took place both within and against totalitarian contexts (Ahn, 2010: 230–231).

Furthermore, the paradoxical juxtaposition of masculinisation and feminisation coexisted in the resocialisation processes the soldiers underwent as a part of military life. Reconciliation of this paradox was enacted by placing the 'comfort women' in a dual feminine position as sexual objects and as 'maternal comforters'. The soldiers' perception of the 'comfort women' has multiple facets. They could displace and project their own emotions onto the 'comfort women' by constructing the women as their 'comforters', like their mothers or lover, or, conversely view/treat them as sub-human 'whores'. The soldiers' contradictory feelings of contempt and intimacy towards the women, which will be explored in the following chapter, are signified in accounts of both 'comfort women' victims/survivors and Japanese veterans.

Moreover, colonial supremacy, based on racial hierarchy, placed the women in a contradictory position whereby they offered complex interactions through which the soldiers could heal their wounded masculinity while maintaining their colonial superiority. In this process, a paradoxical role of the 'comfort women' involved bolstering masculinity through affirming manhood and concurrently endangering it through the transmission of venereal diseases. It is also interesting to note that the comfort stations served two paradoxical and entirely opposite functions: relief from and reproduction of aggressiveness and cruelty. In this context, sexuality was used in both regulating and expressing the aggressive aspects of masculinity.

The military enacted a regime of sexual and identity regulation; the consequences of which demonstrate multiple paradoxes and complexities. This regime served to regulate the Japanese armed forces themselves, ensuring that the soldiers could be continuously sent back to the battlefields. The support the 'comfort women' system provided for the war effort has been recognised in Japanese military documents, and confirms the military's dependency on women. The system was considered an important component of the regime: the women were one of the main incentives the military authorities used to awaken and reinforce the masculine colonial power of the military men. Cynthia Enloe draws attention to this kind of military dependency on women for affirming men's masculinity (Enloe, 1988: 214). A military form of masculinity among the Japanese soldiers was supported by, and constructed in relation to, the roles imposed on the Korean 'comfort women' (Ahn, 2010: 226), as will be further investigated in the following chapter.

In summary, military forms of masculinity are paradoxical, incorporating as they do not only violence, destructiveness, sexualisation and hierarchy but also self-sacrifice and obedience. Resocialisation was important in the army, and allowed for the simultaneous processes of masculinisation and feminisation to produce both aggressive and submissive aspects within military masculinity. To this end, promoting and regulating male sexuality was crucial for gendering the military and assisting the Japanese war project. The particular form of military masculinity generated in Japan at this time lay behind the creation of the 'comfort women' system; a system that was used to reinforce military masculinity. The men's masculinity—produced, damaged or reproduced within hierarchical military practices of power—was thus always shifting in line with the chain of command. The self-positioning of the military men during the war was not fixed but fluctuated between compliance, conformity, consent, inaction, calculation, resistance and opposition. If the temporality and spatiality of their shifting positions are taken into consideration, it is difficult to draw a clear-cut line between 'forced' and 'voluntary' engagement with the totalitarian state programme (Ahn, 2010: 230). Gender and colonialism were embedded in both the versions of masculinity imposed on the servicemen and the versions of femininity imposed on the 'comfort women'. Thus, the following chapter investigates the reshaping of womanhood in the service of colonialism, and particularly of images of the women as 'promiscuous', 'submissive' and 'inferior'.

Notes

1 I do not intend to discuss all extant masculinities in WWII Japan, but look only at the masculinities apparent within the Japanese Army. Though Japan's defeat resulted in sweeping changes to this military masculinity, this book is concerned with the earlier, wartime period.

2 *Kokusaku kenkyukai shuho*, 18 April 1942 in Beasley 1987: 192, 244–245.

3 *Hantojin* means literally people from the peninsula of Korea.

4 *Chôsenjin* means literally 'people from Korea', but it is a derogatory term for Koreans. It is a nuanced term similar to English colloquial expressions such as Paki for Pakistani, Paddy for Irish or Chink for Chinese.

5 During the war, white rice was considered good quality rice and was only available for the rich and those of high status. The vast majority of Koreans had to eat brown rice mixed with other grains.

6 *On* is translated by Ruth Benedict as 'indebtedness' (Benedict, 1946: 98–113). However, Tsurumi criticises Benedict's understanding of it, stating that *on* is better understood as obligation resulting from receiving benevolence from one's superior (Tsurumi, 1970: 93).

7 Tojo Hideki, Army Minister, *Senjinkun* (Field Service Regulations), Tokyo: The Army Ministry, 1941 (reprinted by Boei mondai kenkyukai, Tokyo, 1972) in Cook and Cook, 1992: 164.

8 The pamphlet titled 'The outline for establishing population growth policy' issued in 1942, clearly presents Japan's motherhood politics during the war. See Uno, 1993: 300; Miyake, 1991.

9 On Japanese women's participation in the colonial endeavour, see for example Ryang, 1998.

10 On familial ideology in Japanese society, see Tadashi (1989) and Iizuka (1950).

11 The family-state structure of the Meiji state first took shape in the 1880s, when family-state ideology advocated the merging of the individual stem family with state power and cast the Emperor as the great father of his subjects. This ideology was reflected in both the Meiji Constitution (1889), which defined Japanese people as subjects of the Emperor, and the Imperial Rescript on Education (1890), which taught schoolchildren filial piety and loyalty to the state (Miyake, 1991: 270; Nishino, 1992: 145–146 in Ahn, 2010: 231).

12 The Emperor was simultaneously established as semi-divine father to the national community as well as the head of state (Weiner, 1995: 449).

13 *SEATIC* (Southeast Asia Translation and Interrogation Center) *Air Bulletin*, No. 131, 28 April 1945: 33.

14 I am aware that there are overlaps between traits of masculinities and femininities, and that gender stereotypes are too simplistic to encompass the complexities of constructions of masculinity and femininity in specific cultural contexts. However, in my framework I have fixed the oppositions of stereotypical masculinity and femininity at a theoretical level to demonstrate the interdependence of these

concepts and their contrast, and to show how gender is realised through the 'comfort women' system (Ahn, 2010: 232).

[15] Nakayama, Tadanao, 'Manmô no tabi (3), Tôyô', November 1933: 143 in Yoshimi, 1995b: 47.

[16] Konsei dai 14 ryodan shireibu (14th Mixed Brigade Headquarters). 'Eisei gyômu jumpô', report from March 1933, Kokuritsu kôbunsho kan (Japanese National Archives) in Yoshimi, 1995b: 47.

[17] One veteran made a comment in reference to the fact that some of the surviving 'comfort women' have been asking the Japanese government for reparations, saying that 'the women are materially minded nowadays just as they were in those days' (Senkyûhyakunanajûni, 1992: 303).

[18] Hayao Torao, 1939, *Senjoni okeru tokushugenshŏ to sonotaisaku* (Unique Phenomena On Battlefields And Measures To Cope With These Problems) in Yoshimi, 1992: 231–232.

[19] Koromo dai 3040 butai kinen jigyô jikkô iinkai, 1997: 210–211 in Yoshimi, 1995b: 74.

[20] As for the Japanese soldiers' mental disorders during WWII, see Janice Matsumura (2004). 'State Propaganda and Mental Disorders: The Issue of Psychiatric Casualties among Japanese Soldiers during the Asia-Pacific War', *Bulletin of the History of Medicine*, 78(4): 804–35.

[21] Testimony of a former South Korean 'comfort women', Kimiko Kaneda (South Korea), http://www.awf.or.jp/e3/oralhistory-00.html.

[22] The Korean Council for the Women Drafted for Military Sexual Slavery by Japan 2016, Report submitted to Committee on the elimination of discrimination against women (CEDAW), https://tbinternet.ohchr.org/Treaties/CEDAW/Shared% 20Documents/JPN/INT_CEDAW_NGO_JPN_22816_E.docx.

Chapter 4

Contested Bodies: The Making of Military 'Comfort Women'

T his chapter elaborates on discussions introduced in previous chapters on how gender, national identity and sexuality have been involved in the construction of patriarchal colonial relationships. It is arguable that both gender and national identity were fundamental to the construction of Japanese colonialism, and that the 'comfort women' system helped to produce and reproduce Japan as an imperial state wielding power over the lives of people in its colonies and occupied areas. In particular, the maintenance of the wartime military system depended on the circulation of these concepts of military colonial masculinity and a binary concept of womanhood, 'virtuous' versus 'defiled'. The regulation of sexuality and identities, particularly in the context of the comfort station system, was a crucial means through which Japan's wartime militarism was constituted and maintained.

The following sections look into the making of Korean 'comfort women' through the comfort station system, exploring the way female colonial body and identity politics are constructed through contextualising the victims'/survivors' own narratives of their lived experiences in terms of body, sexuality and subjectivity. A strong focus is placed on exploring the interactions between the micro-level subjective experiences of 'comfort women' and the macro-level forces of masculine colonial policy structure. Through the daily practices prevalent at comfort stations during the war, the construction of these women's bodies and the subjectivity involved with classifying them as 'comfort women', or prostitutes, in the binary opposition between a respectable body and a sexualised one can be discerned. Discussion of complex relationships between the soldiers and the women is followed by setting out the legacy of the victims'/survivors' ordeal during the post-war period. These intricate connections between Japanese colonialism, Korean nationalism and pre-existing concepts of Confucian womanhood in constructing the 'comfort women's' bodies andsubjectivity during and after the war are also explored. The end of this chapter turns to the question of the women's multiple positionalities as both victims and actors facing persistent sexual, physical and emotional exploitation in their interactions with Japanese military personnel during WWII.

Sexual Initiation

Since 'comfort women' had no official status in the Japanese military, procured women and girls were brought to military brothels (or comfort stations) in transports designed for carrying military supplies, such as the tail compartments of trains, or the hulls of ships. When allocated to units of the Japanese forces, their names were recorded on military documentation under the headings 'distribution of supplies' and 'receipt of supplies' (Nishino, 1992: 53, 67). This practice discloses the fact that the women were considered as 'military supplies' provided to the military men as 'stock' required for carrying on the war. Ships transporting them to the far off Pacific Islands even carried notes with a warning 'not for onboard use' (Jûgun ianfu, 1992: 57). Under these circumstances, the women were not only turned into commodities for sexual services, but their bodies literally became the property of the military, thereby depriving them of their humanity.

Upon her arrival at a comfort facility for soldiers, coercion undoubtedly played a role in the sexual initiation a woman was forced to endure. The initiation of a 'comfort woman' usually took the form of rape at her first destination. Kim Ŭllye (1926–2008), who was taken to Nanking, recalled the dreadful day:

> On the second day [of arrival] I was taken into an officer's room. For the first time he penetrated me, stole me. First I

> was frozen with fear and then started battling against him,
> but nothing helped... It was so sore (personal interview,
> 1995).

The women must have been utterly terrified in such situations. Furthermore, a lack of knowledge about sexual intercourse is often revealed in the women's narratives: one victim/survivor, Ch'oe Myŏngsun (pseudonym), describes her first experience: 'something was entering me, and at first I thought it was his knee' (personal interview, 1992).

The forcible sexual initiations that occurred when a woman first arrived at a military comfort station were frequently perpetrated by high-ranking officers (Mun P'ilgi, personal interview, 1992; Dolgopol and Paranjape, 1994: 95), as only high-ranking officers were given access to virgins. Such a practice was conceptualised as allowing men to have the first 'taste' of these women (Jûgun ianfu, 1992: 69 in Ahn, 2018: 5). Furthermore, access to a virgin was commonly thought to bring good luck on the battlefield and act as a talisman for the avoidance of death in battlefield (Hicks, 1995). Hence, superstitious beliefs about virgin bodies were implicit in sexual initiations and almost magical properties were generally attributed to a 'pure' virgin body.

In some cases, sexual initiation took the form of gang-rape, leaving the girls physically and mentally devastated, and consequently serving to reduce any further resistance: 'After the officer had finished, the soldiers began to come into her room and raped her repeatedly' (Dolgopol and Paranjape, 1994: 91). Following this initiation, the women were usually forced to serve rank and file soldiers (Hwang Kŭmju, personal interview, 1995 in Ahn, 2018: 5). The value of the 'virginity' of young girls was lost when they had been more frequently 'used' by soldiers:

> During the first year I [Hwang Kŭmju], like all the other
> Korean girls with me, was ordered to service high-ranking
> officials, and as time passed and as we were more and more
> used, we served lower-ranking officers (UN Commission on
> Human Rights, 1996a: 14).

Strict military hierarchy in the barracks was therefore maintained in defining the men's 'right to sex', as noted in Chapter 3.

The women themselves often interpreted these sexual initiations in terms of 'having lost virginity' or virtue, and considered the experiences very shameful. The cultural code of Confucianism served to intensify this ideology of chastity in the women's minds. The 'castration and theft metaphors', described in Sharon Marcus's work (1992: 398)— the understanding of the sexual organs as objects that can be taken or lost—is graphically illustrated in their descriptions of the initiation. These initiations have been described by the 'comfort women' as 'taking my virginity' (Han'guk chŏngsindae, 1993: 36), 'tearing away virginity' (Dolgopol and Paranjape, 1994: 105; Han'guk chŏngsindae, 1993: 203), 'hurting body' (Han'guk chŏngsindae, 1993: 233). Such losses were considered to dissolve the self (Marcus, 1992: 398). The 'deprived' present themselves as 'the ruined', 'the dead' or 'finished' (Han'guk chŏngsindae, 1993: 219), since the occurrence of rape is evaluated in terms of the destruction of a self-defining chastity. The 'castration and theft metaphor' haunted the women through the whole of their lives, burdening them with lifelong senses of shame.

Routinised Sexual Violence

After the crisis of sexual initiation, being forced to have sex with the soldiers became an ongoing daily routine for the women. Sexual exploitation and violence became an ordinary aspect of everyday life. One typical sight at comfort stations was that of soldiers queuing up for sex, 'their trousers down and underpants already almost off' (Hwang Kŭmju, personal interview, 1995). Many soldiers began to undress outside the door and would come out of the rooms undressed (Dolgopol and Paranjape, 1994: 128). In such instances, each soldier completed intercourse quickly as the ones waiting for their turn were impatient, and they would bang on the doors and tell the occupant to hurry up.

The image of this scene looks very much like that of a queue for a toilet. In fact, in a wartime report written in 1939 by a military medical doctor, Tetsuo Asô (1939), the women were even directly referred to as 'sanitary public toilets' (Asô, 1993: 227). Sakamoto Takao, a right-wing Japanese historian, makes use of this connotation in order to argue against including references to the 'comfort women' in school history textbooks. More specifically, he states that it is not essential for a proper understanding of Japanese history to include references to changes in 'toilet structures' (Sakamoto, 1998: 39, 42–43 in Ahn, 2008a: 42). Referring to the 'comfort women' with such derogatory language (Yoshimi, 1995a: 222; Senda, 1978: 65) is an attempt to discredit their respectability. This metaphor of the women's bodies as being for 'sanitary use' represents them as objects available for public use. The use of such imagery exemplifies in graphic fashion the belief that men's sexual needs are as basic, and even as natural, as the need to defecate.

In the daily lives of the 'comfort women', the most common form of violence employed by the soldiers and military brothel managers or keepers was the use of beating as a means of controlling and subduing the women. When not compliant, the women were even more harshly beaten (Hwang Kŭmju, personal interview, 1995). There were also Korean managers of military brothels, who treated the women with equal violence. Hwang Suni (1922–2007) begrudged the vicious Korean brothel keeper where she was held during the war: 'though as the same Korean [the keeper], how badly he beat me since I was not willing to serve customers' (Han'guk chŏngsindae, 1999: 225). Beatings were routine at comfort stations:

> We were beaten almost every day. If we looked at the moon, we were hit as the soldiers asked what we were thinking of. If we talked to ourselves they hit us again, saying we must be swearing at them (Han'guk chŏngsindae, 1993: 102).

In some places, there were Korean soldiers among the 'customers'.[1] Mun Okchu (1924–1996) encountered a Korean man at the comfort station where she worked:

> One day, a soldier came into my room sobbing, and when I asked why, he said that he was a Korean and had been drafted to the Marusa Unit.... Koreans in the unit brought tickets and condoms and used them just like the Japanese soldiers (Han'guk chŏngsindae, 1993: 157–158).

Kang Muja related the story of two Korean soldiers in her room at the comfort station, who pitied her and spent their time talking instead of making her serve them (Han'guk chŏngsindae, 1997: 57). She hinted that some Korean soldiers may not have had sex with the 'comfort women', and may not have been as violent or brutal as their Japanese counterparts. While I have not come across any reference to violent conduct by Korean military personnel in any of the women's accounts, it would require further research to determine whether this was true of all the Korean combatants.

In the everyday life of comfort stations, women were subjected to various forms of sexualised humiliation and coercion, for example some women were forced to keep the men hard orally (Han'guk chŏngsindae, 1993: 39) and others suffered from genital stabbing, or having burning cigarettes placed on the pelvis (Han'guk chŏngsindae, 1993: 89; Chonggun wianbu, 1995: 6). The North Korean 'comfort women's' testimonial book (Chonggun wianbu, 1995) gives even more gruesome and graphic descriptions of the torture and violence the women were subjected to, such as being forced to eat the flesh of other 'comfort women'. Some of the most extreme forms of violence involved attempted murder, for example Mun Okchu and Yi Sangok (1922–2004) were stabbed with a sword by drunken soldiers (Mun Okchu, personal interview, 1992; Han'guk chŏngsindae, 1993: 174). Chŏn Kŭmhwa (1924–1994) recalled her life at a comfort station in China as being 'less than that of an animal' (personal interview, 1993). Ch'oe Myŏngsun (pseudonym) said that she was beaten so much that she seemed to lose her spirit—she just lay like a corpse, with her eyes open but not focused on anything (personal interview, 1992). In the routinised daily practice of various forms of violence, the women's humanity and individual integrity were denied, and the women were counted only in terms of their corporeal existence.

Elaine Scarry's discussion (1985) of the 'grammar' and logic of torture is relevant here. The point of torture is not just to destroy an enemy, or to force him to yield important information, but also to oblige him to testify to the power and superiority, the 'rightness', of the torturer and his cause. By violating and destroying the women's actual bodies and minds through repetitive sexual coercion, the power relationship between the colonial male and the colonised women was established and reinforced.

In the ordinary routines of everyday life established at comfort stations, the rhythm of violence inflicted on the women was influenced by the military schedule; expeditionary forces, active combat, moving camp and holidays. There was a time-bound pattern in the daily lives of the 'comfort women', punctuated by day and night, weekend and weekday, before battle and after battle, or when a military ship came into harbour and after the ship left. Oh Omok (1921–1999) confirmed how this pattern was determined by the military timetable: 'when the soldiers were away on an expedition it was quiet, but once they returned then again we had to serve lots of them' (Han'guk chŏngsindae, 1993: 88).

In addition, different patterns prevailed during weekends and weekdays. Most of the victims/survivors painfully recalled that they had to deal with harsher circumstances during weekends since greater numbers of soldiers frequented the comfort stations from 8 o'clock in the morning until midnight, or even overnight (Han'guk chŏngsindae, 1993: 113). The women often did not even get time to eat or to go to the toilet, so they ate meals lying on the bed while 'serving' the military men (Jûgun ianfu hyakutôban, 1992: 48) or defecated in their own rooms. Chŏn Kŭmhwa (1927–1997), whose Japanese name at the comfort station was Sumiko, had to eat, defecate and 'serve' the soldiers in the same room: 'The most difficult thing was when I needed to go to the toilet. There was no pot in the room. I had to ask for a pot. Ah.... it smelled [as the pot was not often taken out]' (personal interview, 1992).

Pak Sunae, who was in Rabaul in Papua New Guinea during the war, describes what weekends with the soldiers were like: 'On Sundays there were countless soldiers like ants. We wore something similar to a dress, but we couldn't be bothered to wear underpants. Down there [private parts] was swollen and sore' (Han'guk chŏngsindae, 1993: 246). Son P'anim, recalled that she felt like she was entering a slaughterhouse when weekends were approaching (Han'guk chŏngsindae, 1997: 69).

This weekend exhaustion of the 'comfort women' is confirmed by a Japanese veteran, Matsumoto:

> The woman I had on that day had already been very busy and served numerous soldiers that Sunday. When I entered her room, she seemed too exhausted even to sit up. She was almost falling asleep (Matsumoto, pseudonym, personal interview, 1996).

The men's cycles of exhaustion and recovery, work and leisure were thus inversely related to those of the women.

Changes to the intensity of violence occurred before and after battles, which seem to have had the effect of producing and subsequently releasing the men's military aggression (Ahn, 2010: 226). This pattern and the intensity of violence before and after combat were confirmed by some 'comfort women'. Some soldiers, who were just about to leave for combat, were gentle rather than violent with the women—especially when they anticipated their imminent death. Kim Tŏkchin (1921–2004, pseudonym) shared her experience of such encounters:

> The soldiers who were about to leave for combat were somewhat mild and a few of them would give us their loose change, saying it wouldn't be of use to them any longer.... some were weeping from feeling so scared to go fight (Han'guk chŏngsindae, 1997: 53).

Conversely, Hwang Kŭmju (1922–2013) recalls the opposite reaction: 'The men who were just about to go out in combat were particularly cruel. It was simply unbearable' (Han'guk chŏngsindae, 1993: 103; personal interview, 1995). As Nishino Rumiko, a Japanese author, reports, the military personnel were particularly aggressive when their comrades had been killed in battle. On the war front in China, some distressed Japanese soldiers killed on sight any Chinese person they spotted on the way back to their barracks after combat as their aggression and tension reached a peak. In such moments, sex with 'comfort women' was provided to release their aggression from its high point (Nishino, 1992: 77 in Ahn, 2010: 226). These differing accounts show that under similar circumstances of combat stress, soldiers could display two contradictory attitudes towards the women.

The gross sexual abuse was overlaid by the additional exploitation of the women's bodies as labourers. They were expected to undertake any kind of work needed on the war front, from sexual slavery to supplementary services, especially towards the end of the war. Examples of such services include: cleaning the military bases, washing military uniforms (Jûgun ianfu hyakutôban, 1992: 115), cutting and burning hay for camouflage (Han'guk chŏngsindae, 1993: 90, 142), receiving military training with a spear (Han'guk chŏngsindae, 1997: 177), carrying bullet boxes or bombs (Asian Women, 1996: 10; Han'guk chŏngsindae, 1997: 60), nursing wounded soldiers (Mun Okchu, personal interview, 1992; Dolgopol and Paranjape, 1994: 109, 114), welcoming soldiers back from expeditions (Kim Haksun, personal interview, 1992), making deliveries and serving the forces (Han'guk chŏngsindae, 1993: 88), entertaining troops by singing and dancing, making garters after 'serving' the soldiers (Mun Okchu, personal interview, 1992), washing condoms for reuse (Mun P'ilgi, personal interview, 1995), waving the men off to war, donating blood for the wounded soldiers (Sin, 1997: 383; Han'guk chŏngsindae, 1997: 95) and even spying (Jûgun ianfu hyakutôban, 1992: 115).

The use of the bodies of 'comfort women', for multiple functions as sexual slaves, cleaners, entertainers, and even to carry out paramilitary duties, can be seen as 'super-exploitation' in Blaunt's terms, which means exploitation to the point where continued labour is barely possible, and even in some cases going beyond that point (Blaunt, 1987: 165). The bodies of the women were 'used up' and, once they had outlived their 'usefulness', were discarded in the service of the Japanese war effort.

Endangered Bodies

The women endured bodily injury not only through the routinised violence discussed above, but also by way of disease and the unwanted pregnancy that often occurred. Their health was jeopardised by illnesses such as malaria (especially in Southeast Asia and the Pacific Islands), venereal diseases, malnutrition and physical exhaustion (Zainihon chôsen, 1992: 7). Mostly free of diseases when they were first taken to the comfort station, the women were at a high risk of catching venereal diseases from the soldiers. Syphilis and gonorrhoea reached epidemic proportions among the Japanese armed forces during the war. Consequently, the military authorities provided the comfort stations with condoms and emphasised the importance of sanitation. Yet despite these efforts, venereal diseases were rife among the 'comfort women', and infection sometimes resulted in death (Han'guk chŏngsindae, 1993: 89). Ebado, a Japanese veteran, reported that some of the soldiers who had venereal diseases forced the women to have sex without condoms as they believed that by transferring the disease to others they would be cured (personal interview, 1996).

Most of the accounts given by both the women and the Japanese veterans mention that after an initial check-up for diseases upon arrival, the women had to undergo compulsory, periodical genital examinations from the military doctors.[2] The physical condition of the women was regularly checked, in most cases on a weekly basis, and then reported to the military authorities. All of the women's names were listed in order to record and classify their medical states. The results were distributed to every regiment with ratings given for each woman (Dolgopol and Paranjape, 1994: 33; Mita Kazo, personal interview, 1996). However, this practice of regulation did little to check the spread of venereal diseases because of the sheer number of men with whom the women were forced to have sexual contact.

When the women caught diseases, they were sometimes condemned for being 'polluted', and held responsible for the infection and its spread. As Chŏn Kŭmhwa pointedly asked, 'why were we [the 'comfort women'] blamed for disease when the [Japanese] soldiers were the ones who transferred it to us?' (personal interview, 1994). The image of the women's bodies as sources of 'pollution' led to the view that the women were contaminating the soldiers with the diseases which might endanger their virility.

Treatment for venereal diseases was almost as painful as the infection. A former military doctor, Yuasa Ken, reported that shot 'No. 606', an antibiotic containing mercury and arsenic (Salvarsan) administered to cure sexually transmitted diseases, was very strong and had severe side effects (personal interview, 1996). Yi Yŏngsuk, a victim/survivor, points out that attempts at protecting the women from sexually transmitted diseases were not for the sake of the women's well-being (Han'guk chŏngsindae, 1993: 65) but were, in fact, aimed at preserving the soldiers' strength for combat.

The military authorities were primarily concerned with maintaining the survival and health of the 'comfort women's' bodies — as sexual and in some cases labouring bodies — for as long as they could be useful to the war effort. The women held little value outside their usefulness as sexual bodies, and consequently only the reasonably healthy and disease-free were regarded as useful. When the women caught a serious disease which was untreatable or incurable, they were sold on to civilian brothels, for example in Indonesia and China, or were simply left to die (Jûgun ianfu hyakutôban, 1992: 108). The women were in effect treated as disposable 'objects', to be discarded when no longer useful for 'serving' the soldiers (Hwang Kŭmju, personal interview, 1995). Dead bodies were often cast aside without proper burial or ceremony.

> Those who already became weak without having proper meals turned out to be half dead after serving so many [soldiers]. Then the receptionist dragged her out... and installed a healthier woman in her room... When the shot didn't work any more, soldiers carted her away to the mountain. The dead body was dumped there and barely covered with grass (Han'guk chŏngsindae, 1993: 140–141).

Sexually transmitted diseases had lifelong effects on the women. According to the results of a health examination carried out for the 'comfort women' victims/survivors in South Korea in 1995 as a part of a health services initiative, 10 out of 35 survivors were diagnosed with syphilis originating from their comfort station days. In some cases, the disease was transmitted down to the next generation of the survivors.[3] Ha Pokhyang (1926–2001), who had contracted syphilis at a comfort station during the war, lamented the loss of two sons after birth as a result of the children having been infected via her in infancy (Han'guk chŏngsindae, 2001b: 265).

Pregnancy, also a risk under the circumstances of repeated sexual activity, made the women's lives even more difficult. Because their bodies were valued primarily as objects employable for sexual servitude, and not for their reproductive capacity, the military authorities did not welcome pregnancies or babies. One typical comment from the Japanese men was that 'we don't need *Chôsenjin*⁴ babies who will not give their loyalty to the Emperor' (Zainihon chôsen, 1992: 18). Korean blood was regarded with suspicion and seen as heralding treachery. The descendants of the 'comfort women' from this time period were regarded as 'contaminated' and responsibility for these children was denied by both Japan and Korea.

In most cases, when women fell pregnant, they were subjected to forced abortions by military medical staff (Yuasa, personal interview, 1996; Nishino, 1992: 94–95; Han'guk chŏngsindae, 1993: 52). These pregnancies were seen by the military authorities as 'a matter of the dignity of the Imperial Japanese Army' (Yuasa, personal interview, 1996). Undergoing an abortion in substandard medical facilities, with medicine in short supply, was an extremely hazardous affair, and some women died as a result of such high risk procedures (Yun Turi, personal interview, 1992). Hong Aejin, who remained in China after the war, spoke of her own experience of forced abortion when her pregnancy was discovered by the keeper of the comfort station and her entire womb was removed (Han'guk chŏngsindae, 1995: 48). In some cases, the women were not informed that they had been given a hysterectomy. Kim Poktong, who was taken to Manchuria during the war as a 'comfort woman', was not aware that the procedure had been carried out, even after the war. 'Without knowing about that [removal of her womb during the war], I was crazy to get pregnant, and went to a Buddhist monastery to pray, to get blessed by Samsin [a fertility goddess] and arranged a ritual…' (Han'guk chŏngsindae, 2001a: 212).

When it was too late to abort, pregnancy sometimes led to attempted suicide, as the women could not face the reality and stigma of being a single mother in such a precarious situation or feared what might await them upon their return home (Yun Turi, personal interview, 1992). In other cases, the women were sent to undisclosed areas in occupied territories (Senda, 1992a: 157). The whereabouts and fate of those women who were sent away remains unknown to this day. More often than not, the women's lack of knowledge, their youth and inexperience resulted in them having to give birth under circumstances similar to Midori's case:

> Midori, who was two years younger than me, became pregnant. Without knowing it, she kept on serving soldiers until her tummy became noticeably larger. It was too late, and she had to give birth. She then had to continue to work and had someone else look after the baby, but it died of sickness after just eight months (Han'guk chŏngsindae, 1993: 207).

Among these babies, like the child of Song Sindo who was pregnant twice at a comfort station in Wuchang, China, some were adopted by local Chinese families (Yang, 1995: 37). However, many children are reported to have died, and the location and fate of others remains unknown.

Menstrual cycles were simply disregarded at comfort stations. At some comfort stations, there was a regulation banning the women from contact with the combatants during their menstrual cycles (Allied Translator, 1945: 11). Nevertheless, many survivors have reported that they were required to continue 'serving' the soldiers even during menstruation. Some recall this as one of the most dreadful things they had to endure (Mun P'ilgi, personal interview, 1992). In addition to experiencing continuous abuse during their periods, they were faced with a serious lack of sanitary products, further depriving them of their dignity. Kim Haksun reported inserting self-made small cotton balls inside her vagina so that no blood leaked out. When cotton was not available, she had to cut cloth into small strips and roll this up to use instead (Kim Haksun, personal interview, 1992; Han'guk chŏngsindae, 1993: 39).

> We were given some sort of cotton wool to use during our monthly period. But the supply of cotton stopped after

> a year, and from then onwards we either stole someone
> else's sanitary towel as it was drying on the washing line
> or collected, washed and used gaiters discarded by the
> soldiers. If we were caught taking the gaiters, we would
> be beaten by the men; the soldiers saw this sort of thing as
> unlucky (Han'guk chŏngsindae, 1993: 101–102).

The soldiers' angry and violent reaction to menstrual blood reveals the prevailing myth about it portending death on the battlefield.

In misogynist thought, a virgin body is perceived to be 'pure', and a menstruating body 'polluted'. Ideas of pollution, of purity and danger, focusing particularly on the bodies of women, are commonplace across many cultures as Mary Douglas powerfully highlights in her book (Douglas, 1966). This idea of pollution and impurity can be found in the Japanese soldiers' objection to the usage of their personal equipment as substitute sanitary towels for the women. Women's bodies were considered to be capable of bringing both fortune and misfortune at the front, depending on whether they were viewed as either 'pure virgin' or 'polluted'.

'Defiled' Bodies: Prostitution

The 'comfort women' system imitated, in some respects, Japan's pre-war system of licensed prostitution. In fact, the organisation of everyday life in comfort stations was similar to that of brothels, with men allowed to choose their favourite woman from a line-up (Han'guk chŏngsindae, 1993: 65 in Ahn, 2008a: 40). In some comfort stations, each woman had an identifying nametag or number attached to the wall and the soldiers queued up in front of the room where the number plate they had chosen was hanging (Suzuki, 1992: 130 in Ahn, 2008a: 41).

Concerning payment, most of the military personnel paid for having sex—a system which can usually be observed in brothels. According to regulations presented in the 1945 Supreme Commander for the Allied Powers Research Report: Amenities in the Japanese Armed Forces, 50–60% of gross takings paid by the military men to the comfort stations were theoretically supposed to be allocated to the women (Allied Translator, 1945 in Ahn, 2008a: 40–41). However, most 'comfort women' testify that they were paid virtually no money. The costs of food, clothes, medicines and other daily necessities were charged to the women. If the women caught any sexually transmitted diseases, they also had to pay high sums for medical treatment (Jûgun ianfu hyakutôban, 1992: 43, 108).

Fees were determined by regulations and were primarily paid by means of tickets sold to the troops prior to their visit.[5] A victim/survivor, Kim Tŏkchin, recalled how this transaction operated:

> We collected these tickets brought by the soldiers and gave them to the Korean manager, who recorded them in his notebook each day. He promised to give us a fortune once Japan won the war, but we received no wages (Han'guk chŏngsindae, 1993: 53).

Yi Okpun recounts that the seal of the commanding officer was stamped on the ticket she had received from the soldiers who visited her (Han'guk chŏngsindae, 1993: 141). These accounts underline the fact that monetary transactions were exclusively between the proprietors of comfort stations and the military personnel (Ahn, 2008a: 41), and did not involve the women themselves.

In addition, in some areas it was common practice to retain a substantial part of their wages, if there were any, as part of a compulsory savings scheme (Yang, 1995: 35, 42). Part of these savings were used for military expenses, for example to contribute to buying military armaments (Han'guk chŏngsindae, 1997: 178). Pak Yŏni recalls that her income was put into a bank account and that she had trusted the saving scheme. However, after the war, the savings account book turned out to be just a sheet of paper (Han'guk chŏngsindae, 1997: 132). In 1992, victim/survivor Mun Okchu (1924–1996) claimed access to funds held in a military savings account which she had deposited in field post offices during the war, but her claim was not accepted by the Post Bank in Japan (Mun, 1996: 153, 206–210).

Rewards were counterbalanced with punishments in relation to the number of 'customers' served. Typical punishments were being beaten, confined, temporarily deprived of food or threatened with the prospect of being sold to a private brothel, notably in China. Pak Yŏni reports that the number of soldiers she 'served' was counted at the end of each day, and she was punished by the keeper of the comfort station when she had not 'served' enough men (Han'guk chŏngsindae, 1997: 125).

To further incentivise the women, a sense of rivalry and competition was created by grading or 'ranking' them according to the number of men 'served' per day or week. In some cases, as Pae Chokkan experienced, the women were 'awarded' ranks like those given to soldiers in accordance with the length of their stay in a comfort station and their productivity or 'performance'. Prizes and incentives such as a gold ring, better food, better treatment, sweets or 'promotion' to a higher ranking, were offered when they 'served' more men. Beauty contests were even held to enhance the women's 'performance' and to entertain the military men. At the unit where a survivor, Mun Okchu, was stationed, the military men voted for the two best contestants among the Korean and Japanese 'comfort women' (Sŏultae in'gwŏnsentŏ, 2018: 211).

Another victim/survivor, Pak Yŏni, confirmed the operation of a hierarchical system at the comfort stations: the newcomers had to be submissive to seniors who trained their subordinates how to 'serve' the men, for instance how to use condoms and how to clean themselves (Han'guk chŏngsindae, 1997: 124). Senior ranking women even had the authority to punish others of lower rank (Han'guk chŏngsindae, 1997: 177–178). Another influence on the women's hierarchical rankings was the rank of the military men whom they 'served'. Thus, the prevailing male military hierarchy was reproduced among the women, with the ranking of the men serviced transmitting prestige and hierarchy to the women with whom they were associated. Being connected with high-ranking officers in the military made a measurable difference in the daily lives of the women; a situation that will be further discussed later in this chapter.

The supposed function of the 'comfort women', as inscribed onto their bodies by the colonial power, was to provide 'comfort' for the military servicemen, and prostitution was a way to confine the women to this role. Here, it is worthwhile to draw on the idea of 'sexual scripts' as proposed by Gagnon and Simon (1973)—whereby sexual behaviour is perceived as something that is scripted; a 'sexual script' like the text of a play. Wendy Hollway (1984) brings this concept together with Michel Foucault's theoretical approach in her analysis of the 'sexual scripts' people use in their sexual interactions with one another. The idea of the scripts suggests that in order to follow one's script as directed, one requires a partner/co-actor who plays an appropriate supporting role. This concept also suggests the possibility of disrupting the script by not acting 'appropriately'. Sharon Marcus (1992) offers a contentious analysis of rape and anti-rape strategies by applying the concept of the 'sexual script' to the context of rape. She argues strategies such as verbal self-defence, physical retaliation or refusal to accept the rapist's body as overwhelmingly powerful, and can be interpreted as actions that are able to disrupt the rape script. Marcus's suggestion that rape can be prevented by one's refusal to accept the script of rape victim might be thought to be of limited value in the case of the 'comfort women', where extraordinary levels of serial sexualised violence become 'ordinary' matters of routine to daily life.[6] The women could only play the part of enslaved victim in this particular 'sexual script'. In such a constrained situation, the women were forced to act out the part allocated to them in another's script, and to be categorised as prostitutes by a patriarchal colonial power. At the same time, although sexual violence could not be wholly prevented, the women's nuanced attempts not to act out the pre-set scripts they were forced to contend with will be explored later in this chapter.

The sexual script allocated to the women was that of prostitute— a role created in relation to that of the combatants/'customers' located in a military brothel scenario. In order to keep the women in a constant state of sexual objectification for the men, their bodies were assigned an objectified and commodified form of female sexuality. Concurrently, negative connotations of the prostitute—mercenary, unclean, involved in commercial transactions for sex, and valuable solely by virtue of her provision of sexual services for others—were encoded onto their bodies by language reflecting both a masculine and a colonial perspective in which the women were described as *Chôsenpii* (Korea 'cunts').

Classifying the women as mere sexual objects played a major part in 'fixing' their identity as 'prostitute', so that it became difficult for a woman to ever escape the label. Imposed licentiousness combined with a sense of dishonour, on both an individual and a community level, had deeply demoralising effects. This process verified her position as a sexual object while her power to resist was weakened.

Having been forced into the role of serving for the soldiers' 'comfort', the women were made to feel 'defiled' by the way the men defined them. As a response to this image, many 'comfort women' like Sŏk Poksŏn who was stationed in China, attempted to clean their bodies after soldiers' visits: 'In the beginning, I had no idea about washing there [private parts], but I did so, and why? Because I became dirty... Even though nobody told me to wash it, naturally I did so because... it was dirty' (Han'guk chŏngsindae, 2001b: 103). This action could be interpreted as a daily ritual of cleansing her body in order to cleanse her mind in an effort to live through the ordeal she was enduring. Furthermore, what she wanted may not have been only to cleanse her own sense of inhabiting a 'dirty' body, but also to erase the evidence of the 'dirty' behaviour committed by the soldiers on her body.

Another source of this image of an unclean and contaminated body comes from the venereal diseases the women were infected with, and from the negative perception of women's menstrual blood as 'contaminated', as mentioned earlier in this chapter. Sexualised, contaminated and lewd descriptions of the bodies of the 'comfort women' were shaped, reproduced and imposed on them through sexualised and violent daily practices at the comfort stations. These negative social and cultural views of prostitution played a role in the women's thinking and fostered a negative view of their own selves and bodies, even though they were actually the victims.

Describing the military 'comfort women' as prostitutes on the basis of commercial transaction is a hegemonic discourse emanating from the conservative post-war Japanese state. This view transforms the act of sexual coercion into one of 'whoring'. Many Japanese neo-nationalists maintain that 'comfort women' were professional prostitutes motivated by money and earning high incomes (Fujioka, 1996; Nakamura, 1996; Takeda et al., 1997). Hata Ikuhiko describes the work as 'high risk, high return' (Hata, 1997 in Ahn, 2008a: 40). The neo-nationalist spin thus appears to exempt Japan from responsibility for the system: the victims are held to be responsible for what happened to them and this serves to legitimise the right of the combatants to procure sex from them. In this way, the 'comfort women' system is defined by an androcentric coloniser's view (Ahn, 2008a: 42).

As the Japanese neo-nationalists have claimed the 'comfort women' system to be one of prostitution, associating these women with any mention of the term has become a rather sensitive issue in the post-war debate on the issue. The majority of Korean and Japanese intellectuals and activists (with the exception of Japanese right-wing authors) engaged in this debate see the women as sexual slaves, and strive to draw a clear cut line between sexual slavery and prostitution. For example, Kurahashi Masanao distinguishes two types of 'comfort women', sexual slaves and prostitutes, according to the way they were recruited—either by force or by their own volition for financial gain (Kurahashi, 1994: 68–72). This differentiation draws a line between Japanese 'comfort women' who were mostly professional prostitutes and their Korean counterparts, who were mostly taken against their will or lured with false promises. Thus, Kurahashi (1994: 37–38) and most Korean activists and scholars (especially those who hold nationalist viewpoints) distinguish pre-existing licensed prostitution in Japan from the type of sexual slavery found in the 'comfort women' system.

Kurahashi's distinction might be useful in providing a framework for understanding that a potential variety of categories of 'comfort women' may have existed. However, such differentiation does not take into consideration the fact that there could have been an element of continuity or overlap between the categories of sexual slavery and prostitution in terms of the way the women's lives were managed. Furthermore, this view excludes the Japanese 'comfort women' from being categorised as victims of the system since they had previously been prostitutes in civilian life. The concept of prostitution as an active choice representing voluntary involvement motivated by economic reasons is problematic. It cannot always be said to have been a free choice. Economic pressures such as poverty should also be taken into account as forces that drive women into prostitution. The idea of 'force' needs to be reconsidered where extreme economic pressures are involved—as was the case with many Japanese women involved in pre-war licensed prostitution. Hence, the line between being trafficked by force and being motivated by 'free' choice is, in practice, blurred. Instead of concentrating on the question of whether or not the 'comfort women' might properly be described as prostitutes, it is the question of how the connotations and effects of classifying them as such is related to questions of responsibility that demands investigation.

The sexual regime of the comfort stations drew a line between the 'chaste and virtuous' woman and the 'debased, sexualised' woman personified by the prostitute. The 'comfort women' were forcibly positioned as the latter. What is particularly tragic and unjust is that this understanding of their feminine identity has been partially shared by other Korean citizens and by the women themselves in post-war Korean society. In their narratives, the women draw at times on the language of prostitution in describing their ordeal. A substantial number of my female respondents still refer to the soldiers as 'customers'. Pak Turi, a victim/survivor, still referred to the comfort station she was taken to as 'the house to sell a body' (Han'guk chŏngsindae, 1997: 33).

The testimonies show that many of the women have felt themselves to be morally and socially degraded or stigmatised by their enforced sexualisation. Former 'comfort woman', Yi Okpun, used the metaphor of 'a rotting pumpkin left out in summer' in her self-representation (Han'guk chŏngsindae, 1993: 143). 'Pumpkin' is used as a metaphor for an ugly woman in a Korean context. The rotting pumpkin is thus a striking image of her perception of her own body as 'defiled' and ugly. In viewing their experiences through a patriarchal lens, the women deemed themselves to be 'dirtied' by rape, or 'unclean' (Han'guk chŏngsindae, 1997: 115). Accordingly, many of them developed a sense of self-loathing. It is a paradox that on the one hand, in their personal narratives, the women strongly refuse to accept the label of 'prostitute' and, on the other hand, that their own senses of personal defilement are equally strong. Lived experiences of their own bodies as former 'comfort women' are therefore deeply embedded in their sense of self. Social stigmatisation of the 'fallen' woman's body pervasively influences their embodied subjectivity. Before examining in detail the implications of positioning them as prostitutes, Confucian ideas of womanhood deserve exploration as this pre-existing ideology and set of practices have had long-term, deep effects on the 'prostituted' women's lives.

Womanly Virtue in Korean Confucianism

Regardless of their will, the women were supposed to act out enforced scripts of prostitution that they had no part in drafting. On the other hand, although the form of 'defiled' body imposed on them is demeaning and oppressive, the ability to impose it is also partly represented by its overlap with the pre-existing Confucian concepts of womanhood in Korea.

Pre-existing Korean ideas of femininity stemming from Confucian social ethics highlight chastity, docility, submissiveness, compliance, self-sacrifice and devotion. The Chosŏn dynasty (1392–1910), the last Korean kingdom in history, saw the establishment of Confucianism as the ruling state ideology. It constructed an ideal Confucian society in politics, economics, culture and belief systems which separated it from the Buddhist tradition of the previous dynasty, Koryŏ (918–1392) (Min, 1987).

Women were deeply affected by the enactment of the socio-cultural practices of Confucianism in the late Chosŏn period. In the Confucian conceptualisation of female virtue in hierarchical relations between the sexes, a woman holds inferior status to that of a man, and must submit to a man in every field of social action and at every stage of life. A woman and a man are differentially positioned in their roles and place in society according to *naeoebŏp*, which is a Confucian code of sex segregation delineating an inner world for a woman and an outer world for a man. (Han, 1983: 65; Han, 1986: 38–39). The conventional division between the public sphere for men and the domestic sphere for women, which reveals the clear demarcation between male and female roles, is fundamental to Confucian ethics. An influential Confucian text titled *Lichi* (Book on Confucian Morality) states that segregation of the sexes begins from the age of seven. It then identifies three subordinations of woman (*samjongjido*): to her father before marriage; to her husband during marriage; to her son after her husband's death. Next, it posits the seven evils of a wife who is expelled from her husband's home (ch'ilgŏjiak): disobedience, infertility, lewdness, jealousy, disease, gossiping and stealing (Kim, 1976: 52–53). Finally, it prohibits the remarriage of widows (Pak, 1985: 36–38). The spatial and temporal aspects of a woman's whole life can therefore be regulated and bounded by her position within Confucianism.

Confucian ideology was embodied in an intense preoccupation with woman's sexual conduct. Confucian patriarchy in the middle of the 17th century entrenched the doctrine of female chastity through the legal code of the Chosŏn Dynasty (Ch'oe, 1983). A woman was required to guard her chastity more dearly than her life itself.[7] Self-censorship was imposed by the Confucian ideal of the virtuous woman:

> Upper-class women in Confucian Korea often carried a small dagger in an ornamented casement as part of their attire as a signal of their willingness to take their own lives, if and when their bodies were violated by men other than their husbands, especially by invading foreign soldiers (Choi, 1992: 13).

The ideology of chastity positions a woman, particularly her body and sexuality, as the property of one man, the husband, and this ideology is also employed to define the respectability of a woman. Accordingly, remarriage of a widow was prohibited since a woman of true Confucian virtue was supposed to devote herself to only one man throughout her whole life. Special recognition was awarded to a woman who upheld her chastity by ending her own life, while punishments, ranging from corporal punishment to the death sentence, were imposed on a woman who had sullied her chastity through extramarital or premarital affairs.

Positive and negative sanctions on women to ensure they conformed to this ideal were developed in the late Chosŏn Dynasty in order to institutionalise female chastity: for instance, women's adherence to chastity could assure the growth and prosperity of the family household, or deliver rehabilitation for a family which had declined. Exemption from compulsory military or labour service of their male family members, and release from slave status were used as enticements for females of all social classes to fulfil societal expectations in the dynasty. These measures drove a daughter into self-sacrifice with the motivation of elevating the status and standing of her family in Confucian society. The ideology of chastity was further reinforced through punishment[8] and education, (Yi, 1985: 45–52) with women indoctrinated into the ideology by way of family and community pressure. These devices of incentives and punishments served to bind the women to the particularistic norm of female sexuality in Confucianism.

In Confucian morality, womanly virtue is solely constituted through the maintenance of her chastity. Such an ideology results in the binary classification of women into two groups, 'the virtuous' and 'the fallen'. The opposition between these two groups is a mechanism for regulating the sexual behaviour of women. To conform to the norms of respectability is to recognise the sexualised woman as degraded. Women are set against women: the 'good wife' against 'the prostitute'. Hence, the construction of respectability inherently marginalises one other group of women. The contrast between 'virgin' (as the paradigm of the good woman) and 'whore' (as the representation of the bad), controls women most effectively when it is deeply internalised. Confucian patriarchal ideology permits a woman only a contingent identity as a wife and mother: that is, as an instrument that perpetuates the patrilincage (Choi, 1992: 107). On the other hand, the prostitute is available for the sexual pleasure of a man, unlike his wife who is reserved for the function of reproduction. The sexual double standard is starkly visible. No such dual classification of 'fallen' and 'respectable' is attached to the 'chaste' versus the sexually active man.

Asô Tetsuo, an ex-military Japanese medical doctor, reported that more Japanese than Korean 'comfort women' had venereal diseases as they were recruited from among prostitutes. In contrast, most of the Korean women and girls were not infected at the time of their recruitment. Asô emphasised the hygienic 'quality of comfort women' in preventing the spread of sexually transmitted diseases amongst the armed forces (Asô, 1939 in Nishino, 1992: 44, 50). This difference between the Japanese and Korean 'comfort women' was confirmed in testimonies by veterans and a former typist in the forces (Jûgun ianfu hyakutôban, 1992: 26–27).

I do not intend to reproduce the dichotomy between virtuous and 'loose' women which I am currently critiquing, by saying that the Korean 'comfort women' were 'innocent virgins' and therefore respectable ladies, while the Japanese women were 'fallen prostitutes'. In fact, the dichotomy between 'defiled' prostitute and 'innocent virgin' has prevented most Japanese victims/survivors from coming out in public because 'many Japanese ex-comfort women had been recruited to war front military comfort stations from various kinds of sex related businesses' (Muta, 2016: 627 in Norma, 2017: 117). When the biography of Shirota Suzuko, a Japanese victim/survivor, was published in Japan in 1971, the public did not pay much attention to her story. Androcentric discourses on the 'comfort women' issue considered her story as belonging to the genre of wartime nostalgia or sentimental entertainment (Yamashita, 2012: 250). What I stress here is that since premarital or extra-marital sexuality was so strongly discouraged in Korea, the strict sexual norms of the ideal Confucian woman's virtue served to supply 'clean' bodies of women and girls as especially valuable recruits to the comfort stations. The young Korean 'virgins' who were the preferred source group of recruits were destined for a life of sexual slavery masquerading as prostitution to minister to the soldiers' needs, and therefore denied the opportunity of ever achieving the status of 'respectable' womanhood as described in the Confucian code.

The Confucian code of womanhood prevalent in Korean society paved the way for developing the script of a sexualised, promiscuous and submissive femininity, and is paradoxically replayed in both Japanese colonial and Korean nationalist tropes and practices. In this way, Confucian female virtue in colonial and post-colonial Korea was imposed upon, and internalised by, the Korean 'comfort women', and led the victims/survivors to harbour feelings of shame and stigma after the war.

'Inferior' Bodies

Japanese construction of Koreanness

This section explores the Japanese construction of the Korean identity of the 'comfort women' through the use of protracted sexualised violence, and the manipulation of Korean women's image as prostitutes. One of the key factors in this process was the identity imposition brought upon Koreans through Japanese colonial rule (1910–1945), under which they were regarded as 'an inferior race'.

Richard Mitchell (1967) acknowledges that centuries before colonisation, Koreans were historically deemed to be the bearers and transmitters of an advanced culture and technology. As a result of colonisation in the 20th century, however, this viewpoint faded and was replaced with an idea of Koreans as uncivilised, irrational and unruly. For example, in Michael Weiner's work on Korean labourers in pre-1945 Japan during Korea's colonial period (1919–1945), he reports:

> Koreans were accused of being emotionally volatile, indolent and unstable, while the community was perceived as being largely composed of ignorant, filthy and morally deficient paupers who were prone to criminal behaviour (Weiner, 1994: 214).

Even before the colonisation of Korea by Japan, the lives of Korean women were depicted as 'uncivilised', 'pitiful and sad, like those barbarians', and as 'merely men's playthings' in articles in the Japanese magazine, *Fujin shinpo*, issued in 1894. Consequently, some articles in the women's magazine urged Japanese women to act as missionaries in guiding other Asian women to civilisation and independence:

> It is because, like our country's current effort to assist their civilization by lending them military power and by helping with their independence, we want to help them by using as much as possible the power of our women in looking at this situation.[9]

The Japanese construction of Korean identity that was imposed on the Korean 'comfort women' followed the lines of such racial prejudice.

The subjugation of the colonised was represented and understood to be a particular quality or characteristic of a people judged to be inferior by nature. Craven submissiveness was attributed to the 'national character' of the Korean women. The newspaper, *Donga Ilbo*, reported that according to a survey carried out by the Japanese colonial government, Japanese manufacturers in Korea had a preference for young Korean girls since they were docile and not difficult to handle.[10] In this way, the Korean 'comfort women' were framed, defined and understood as 'docile' and 'uncivilised' through the needs and projections of masculine Japanese colonialism which served to naturalise Japanese domination over them.

In constructing the women's identities, gender was also a key for creating a colonised identity rooted in power relationships. The restructuring of the Korean identity of the 'comfort women' was allied with the patriarchal Confucianist gender relations in which it has traditionally resided. Control of sexuality is deeply embedded in colonial politics, where masculine and colonial dominance were associated with the comfort station project. As Nira Yuval-Davis and Floya Anthias (1989) plausibly argue, the control of women through their sexuality is essential to both national and colonial processes. The 'comfort women' system is then a true demonstration of the ways in which sexuality was utilised in the colonisation of Korea.

This represents a gender-specific strategy to undermine national identity through sexual debasement. Xenophobia and misogyny merged in the practice of routinised sexual violence against Korean 'comfort women', which was a highly sexualised form of xenophobia which stripped them of their dignity. The representation of ethnic hatred towards women was manifested in derogatory words such as '*Bakayarô! senpiino kuseni!*', which literally means 'Idiot! nothing but a Korean cunt!', or '*kisama yaro!*' meaning 'You, bitch!', (Han'guk chŏngsindae, 1993: 89) words often heard at comfort stations. The sexualised violence, and manipulation of Korean women's image as prostitutes in and through the daily routines of the comfort stations, was an expression of domination of men and colonisers, as well as an apparatus for creating a subjugated sense of self. The identities of the powerless and subjugated and of the powerful were forged together. These two complementary and interdependent positions were translated into the political process. The humiliation of the 'comfort women' confirmed and reproduced the sense of power and superiority of the Japanese soldiers. Thus, the positioning of the bodies of the women as a sexualised, inferior and defiled site represents a ground of identity formation and an essential move in the power configurations of the coloniser and the colonised. Consequently, highly asymmetrical forces of domination and subordination worked together in a cyclical fashion to normalise the suppression of the Korean 'comfort women'.

Assimilation

Ideological themes become most effective as social forces when they are embedded in everyday social practices. For this reason, a policy of systematic deculturation was implemented in daily practices in colonial Korea alongside a policy of assimilation. Expression of Korean culture was forbidden while Japanese culture was imposed. This practice was in line with the ordinance banning the use of both Korean surnames (*sôshi kaimei*) and the Korean language itself. The order was issued for the purpose of promoting assimilation by the Japanese colonial government in Korea in 1940 (Sŏ, 1989: 33; Yi, 1996: 246). Assimilation policies promoted the adoption of a pseudo-Japanese identity as a strategic first step in the destabilisation of the social values of the colony.[11] It became mandatory for educational instruction in Korea to be given in Japanese, and worship at Japanese shrines was made compulsory (Pak, 1986: 389–390; Kim, 1986: 500–501; Yi, 1987: 495). Michael Weiner stresses that the construction of an ethnic hierarchical order involved the suppression of Korean institutions and language, and strict adherence to patterns of thought and behaviour which encouraged obedience to the master race (Weiner, 1994: 31). Deculturation policy and practices placed the colonies at the bottom of the pyramid of the Japanese family-state system under the umbrella of the Emperor system (*tennôsei*); a pattern to which the comfort station system conformed.

Likewise, policies supporting systematic deculturation were put in place in various daily practices. While obliteration of Korean culture was implemented by forbidding use of their language, songs and clothes, the imposition of Japanese culture on the 'comfort women' was a core colonial policy. Individual Korean names were changed to Japanese versions, denying their personal identity, and they were expected to speak Japanese. Every effort to retain Korean culture was suppressed in order to destabilise the identity of the women and weaken the foundations of solidarity amongst them. The women were subject therefore to not only physical but also cultural dislocation.

The imposed assimilation policy was designed to implant a recoded Japanese mentality, 'the values and institutions of the Imperial core' designed to 'make the Koreans into imperial subjects of Japan' (Weiner, 1994: 155). This policy was accompanied by propaganda promoting racial harmony and racial community within the framework of Japanese domination. A myth of common destiny under the Emperor was vigorously propagated through the mobilisation of Korean women for Japanese war projects. A substantial number of the 'comfort women' reported that there was a regular recital of the Oath of Imperial Subjects (*shinmin no seishi*), which is a pledge of imperial loyalty, at every morning assembly. The Korean women also had to promise to be loyal to Japan, recite the Oath and sing Japanese military songs (Mun P'ilgi, personal interview, 1992). They were told to dedicate themselves to the Emperor, adopt Japanese names (Zainihon chôsen, 1992: 14) and were thereby forced to become 'pseudo-Japanese'.

However, this common identity as subjects of the Japanese Emperor was imposed without the loss of their inferior status as Korean, and by no means conferred the same rights upon Koreans as it did upon the Japanese. A paradox is involved in this procedure. In order to subjugate the 'comfort women', as noted above, they were refused all the markers of their 'Koreanness'—dress, speech, cultural expressions—and told that they were in fact Japanese. Yet the differences between the Koreans and the Japanese were also never entirely forgotten. If to be Japanese was to be 'superior', then to be Korean was to be defined as the 'other' and by implication as 'inferior'. A non-traversable boundary of race was drawn in order to formulate and legitimise stratification and hierarchy between the coloniser and the colonised. In other words, their 'Koreanness' was simultaneously denied and affirmed. The enactment of practices of deculturation and assimilation was legitimised through ideologies of a 'natural' ethnic/racial and gender superiority, expressed in a language of affiliation and loyalty. Bodies, ethnic/racial boundaries, violence, power and sexuality are combined in the colonial power's project of identity formation. Subject peoples were regarded as passive, in need of guidance, incapable of self-government, unruly and uncivilised, thereby normalising and legitimising colonial endeavours.

'Pseudo-Japanese' Identity

The reconfiguration of national identities was instituted through everyday practices. The actual practices for restructuring identities demonstrate the relationship of the women and the soldiers to the colonial state. Anne McIntosh (1978) and Margot Lovell (1989) assume that the relation of women to state is 'much more often indirect than that of men... While men were directly controlled within the wider 'public' sphere, the state sought to regulate women indirectly through the language and authority of kinship' (Lovett, 1989: 28). However, this assumption does not quite fit into the context of Japan's military comfort station system. Even though the women were subject to a range of indirect controls, their sexuality and bodies were under the direct control of the colonial government.

The assimilation policy of the colonial state was intended to promote collaboration from the women through projecting an illusion of common destiny for their future with that of the Japanese nation. There is some evidence that the 'pseudo-Japanese' identity which was pressed on the women may have had some effect. A few women seem to have accepted this 'pseudo-Japanese' national identity, either because they believed the colonial propaganda, or more commonly, to avoid the shame with which they were tainted in Korea after their return. Some of the women even expressed the wish that Japan had won the war, as they believed this was the only way they could both survive and put an end to their sexual objectification.[12] The women may have understood that bridges had been burned as far as achieving the identity they wished for in terms of being 'virtuous' Korean women was concerned. It might have been thought that there would be relatively less shame attached to 'becoming Japanese'. One of the common effects of oppression is the desire to become members of the dominant group through sharing in the dominant identity. It can be said that the construction of a particular kind of subordinated identity creates its opposite in the form of the taking on of cultural and social characteristics of the dominant. 'Doubleness' is most characteristic; a gesture through which the subjugated Korean 'comfort women' learn to see themselves both in the terms in which they are viewed by the dominant, subjugating group, and in opposed, self-derived and more self-respecting terms.

On the other hand, in spite of these attempts to turn the colonial subjects, Korean women, into 'pseudo-Japanese', some women attempted to contest this imposition. They struggled in a myriad of ways to maintain their own identities. The identity persistently imposed with such brutality upon the Korean women, and which they were forced to enact every day, on pain of death, did not entirely uproot the sense of subjectivity to which many of the women clung. There is often a gap between the positioning imposed on subjugated peoples by the dominant and their own self-positioning, although the daily enforced enactment of subjugation, degradation and dishonour has inevitably deeply permeated the bodies and the beings of these women. The various ways in which they did contest are explored in detail later in this chapter.

Ethnic hierarchies among 'comfort women'

The preservation of an ethnic hierarchy among the 'comfort women' maintained distinctions even among women sharing a common experience of gross sexual exploitation. There were variations in how they were distributed according to how risky an area was perceived to be. The stratification along the lines of ethnicity and gender existed not only between the Japanese military men and the Korean women but also between the Japanese and other Asian 'comfort women'. This separation between Japanese and Korean individuals, and the dispatch of the latter to more dangerous places, was clearly discriminatory:

> There was obvious differentiation between Japanese and Korean 'comfort women'. The Korean women were allocated to the dangerous places for example, near

> battlefields. Surely, the women near the battlefields were always under as much threat of being killed as the soldiers were [in these places]. The Japanese military authorities were involved in this distribution (Goyama, personal interview, 1996).

Concerns that Japanese women were being placed in danger at the front lines led the military authorities to put forward the alternative option of sending Korean women and girls to such stations (Yun, 1997: 291; Jûgun ianfu hyakutôban, 1992; Bang, 1997: 236). Security was given as a reason for choosing Korean over Chinese women on battlefields in China. Korean women were preferred due to fears of potential connections between Chinese prostitutes and local guerrillas. Nakano Takashi, a former officer, reported that Chinese citizens were not regarded as belonging to Japan, unlike Koreans, who were, at that time, seen as representing less of a risk (Nakano, personal interview, 1996).

Different rates for 'service' were determined by the ranks of the military men the women served, and the ethnicity/nationality of the women. Miyamoto Shizuo, a high-ranking military officer who served in Indonesia during the war, confirmed the operation of a racial hierarchy:

> Among 'comfort women', there were Japanese, Korean, and local women [in Indonesia]. Comfort stations with the Japanese women charged customers most, and then the price was this order; Korean, Chinese, mixed Chinese and native Indonesians, and the cheapest were the natives. But those who were mixed Chinese and a Dutch, or mixed native Indonesian and a Dutch were more expensive than the Chinese or the natives, as the soldiers preferred the mixed (Miyamoto, personal interview, 1996).

According to an Allied report, Pacific Islanders were the lowest paid (Allied Translator, 1945).

The ranks and the officer corps were expected to consort with different ethnic groups; the former with either Korean, Chinese or local women in occupied areas and the latter with Japanese.[13] Hence, the

Japanese 'comfort women' mostly 'served' military officers and did not have to be harassed by as many men. They were often granted special status and privileges such as freedom of movement and were subject to less strict control by the military authorities (Ropers, 2014: 9, 12). The ethnic hierarchy of allocating Japanese women to officers and Korean women to rank and file soldiers created the illusion of different degrees of 'promiscuity'. The prevalence of hierarchical relations among the women and discrimination based on their performance and racial attributes served to foster disunity among them, and promote 'a divide and rule' approach used to keep the women under control.

There are commonalities and differences in the experiences of Japanese 'comfort women' and their Korean counterparts. Both groups had their bodies mobilised for colonial expansionism, and were positioned within a devalued sexualised femininity. The Japanese were marginalised in terms of sexual politics along the lines of gender and class. In terms of Japanese class and gender politics, their bodies were conceived as subjects to be offered up for the nation in wartime. They had become professional prostitutes before they came to the comfort stations (Yoshimi and Hirofumi, 1995: 88). Many were forced into the sex industry as a result of being sold to recruiters by peasant parents because of destitution in their home villages. Economic hardship that impelled individual women into prostitution constituted another kind of coercion. There may have even been a sense of shared oppression among the women in terms of a common experience of sexual exploitation, regardless of one's recruitment route to the station.

On the other hand, the Japanese women might have shared interests and benefited from maintaining a superior national identity with the men of their group (as Japanese); a situation which may have led them to join in supporting the war project. Japanese women were mobilised under the slogan of 'a final devotion for the nation', or 'for the sake of the Emperor' (Suzuki, 1992: 43). 'They [the Japanese 'comfort women'] were told that if they died, their spirits could be enshrined at Yasukini Shrine, the Japanese national shrine where spirits of the war dead are enshrined and worshipped' (Tamai, 1984: 24 in Yoshimi, 1995b: 101). Such war propaganda applied to both men and women, but it demonstrates the gendered language of war. Women were supposed to dedicate themselves to their nation through 'serving' men in accordance with the slogan hung in front of the comfort stations: 'Service by dedicating body and mind of Japanese women!' (Yun, 1997: 292). For example, Shirota Suzuko, a Japanese victim/survivor, recalled that she felt an inclination to console the men who served the nation to the point of death, in addition to wishing to earn money (Yun, 1997: 280).

While the Korean 'comfort women' were positioned as treacherous, damaged and dirty 'whores', their Japanese counterparts were seen as patriots, rather than degenerates, and their work praised as an altruistic effort to serve their country. Any resistance on the part of the Korean 'comfort women' represented not a sign of womanly virtue, but signified a refusal to perform as 'daughters of the Emperor' like their patriotic Japanese counterparts. This positioning reinforced ethnic hierarchy and vice versa. However, unlike veterans in post-war Japanese society, the surviving Japanese 'comfort women' have faced social stigma. This stigma might represent one of the reasons why the issue of Japanese 'comfort women' has not been actively addressed in the post-war period. This section has examined the forced enactment of 'inferiority', degradation and submission to create and bolster the national characteristics claimed by the Japanese colonial power. The following section probes Korean nationalists' views in the post-war debate surrounding the issue, focusing on their problematic conceptualisations of women's bodies as collective national property.

The Body of the Nation

The patriarchal ideas of Korean womanhood rooted in Confucianism, and ideas of degraded femininity as imposed by colonial power formed the foundation of colonial control and gender oppression in the Japanese Imperial Army's comfort stations discussed above. Pre-existing Confucian characteristics of idealised womanly virtues such as docility, submissiveness and acquiescence, along with the dichotomy between 'respectable' and 'loose', were maintained and consolidated in the colonial context through the comfort station system. Though colonial politics appeared to mobilise female labour and sexuality in ways that transgressed indigenous gender divisions of domestic and public spaces—like those created by Confucian ideals—they simultaneously sought to reinforce the traditional roles of women. The colonial policy recodes, and is itself recoded by, pre-existing and established gender relationships.

Ties between the 'comfort women' system and Korea's existing patriarchal structure have remained relatively untouched in Korean nationalist literature. In Yi Manyŏl's article (1997) about the historical background of the comfort station system, the question of the pre-established patriarchal system and ideology in which women's bodies and sexuality are regulated is not addressed. Rather, he only provides a brief political and economic background of the project, mentioning that rendering peasants destitute together with systematic organisation and mobilisation of the human resources of Korean women became a major background for the launching and enforcing of the 'comfort women' system (Yi, M., 1997: 97). Yi's article is representative of typical analyses on colonial domination which fail to consider how indigenous views of women may have played a role in colonial policy. This approach does not engage with the question of why colonised women were exploited in gender-specific ways, and appears to neglect the particularity of women's experiences in a colonial context while universalising the experiences of the colonised regardless of gender; leaving unanswered the question of why women's sexuality was used for imperial purposes. As a result, the Korean nationalist view has neglected to explore the whole picture in its examination of the background of the 'comfort women' system by failing to adequately incorporate theories of gender and colonialism into the debate around the issue.

As is the case in colonial gender politics, Korean nationalist ideas also inherit Confucian notions of womanhood as chaste, virtuous and maternal and are preoccupied with the Confucian polarisation between the 'respectable' and the 'defiled'. Here gender roles in the context of the nation fix women as 'reproducers of the collectivity' (Yuval-Davis and Anthias 1989 in Alison 2007: 80). Women's bodies and sexuality, especially women's chastity, are conceptualised not only as the property of a man but also as a metaphor of 'homeland' (Parker et al., 1992: 9).

Therefore, positioning the 'comfort women' as prostitutes, or even as 'public toilets' by the Japanese colonial power, has striking consequences for both the individual woman and the nation to which she belongs. This ordeal is transformed into a matter of (Korean) men's honour and national collective honour. The problematic symbolisation of women as markers of the boundaries of national belonging is superimposed on the familiar split between those women who are regarded as 'honourable' and those who are perceived as 'shameful' to their nation. There is always a proper place where female sexuality is supposed to belong. A woman's sexuality is thus alienated from herself by its belonging to both men and nation (Yang, 1998: 131). The Korean 'comfort women' whose bodies were mobilised for Japan's imperial war project became outcasts: each occupied a nation-less body unacceptable either to 'respectable' men from her community or to her nation overall, thus not deserving of protection.

Institutional concern with chastity in this nationalist trope represents sexual violence as the violation of chastity or 'national purity', instead of a general violation of human rights—meaning that rape becomes an act that undermines the essential identity of the Korean nation. In fact, in post-war Korea the 'comfort women' episode has been read as a matter of 'national pride',[14] hence one of 'national humiliation' at the hands of the coloniser. This trope of the female body as guarantor of 'national purity' is linked to the converse image of an 'impure body' which has been violated by Japanese men.

The trope of the women's body as metaphor for the integrity of the nation, when taken together with the Confucian ideology of chastity, is a dangerous one for women. Such ideals of 'chastity' and 'virtuous' female sexuality in relation to 'national purity' permitted the silencing of the women for 50 years after the war had ended. Korean national pride, and the sense of shame that many of the victims/survivors themselves felt, combined to collude with the interests of the Japanese in denying what had taken place and in silencing the women into a state of 'collective amnesia'. Social stigma is thereby simultaneously produced and reproduced on their bodies by Korean nationalist discourse and Confucian ideology.

The bodies of the 'comfort women' have also become sites of contestation where Japanese colonialists and Korean nationalists stage their battles over the remembrance and repercussions of history. Yet the Japanese colonialist endeavour to define the women as prostitutes, and the Korean nationalist insistence that women's bodies are vessels of uncontaminated national purity, in fact mutually reinforce each other in a paradoxical fashion. A South Korean newspaper article from 1997 emphasises the women's roles as 'a carrier' of the nation:

> It is the work of women to carry on the life of the nation, and if the women are trampled upon because of the loss of their country, the nation will be destroyed. The mobilisation of the Korean women for comfort women by the Japanese invaders was one of the planned conspiracies of the Japanese government to derail the succession of the Korean people.[15]

Women's bodies are paradigmatic sites in creating gender and national identity. In this context, attention should be drawn to the fact that in both Japanese and Korean nationalism, Korean women are represented as men's property. Japanese men's sexual coercion and use of Korean women was a daily enactment of the Japanese men's possession of the Korean nation and Korean men's inability to keep Korean women for their own use—thus recapitulating Japan's dominance and Korea's subjugation. It also represented the weakness and emasculation of Korean men in contrast to hegemonic masculinity of the Japanese men. The preservation of traditional concepts of womanhood is believed to be the 'only way to resist foreign intrusion—a communal identity marker against outsiders within nationalist ideologies' (Kandiyoti, 1993: 384) and also to repair damaged masculinity.

This explains why research related to the Japanese colonial rule in post-war Korea has been focused on forms of resistance, such as the independence movement. A leading dissident South Korean historian, Kang Man'gil, admitted that 'Korean historiography has made slow progress in research on the history of victims like the 'comfort women', since conducting research and education on the issue of the independence movement were considered more urgent'.[16] Focusing on the history of resistance and hegemonic masculinist narratives of 'national heroism' may succeed in reclaiming the masculine power and Korean national identity that had been stripped away by the colonial power. Yet in the context of this masculinist and nationalist rhetoric, the female body is continuously appropriated either as a kind of national resource, or conversely as a national threat.

Redefining women's bodies has been a regulatory practice of both Korean nationalist power and Japanese colonial power. Reclaiming lost Korean masculine power meant reinstating femininity in 'traditional' Confucian terms such as chastity, docility, self-sacrifice and devotion to counteract the colonists' destabilizing construction of the women's identity as prostitutes. Constructions of womanhood by Korean nationalists and Japanese colonialists have a commonality in terms of interlocking tropes of female sexuality, fertility and motherhood into the formation of national projects. Therefore, the bodies of 'comfort women' have been treated as metaphor and restated in a doubly colonised way.

Parallels can, paradoxically, be found in these two nationalist approaches in the 'comfort women' debate. The Korean nationalists and their Japanese counterparts share a degree of blindness on gender issues, ignoring the gendered nature of colonial rule and patriarchal sexual norms, especially a double standard of sexuality. This excludes a consideration of gender as a set of power relations. Another parallel can be drawn in that these two nationalist approaches tend to generalise the dichotomy between the colonising and the colonised since both approaches are ethnocentric. For both Korean and Japanese nationalists, the issue of the 'comfort woman' has been abstrusely reasoned through frameworks of either victimisation or prostitution. The intention behind this reasoning has been to serve the political agendas of the nationalists within both groups in their attempts to resolve the issue either through apology and reparation from a Korean perspective, or through the legitimisation of colonialism from a Japanese viewpoint. The very foundation of the process of victimisation or prostitution by both groups of nationalists is based on, and bolstered by, Confucian norms of womanhood. Therefore, the rhetoric, distinctions and parallels between these two nationalist narratives both challenge and, paradoxically, reinforce each other.

As a result of these nationalist agendas, ample evidence of coercion and violence as seen earlier in this chapter on Routinised Sexual Violence is ignored by the Japanese nationalists' representation of the 'comfort women' system as prostitution, while narratives concerning personal relationships between the women and the soldiers remain absent from the Korean nationalists' view. In the following section, the complexity of personal encounters between the colonised and the coloniser is examined in greater detail.

Complex Relationships[17]

Discussion of the issue of personal relationships between Japanese military men and Korean 'comfort women' is politically sensitive in both Japan and Korea, as it can be easily misused to support Japanese neo-nationalist romanticisation of sexual enslavement within the comfort station system. Given the highly delicate and contentious subject matter and the denial of sexual slavery by the Japanese Right— who seek to rebrand the women's enslavement as a series of romantic, consensual relations—hardly any academic work on the subject has been published in South Korea. Park Yu-ha (2005, 2013) and Yamashita Yeong-ae (2012) briefly mention the existence of intimate ties between Korean 'comfort women' and Japanese soldiers. In her two controversial books, Park speculates that affectionate and compassionate relationships between the women and the soldiers existed because both were situated in comradely relations, as equal 'Japanese' (Park, 2013: 67, 137–139). She claims that the 'comfort women' might have been able to offset the violence committed on them by the soldiers by engaging in emotional exchanges with their assailants. Furthermore, it is argued that the soldiers should be primarily seen as human beings before being considered as military personnel (Park, 2015, 98–99). Park seems to place more weight on the soldiers' accounts and memories than on those of the women, and gives the female voices and pain only minimal acknowledgement in her discussion. Consequently, her work fails to present a balanced picture of the relationships and does not discuss the power imbalance that certainly existed. In contrast, Yamashita argues that the women were placed into circumstances where they faced sexual exploitation and were victims of sexual violence (Yamashita, 2012: 227), but her work offers only a limited engagement with the complexities and reciprocity of bonds between the 'comfort women' and military men.

Three books published outside Korea, by Sarah Soh (2008), Mun Okchu (1996) and George Hicks (1995), include examinations of these personal relationships. Mun relates her experience as a 'comfort woman' survivor who had been in Rangoon, Burma (now Yangon, Myanmar) during WWII. She recalls her own involvement in intimate relationships, and gives the reader a glimpse into the type of complex relationships that some of the women might have had. Soh presents the personal bonds of affection between 'comfort women' and soldiers from an anthropological perspective. Her interviews with victims/survivors guide readers through what she calls 'private memories of genuine affection and personal compassion towards individual Japanese soldiers' (Soh, 2008: 181). Taking a similar approach, Hicks presents their stories of 'love and kindness' (Hicks, 1995: 51–54). Yet neither Soh nor Hicks seriously address the intricate dimensions of this emotional world, nor the juxtaposition of abuse and affection that occurred, and consequently neither writer reconciles this shared intimacy with the reality of the sexual violence the women had to endure. The accounts from both parties in this volume juxtapose the fact that the soldiers often romanticise their memories of encounters with the women in their interview narratives by focusing on emotional affection, whereas the 'comfort women's versions often refer to pain and violence while expressing a sense of sympathy for the soldiers.

Moving on to a historical discussion of the issue, personal relationships between Japanese military and 'comfort women' were officially banned by the Japanese military authorities. Rule 1 of the Appendix on discipline in the Serviceman's Club Regulations, set out by Unit Yama 3475, stationed in Okinawa and implemented in December 1944, states that the concept of common possession of the 'female staff' is to be consistently applied, and the status of special appropriation is strictly prohibited (Kawata, 1987: 81 in Ahn, 2010:

220). Despite this regulation, a number of military men, especially high-ranking officers, defied the ban on special appropriation and became emotionally involved with, or developed mistress–lover relationships with, individual 'comfort women'. Foot soldiers not in a position to have a mistress had their 'steadies' for regular visits at the comfort stations, again in contravention of the rules.

Meetings between a Japanese military man and a Korean 'comfort woman' occurred in various settings, with varying degrees of violence and intimacy. In Japanese veterans' accounts of the encounters, great emphasis is placed on describing interactions with the women as romantic in nature. The implication here is that these feelings of affection were both mutual and consensual:

> 'Kaoru [a Korean 'comfort woman'] and I got on well with each other. I might have married her.... When I moved to Guangdong, she came to see me. So I am sure she loved me, too' (Dokoda, personal interview, 1996).

Such romantic references also appear frequently in soldiers' wartime diaries published after the war (Takahashi, 1988: 107). However, these accounts rarely make reference to the soldiers' violence and brutality towards the women.

The Japanese men's interactions with the Korean women were not always consistent, ranging from kindness to ruthlessness, resulting in diverse sets of relations. A single soldier could treat a woman both with brutality and sympathy, his behaviour fluctuating depending on the time and the context, such as the prevailing situation on the battlefield or his recent experience in the army barracks.

Individual combatants' hunger for intimacy, love and nurture via a real human relationship seems to have coexisted alongside the violence and contempt shown towards the women. The coexistence of this ambivalence and the complexity of both the women's and the men's affections are common themes running through all narratives. In the women's accounts, two contradictory yet coexisting stances towards the men are apparent: the soldiers are regarded as 'crazy dogs' or 'brutal beasts', or alternatively, as 'kind saviours' (Chŏn Kŭmhwa, personal interview,

1993; Dolgopol and Paranjape, 1994: 79, 91, 109). Yun Turi (1928–2009), who was taken to a comfort station in Busan in 1943, recalled a warm-hearted navy officer who consoled her and expressed sympathy for her in light of the rough life she had to endure: 'He often told me "you poor thing" and didn't touch my body, and brought me candies and money' (personal interview, 1992). Hwang Suni also positively recalls a kind high-ranking officer, Ikeda: 'He took pity on me and adored me, he didn't treat my body to his will, he just laid down next to me when he came to me' (Han'guk chŏngsindae, 1999: 228). 'Comfort women' like Yun and Hwang expressed gratitude when they were desexualised in a sense, and perceived not just as bodies for functional intercourse, but as human companions. The women often disclosed that they had a 'patron' with whom intimacy was exchanged sporadically or over a long period of time.

Considering the harshness of their circumstances, including the violence and coercion to which they were subjected, any words of affection towards the women must have been immensely valued and greatly appreciated. Han Oksŏn recalls warmth and sympathy from Haga, a Japanese Imperial Army doctor stationed in China during the war. She became his mistress and had two children with him:

> When I became tipsy [from drinking], I was sobbing. As I missed home.... Then he tried to soothe me, saying not to weep.... And gently patted me like that and calmed me saying 'yoshi, yoshi' [all right, all right] (Han'guk chŏngsindae, 2001a: 84).

This tenderness had a powerful impact on softening the women's remembrance of their daily encounters with violence as the sense of sympathy sometimes developed into personal ties which offered respite from the brutality. Several former 'comfort women', such as Yun, even accepted marriage proposals from the soldiers with whom they had experienced an emotional closeness: 'He promised me he would marry me if Japan won the war. He left when the war was over and took my photo with him' (personal interview, 1992). Marriage to a Japanese soldier might have been a way to escape one's fate as a military 'comfort woman'.

Considering that the women would face serious social stigmatisation upon returning home, the prospect of marriage and settlement in Japan may have seemed more desirable than returning to Korea. However, very few of these unstable wartime relationships seem to have later developed into marriage.

The racial dynamic of these relationships is worth discussing here. While a Japanese officer or soldier's development of intimate bonds with a Korean 'comfort woman' may have transcended the boundaries of race, the racial hierarchy was never forgotten and continued to exist even within ties of affection. The soldiers' position of masculine colonial power was ever-present in their intimate interactions and continued to be exercised over the woman's bodies and minds at the comfort stations. Kim Yŏngja, who was taken to Manchuria during the war, still has a tattoo on her right arm of the officer's name, Mitaka, for whom she was a 'shadow wife'. She explained: 'He and I… I was quite young. His name is here [showing tattoo of 'Mitaka' on her right arm] Mitaka in Japanese language… in order not to serve others [other military men]' (Han'guk chŏngsindae, 2001a: 105). Having his name ineradicably tattooed on her arm can be interpreted as a gesture claiming his exclusive power over and ownership of her body and life. Thus, the structural forces of the women's relationships need to be contextualised within the grid of gender and racial hierarchy and the military culture of the Japanese Imperial Army.

Although the women's position during the war was not by any means equal to that of the Japanese soldiers, numerous 'comfort women' showed sympathy towards the military men. Kim Ŭllye, who was taken to a comfort station in Nanking at age 17, considered newly-recruited foot soldiers, in particular, to be 'poor things', since the men were often beaten by their superiors (personal interview, 1996). When the men expressed pain or grief during their encounters, some women responded with great empathy. Hwang Kŭmju, who was taken to a comfort station in Jilin, China in 1941 and then to Rangoon, Burma in 1942, tried to console the soldiers when they cried in her presence before going out to battle (personal interview, 1995). The violence and humiliation inflicted on both groups formed a shared sense of vulnerability between them.

Other narratives, like that of Mun P'ilgi, who was taken to Manchuria in 1943, reveal that the women's sympathy often coexisted with feelings of ambivalence or doubt. Upon her arrival at a comfort station, Mun was examined and then saved from being forced to 'service' men by a military doctor, who said she was too young to serve a man. Nevertheless, he slept with her a week after she arrived at the comfort station (personal interview, 1992). He displayed warmth and sympathy but simultaneously took advantage of her. The complexity of the situation is also evident in how she later recalled him as being a kind and considerate person whom she trusted (personal interview, 1992). She considered his place—where she lived the first couple of years, before she had to serve many soldiers—to be a space of safety, where she felt protected in the midst of despair and fear. Her narrative reflects the complex feelings of the 'comfort women' towards the Japanese military men, which encompassed gratitude and pity, but also anger and frustration.

'Shadow family'

The military authorities did not welcome the pregnancy of 'comfort women', since this interfered with performing their role in sexual servitude. In order to prevent pregnancy and sexually transmitted diseases, the military authorities required soldiers to use condoms at comfort stations, but in affectionate encounters where the woman was considered a 'mistress' or a 'steady', this regulation was not always obeyed. Therefore, personal relationships often resulted in pregnancy from unprotected sex. Han gave birth to two children by Haga, a military medical officer, in his absence and without proper arrangements for childbirth: 'A couple of months after giving birth to my first child I got pregnant again. He was on the front line… so he was not there with me when I gave birth' (Han'guk chŏngsindae, 2001a: 82). For those who cohabited with a member of the military and had children from the relationship, the place of dwelling became an intimate space and pseudo-home on the war front. I term this kind of family situation a 'shadow family'. Consisting of a couple, in some cases with children, which functions much like a family with a sense of occupying intimate, private space; not unlike what might be a domestic household at home.

Yet because these 'shadow families' were not officially permitted by the military authorities, they were neither acknowledged nor legitimised. The offspring were considered illegitimate and contaminated—'othered' by both Korean and Japanese society. The 'shadow family' acted as a substitute for one's real family and may have provided both the man and the woman with human contact and the semblance of an ordinary life. This safe refuge from the uncertainty and the physically and emotionally damaging experience of the war allowed them to maintain a sense of normalcy on the war front, where life was constantly threatened. In this imagined home, the woman, as a 'shadow wife', performed her role as caregiver, nurturing and providing a home-like environment, while the man performed his role as provider or protector. In the absence of any proper arrangement for maintaining family life, this set-up became more complicated over time, especially given the difficulty of raising children in the midst of war on the front line.

Whether the woman was a temporary 'steady' for occasional indulgences or a 'shadow wife' in an ongoing relationship, she must have needed to make sustained efforts to hold her partner's attention and sympathy by fulfilling the expected roles of providing emotional support and sexual gratification. The women's narratives reveal cases of genuine feelings of attachment towards the men. Kim Tŏkchin (pseudonym), who developed an intimate closeness with an officer, Izumi, shared her story with him and with his help she managed to return to Korea in 1940.

> As I had often met Izumi, I considered him as father and husband all in one as one family. He taught me numbers and Japanese language while holding my hand. So his affection towards me was profound. He told me every day that he loved me. And he told me that when the war ended, he would take me to Japan with him where we could live together without hardship and he promised to send me to school. We exchanged letters after I returned to Korea (Han'guk chŏngsindae, 1993: 54).

It seemed that she still cherished him in her memory as a caring protector whom she wanted to see again even after so many years. Yi Yongsu, who was emotionally involved with one of the *Kamikaze* Corps, 'consummated her cherished love for him in the rite of "spirit marriage" fifty-three years after the war ended' (Soh, 2008: 188) at the comfort station in Taiwan where she was living during the war. In a newspaper interview, she expressed her feeling that by carrying out this ceremony she wanted 'to commemorate his love for a human being' which, she considered, 'could not be erased with any kind of ideology'.[18] This expression reveals her long-cherished desire to tie the knot with him even though he was no longer alive and to console the spirit of a man who had died as a bachelor. These experiences display a continuum in the women's lives, ranging from sexual slaves to 'shadow wives', in which the boundaries of exploitation and compassion are blurred. Considering the women's complex positions in this space of intimacy, when sexual servitude is transferred into the private sphere, it becomes difficult to view the abusive and unequal aspects in their relationships as altogether different from those often abusive and unequal aspects of the conjugal relations of a conventional monogamous marriage.

Relationships risked becoming another casualty of war at any moment. Stories of a Japanese military man abandoning his promise to a 'comfort woman' were commonplace among the narratives. Naturally, the woman concerned experienced a sense of grief when her partner was killed in combat, and a sense of abandonment when either left for a newly-recruited younger woman (UN Commission on Human Rights, 1996a: 14) or left behind at the end of the war. The children born to 'shadow families' were deserted as well, and were often adopted by local people from nearby areas, as was the case with the sons of Kim Yŏngja and Han Oksŏn (Han'guk chŏngsindae, 2001a: 86, 105). The experience of losing a close partner to war had deep and lasting effects on the 'shadow wives'. It was not uncommon that, having experienced trauma and death so continuously, the women were left quite vulnerable and found themselves unable to keep the children born of these relationships. Such abrupt endings conveyed the transience and instability of the relationships as well as the disposable position of the women themselves.

Traumatic bonding and power

There are parallels but also differences between 'transactional sex' and the personal ties that evolved between 'comfort women' and military personnel during WWII. Transactional sex is the exchange of sex for material reward, which recognises the 'fundamental economic inequality' in the relationship (Swidler and Watkins, 2007: 147), and thus is linked to needs for survival or desire for consumption (Hunter, 2002: 101). Many scholars observe that transactional sex is found in different kinds of relationships of different durations, including marriage and long- or short-term extra-marital affairs (Ankomah, 1992; Caldwell *et al.*, 1989; Hunter, 2002, 2005; Johnson-Hanks, 2006; Kaufman and Stavrou, 2004; Poulin 2006; Swidler and Watkins, 2007). Stoebenau *et al.* (2016: 187–191), who focus on the sub-Saharan context, distinguish between the categories of 'sex for basic needs; sex for improved social status; and sex for material expressions of love', while pointing out that these different categories often overlap.

From the anecdotes of the 'comfort women', we learn that tangible rewards or gifts were given to the women in the form of food that the men had saved from their rations (Soh, 2008: 192). Intangible benefits included outings, protection and even compassion. The women's personal relationships could provide access to the power or authority possessed by a man if he held a high position in the military hierarchy, and this power or authority could act as a shield from further sexual exploitation. Several women, such as Yi Sunok and Mun Okchu, made use of their relationships to obtain a travel permit to escape from the comfort stations and return home to Korea (Han'guk chŏngsindae, 1993: 154, 177–178). Even though, as Stoebenau *et al.* (2016: 188) mention, transactional sex is not only for the 'provision of resources in exchange for sex', but also applies to emotional interactions, its defining characteristic lies in receipt of material resources in exchange for sex or companionship. The literature on transactional sex focuses more on material rewards than on emotional exchanges (Ankomah, 1992; Okigbo *et al.*, 2014; Robinson and Yeh, 2011; Swidler and Watkins, 2007; Wyrod *et al.*, 2001). Unlike transactional sexual relationships, given the scarcity of resources during the war, material exchanges in the personal interactions of the 'comfort women' and the Japanese servicemen appear to have been marginal; instead, the key factors in maintaining personal bonds were protection and/or power, along with emotional support. The ties were often based on a reciprocal need for intimacy and an emotional outlet rather than on the pursuit of material gain.

In order to be spared from daily violence and repeated sexual abuse at the hands of numerous soldiers, some 'comfort women', such as Kim Poktong, welcomed the protection granted by her personal bond with an officer (Han'guk chŏngsindae, 2001a: 209). Some 'comfort women' keenly sought to shape personal ties with powerful men as a survival strategy. It is worth considering that they may well have consciously cultivated their intimate ties with officers as a means of escaping their perilous situation. By making efforts to form and maintain bonds of emotional closeness with a serviceman, the woman who was engaging in this traumatic bonding actively participated in and disrupted the power structure by which she was oppressed. Such women persisted in negotiating their positions through their everyday interactions with the Japanese servicemen.

Through her relationship with a powerful individual, a woman may even have felt a sense of power herself—a feeling which demonstrates that military hierarchies were reflected in the relationships. Han Oksŏn confirms the presence of a perceived power gained through such closeness: 'Since he [Haga, a military medical officer and second lieutenant] had visited me, I took my liberty to attend to only those who I wanted' (Han'guk chŏngsindae, 2001a: 79).

Whether these bonds were an illusion of affection or an authentic feeling, it can be observed from the women's narratives that their interactions helped them deal with isolation and feelings of despondency. Protecting their emotional stability during their sexual slavery went some way towards alleviating their despair and improving their chances of surviving the precarious circumstances of war. This situation might have created a feeling of dependence on the men with whom the women felt intimacy. At times, highly codependent bonds based on emotional attachment were forged. This bonding can be more accurately defined as 'traumatic bonding', which means constructing ties of extensive interdependence in the face of emotional crisis and trauma. In such bonding, flows of emotional attachment can often be bi-directional.

The next question to explore is in what contexts 'traumatic bonding' took place between Japanese servicemen and Korean 'comfort women'. To answer this question, it is worthwhile, as John Tosh (2004: 55) and Lynne Segal (2008: 31–33) observe, to consider the burdens of war felt by these men, such as trauma, vulnerability, physical injury and even death. As discussed earlier in Chapter 3, the provision of the women as 'comforters' offered an emotional outlet for the combatants to release their own feelings of vulnerability, fear and tension and ease or to divert the effects of the extreme regimentation to which they were subjected (Ahn, 2010: 227; Yoshimi, 1992: 53).

In the accounts of both Japanese veterans and former 'comfort women', attempts to cope with the violence, frustration, fear and dangers of warfare intensified individual searches for an intimacy that could offer transient reassurance and solace in their extreme circumstances. The men's and women's shared sense of vulnerability and crisis laid the foundation for a trauma-based bonding within the cruel context of war. Similar to the battered women featured in Judith Lewis Herman's work (1997), the 'comfort women' came to perceive the feeling of intense, strong dependence on authority, and especially that of high-ranking officers, as representing their own source of power. Their partners, Japanese military men, were sometimes seen as saviours from their plight as sexual slaves. Thus, the Korean 'comfort women' under Japanese colonial rule acknowledged and/or benefited from their partners' embodied power as colonisers and as men. For the women, this bond juxtaposed care, devotion, benefit and appreciation with pain and hardship. This indicates that there existed interdependency and complexity to this 'traumatic bonding' in the context of the crisis of war and the loss of the servicemen's own autonomy.

As demonstrated above, the paradoxical juxtaposition of intimacy and contempt, protection and exploitation within ties of affection for their partner(s) is revealed in the women's personal anecdotes. The binary perception, on the part of the military personnel, of the women as both consolers and promiscuous 'whores' and, on the part of the 'comfort women', of the soldiers as both 'crazy dogs' and 'kind saviours', is not only indicative of the challenging and intricate nature of their interactions, but is also symptomatic of codependency. This mutual dependency, which may often have superficially appeared to transform sexual exploitation or traumatic emotional ties into romance was, in reality, masking a power disparity. Although both parties shared trauma and reciprocity in their exchanges of intimacy and emotional support, the women's power within these relationships was limited by their asymmetrical access to resources and authority when compared with their Japanese soldier counterparts.

This power asymmetry between the Korean 'comfort women' and the Japanese military men is rooted in gendered and racialised hierarchies interwoven in the women's identities and inherent in their relationships with the combatants. Colonial visions of Japanese superiority were reinforced in this context by the positioning of the Korean 'comfort women' as 'promiscuous' and 'inferior'. As noted in Chapter 3, the newly-recruited rank and file were vulnerable and were expected to display absolute obedience towards their superiors, but they 'were not at the bottom of the punitive military hierarchy: the "comfort women" were a step further down in the hierarchy than the rank and file' (Ahn, 2010: 224). Even newly-conscripted men wielded power over the women in their intimate space. The subordinates sought to retrieve their power through dominance over the women at the comfort station.

In this context, a Korean 'comfort woman', situated in the most subjugated position, pursued power or protection through her ties to a higher-ranking man in order to offset the violent and ruthless power the foot-soldiers held over her. The pseudo-power she held through ties with her officer-partner reflected the power and authority he possessed in the military hierarchy. Through engaging in these intimate bonds, the woman was simultaneously involved in sustaining the hierarchical practice of power in the military forces and engaged in disrupting the 'chain of power'.

This 'chain of power' started with a higher-ranking officer exercising power over his subordinates, eventually cascading down to the foot soldiers at the very bottom of the military hierarchy and, by association, to the 'comfort women' themselves. Although the chain was usually one-directional, it was not simplistic and could become disconnected or entangled by the women's exercise of pseudo-power. Two different levels of gendered and racialised power overlapped in a single intimate space, the comfort station. Here, spaces of intimacy such as the 'shadow family' created both disruptions and reproductions of different power hierarchies through the creation of personal bonds. The interplay and disruption of power structures further entrenched the women's complexity of feelings of affection, intimacy, protection, pity, remorse and contempt. Dimensions of power—hierarchy, exploitation, dependency and affection—were entangled in the 'traumatic bonding'.

This section has analysed the complex and contentious issues of 'traumatic bonding' where mutual affection and codependency between Korean 'comfort women' and Japanese soldiers were enacted during WWII. The arena of interpersonal relationships represents the delicate, micro, emotional level of the Japanese Imperial Army's 'comfort women' system. To this end, the way in which both groups utilised traumatic bonding as a means of coping with war has been discussed. Beneath the yearning for human connection, these relationships were highly complex and deeply affected by the overarching power dynamics of gender and the racialised colonial hierarchy. The following section investigates evidence of contestation and additional coping strategies which the women employed to survive and maintain their sense of subjectivity during their precarious wartime ordeals.

Coping with the Unbearable: Contestation

This section illuminates the ways in which the 'comfort women' coped with the colonial masculine power's reconfiguration of their identities and bodies and their subsequent self-positioning. A sense of female solidarity and ethnic awareness is another focus of this section. As noted earlier in this chapter on Routinised Sexual Violence, the circumstances of routinised sexual, physical and reproductive violence in detention allowed very little room for contestation of the women's enforced role of sexual enslavement. However, they engaged in various acts ranging from subtle, nuanced behaviour to direct action to maintain their dignity and integrity as human beings. For example, some women fought back or even attempted to kill the soldiers while defending themselves. To escape their harsh reality, strategies ranged from taking drugs or drinking, to becoming mentally ill or even attempting suicide. Some tried to run away from the comfort stations, while others took the pathway of cultivating closeness with officers. Less risky strategies than direct confrontation included pleading or pretending to be ill, claiming to have caught venereal diseases, or feigning menstruation where the regulation of not having to serve during one's period was enforced.

After countless exhausting days at the comfort stations, many of the women developed their own ways of dealing with the soldiers' excessively abusive demands. One important long-term coping strategy was to attempt to keep one's self in reasonable physical shape, by taking extra precautions not to become infected with sexually transmitted diseases and doing one's best to avoid being beaten (Han'guk chŏngsindae, 1993: 206). The ability to live through sexual abuse may itself be seen as a form of resistance. As noted earlier, they used their bodies to resist exploitation, so that their bodies represented a means of resistance as well as a means of imposing positionality.

Pleading with, or even threatening, the soldiers was a method sometimes employed to handle the men without having to oppose them directly. When the soldiers violated a regulation at comfort stations, for example, not using condoms, the women sometimes resisted by pleading with them to use one and/or threatening to report them to their superiors. Physically hiding themselves somewhere like a backyard or a toilet was another tactic used to temporarily avoid the soldiers. However, when the women were found out to have behaved in this way they were severely punished (Han'guk chŏngsindae, 1995: 142, 229).

Another coping strategy was 'going slow' to reduce the number of men they had to serve, for instance prolonging the span of time allotted to serving each man, or taking extra time washing oneself between sessions (Han'guk chŏngsindae, 1993: 141). Yi Yŏngsuk recalled:

> After one year at the station, I realised I should look after my own body a little better. Sometimes I would pretend to be ill by stepping on to the examining table without having washed myself [my private parts]. Then I had to go through a period of treatment, during which I didn't have to work (Han'guk chŏngsindae, 1993: 66).

Since physical violence was the greatest threat the women faced, some women feigned submissiveness to avoid violence. In the face of such brutality, it is not surprising that many women were too terrified to resist. In this context not displaying resistance may be interpreted as a survival strategy:

> I gave up resisting and did whatever I was told to... and I was so scared that I would even have pretended to die if I had been told to do so. Maybe because of this, the soldiers didn't treat me cruelly (Han'guk chŏngsindae, 1993: 52).

Public displays of violent punishment, such as the beating or even murder of a rebellious woman, or the burning of the corpse of a woman who had taken her own life demonstrated to the women the consequences of resistance, in order to deter them from any defiant behaviour (Yun Turi, personal interview, 1992). Yi Tŭknam recounted how she had to make an effort to please Captain Sakai, who was violent, as she felt that she had no power to stop his regular visits (Han'guk chŏngsindae, 1993: 206). Compliance could therefore be an act in the interest of one's long-term survival. A 'fake-smile' was used to avoid violence as in Yi Okpun's case:

> If you didn't want to die there, you had to do things tactfully. If we made faces at the men we were taken to a confinement room by Nakai [the receptionist], so we smiled regardless

of whether we felt like doing so (Han'guk chŏngsindae, 1993: 141).

These strategies for avoiding violence meant that the women needed to suppress their anger or 'desire for revenge' (Yi Yongsu, personal interview, 1996). However, suppression did not amount to acquiescence, and the women waited many years before their pent-up anger and desire for revenge could be vocalised. Yi Okpun expressed her rage towards the violent soldiers:

> Whenever any of us was beaten by the soldiers, I used to grind my teeth together, saying to myself; "One day I am going to prey upon you all. I will wipe out all seeds of your offspring" (Han'guk chŏngsindae, 1993: 144).

Many women adopted strategies for retaining their self-respect by refuting the judgements made about them by the military men. The men viewed the women as degraded, contaminated and inferior. However, many of the women vehemently argued in their narratives that it was the soldiers themselves who were 'filthy' and defiled. To reversely label the men as 'filthy' was to challenge their pretensions of masculine and colonial power and superiority.

A form of resistance which carried more risk was to directly refuse the men's requests. The women who fought the soldiers were ready to die, like Hwang Kŭmju when she was forced to engage in oral sex: 'I shouted at him, "I'd rather eat your shit than suck you!" This made him very angry. He beat me and threw me about, shouting *Konoyaro koroside yarôka*, something like "I am going to kill you, you bitch"' (personal interview, 1995).

Some women like Mun Okchu, who defended herself from a drunken soldier threatening her with his sword, reacted with force against her assailant. When pleading with him had no effect she went on the attack:

> At the moment I flung myself at him, ready to die, his sword fell from his hand, he was so shocked at my reaction. So

> I grabbed it [the soldier's sword] and stabbed him in the chest without realising what I was doing. He was bleeding and taken away by car. I was arrested by the military police (Han'guk chŏngsindae, 1993: 160).

Although such resistance could not be sustained for long in the conditions of sexual slavery in which the women were held, this direct form of resistance nevertheless represented a woman's ultimate refusal to be exploited as a sex slave.

One of the most extreme measures one could take to escape one's precarious situation was suicide. Committing suicide may be seen as a passive yet powerful form of refusing to accept an oppressive situation. 'Comfort women' tried to escape the unbearable and ongoing violence they were experiencing through a self-imposed death by drinking poisons such as disinfectants, hair dye or creosote,[19] or by jumping into the sea, or leaping from a high place. However, attachments to homeland or family often deterred the women from killing themselves (Dolgopol and Paranjape, 1994: 115; Han'guk chŏngsindae, 1993: 207). Even then, some attempted suicide on the way back home to Korea or even after their return, fearing the shame and stigma they knew they would have to face. For example, when Kang Tŏkkyŏng (1929–1997) learned of her pregnancy she tried to throw herself off the ship as it crossed the sea to Korea on the return voyage after the war (personal interview, 1995).

Feminist author Phyllis Chesler views women's suicide attempts, especially those carried out in an oppressive context, as a sign of their powerlessness and psychological martyrdom. She argues female suicide attempts function not so much as calls for help, but rather as 'the assigned baring of the powerless throat, signal of ritual readiness for self-sacrifice' (Chesler, 1972: 49). Laura E. Donaldson argues self-imposed death, in the context of *sati*,[20] as an assertion of resistance rather than admission of defeat and as providing a presence that counters the invisibility of women (Donaldson, 1992: 30–31). The ultimate and shocking thought of suicide in oppressive circumstances signifies more than just relinquishing life. A last outcry of resistance by a 'comfort woman' in the form of self-inflicted death can therefore be seen not only as an individual action of personal despair, but also as a way of escaping sexual enslavement by terminating her imposed role as a powerless sexual object in the comfort station while simultaneously taking revenge on her tormentors.

Other reactions the women had to their precarious situations were to develop mental health problems, which may also be seen as forms of contestation. Im Kŭma, who remained in China after the war, presents her experience of insanity three months after she arrived at the comfort station, since she found it too 'horrendous' to 'serve' the soldiers (Han'guk chŏngsindae, 1995: 104). Some of the women went mad after they returned to Korea because of the lasting trauma from which they continued to suffer (Ch'oe Myŏngsun, personal interview, 1992).

Jane Ussher convincingly proposes that madness stems from women's powerlessness, and argues that it is the inevitable outcome for women trapped within a culture of incarceration and oppression (Ussher, 1991: 20, 299). This insanity might have been a way for the women to shut themselves off from situations where they were ceaselessly forced to have sex in a confined military brothel, and to remove themselves from the control of masculine power. Madness may thus be viewed as a form of expression of opposition from those who were unable to contest their oppressive situation in other ways.

Taking drugs, especially opium, or drinking alcohol (Jūgun ianfu hyakutōban, 1992: 105) can also be identified as coping strategies. Yi Ponghwa, who remained in China after the war, reported that she started to drink and smoke at the comfort station, otherwise she would not have been able to bear life there (Han'guk chŏngsindae, 1995: 90). Ch'oe Illye became an opium addict shortly after arriving at a comfort station (Han'guk chŏngsindae, 1997: 193). Such coping strategies may have enabled the women's short-term survival, however, drug overdoses were occasionally fatal (Han'guk chŏngsindae, 1993: 81).

One case reported that a Hygiene Sergeant was arrested after he was discovered to have given or tried to give morphine to 'comfort women' who had requested it from army supplies.[21] Yet drugs such as opium or morphine were often tolerated, or in some cases even encouraged, by some of the proprietors of comfort stations. Victim/survivor Chŏng Soŭn recounted her experience with drug injection:

> When I was too exhausted after being harassed by uncountable soldiers to serve more, then a drug was injected into my arm so I could carry on. Especially on weekends, I had to get an injection before the soldiers came to the comfort station (Yun, 1997: 290).

One former officer, Goyama, alleged that proprietors made a profit working with the military authorities in opium dealing (personal interview, 1996).

Some women attempted to escape from comfort stations; feeling that if one way or another they were going to die, they might as well risk death by trying to flee. Kim Haksun constantly contemplated running away from the comfort station where she was held:

> Since the time I got there, I had a single-minded goal to find out how to get out of there [comfort station]... Though Emiko and I thought about many different ways, I didn't know where to go even if I did manage to get out, because I was not familiar with that area at all. We promised each other to escape together when an appropriate time came (Han'guk chŏngsindae, 1993: 40).

Escape was made even more difficult as the women were kept under close surveillance. Chin Kyŏngp'aeng said that she was constantly under the watch of military police who were meant to keep her from running away or attempting suicide. She reported that 'I had no freedom; even to die' (Han'guk chŏngsindae, 1997: 24). Military documents such as *Tsucho* (military communication) and *Jinjunissi* (military daily records) instructed that surveillance at the comfort stations should be carried out by the district military chief and by military police.[22] It is reported that the letter signifying 'comfort' was tattooed on either the bellies or arms of some of the women held in China to discourage them from running away as they would be easily recognisable as 'comfort women' (Jûgun ianfu hyakutôban, 1992: 42). In general, displacement from their hometowns to an unknown area where regular war or guerrilla fighting was occurring, and isolation from the local population, made escape almost impossible. Furthermore, there was a language barrier between the women and the local people which limited their chances of receiving help from the local population (Han'guk chŏngsindae, 1993: 80).

Most of the Korean 'comfort women' were housed either on or near battlefields, meaning that circumstances might have been even more dangerous outside the military brothels. 'In order to travel through Japanese occupied territory, one needed the permission of the Japanese Army' (Yoshimi, 1995b: 145). Most attempts at taking flight therefore failed, unless the women had help from someone who was able to arrange a travel permit and transportation.

Korean 'comfort women' who were taken to Japan or to stations within Korea tried to escape more often than those stationed in other areas, like Yun Turi (personal interview, 1992). At least they could communicate with the locals, and there might be people around who could help the women flee farther away from the comfort station where they had been taken. But escape attempts were risky as those who were unsuccessful suffered severe punishment.

This range of varied coping strategies, and the utilising of whatever limited resources were on hand, is evidence of the women's resilience and ongoing struggle to maintain a sense of self, and prevent the complete reshaping of their identities and bodies by the masculine colonial dominance. While the women may have adopted the subject-positioning imposed by the institutionalised social scripts as 'comfort women', it does not mean that they necessarily accepted these scripts as a core component of their identities. Some enforced subject-positioning was taken up by the women when they saw themselves as 'dirty' and 'impure' and thus not fit to return home. On a societal level, the women had been rendered invisible, silent and powerless. However, even in such adverse circumstances they were not entirely reduced to the position of passive or defenceless victims. Thus, their bodies cannot be reduced to the status of vehicles for the mere inscription of androcentric colonial power, as they were also tools for the disruption of colonial power when they refused to act out the imposed sexual scripts. The women's bodies became sites for both the enactment of colonial power, and sites for the production of resistance against this same colonial power.

In much of the work on war, militarism and women, women are depicted as defenceless victims of male violence particularly in terms of their sexuality. For example, in her pioneering work on wartime sexual violence, Susan Brownmiller appears to consider a woman only as booty or 'a tangible reward' of war (Brownmiller, 1975: 35). She assumes women are endowed with a 'structural vulnerability to be raped' (Brownmiller, 1975: 13). Similarly, Kate Millett also describes women as 'victims' (Millett, 1969). In Millett's explanation of how a man uses his sexuality as a way of controlling and degrading women, women are identified as 'legitimate victims'.[23] Yet these studies do not take into account women's self-positioning under circumstances such as colonialism or militarism within which their human rights are severely suppressed. The dichotomised gendered position of women as victims and men as perpetrators of violence in war, the binary notion of victim versus agent (Coulter, 2009) and an inherent linking of masculinity to violence are contested in the recent works by Segal (1990, 2008), Moser and Clark (2001), Tosh (2004) and Zarkov (2007).

The 'comfort women' both conformed to and contested their imposed position as victims of multiple forms of violence. Certainly there is evidence, as indicated in the women's narratives, of coping strategies and struggles between the Japanese colonialists and the Korean 'comfort women': the former utilising all means within their power to deny the women's ability to define themselves, and the women trying their hardest to cling to their personhood and use it as means of coping. The women's counteractions constitute contestation and/or negotiation of their positioning as colonised subjects and also, at times, of the patriarchal codes of virtuous womanhood.

They both overtly and covertly negated the fixed notion of themselves as inferior beings possessing subjugated bodies and subjectivity. Many kept alive a sense of their own identification as Koreans. For example, Ha Kunja (1928–2017), a victim/survivor, recalled her expression of anger over negative comments on

Koreanness, saying, 'do you know *donggarashi* (chilli)? I am a *Chôsenjin*',[24] (Han'guk chŏngsindae, 1995: 69). Here, *donggarashi* (chilli) represents a distinctive marker of Koreanness and is a typical ingredient in Korean cuisine. Ha's emotional attachment to her origins and culture revealed itself in her longing for home and family, especially mother, and in her references to Korean culture.

Collective efforts towards the preservation of identity gave strength and resilience to the women, to help them to survive their ordeals. The women's shared experiences of suffering and being marginalised, despite a divide-and-rule strategy implemented by means of the hierarchy the military tried to establish among the 'comfort women', served to create firm bonds and shared sources of strength among them. Solidarity and shared ethnic awareness were clandestinely anchored to their everyday lives, and were used to distinguish the Korean women from the Japanese. In particular, the women practised solidarity through caring for each other. Yi Yongsu, a 'comfort women' victim/survivor recalled:

> One day, one of the older girls who was normally quiet told us that she, too, was Korean when the war was over. We hugged each other and wept with joy. She held my hand tightly and told me I must go back to Korea alive (Han'guk chŏngsindae, 1993: 93).

Such solidarity in terms of identity was a response to the hierarchy the military tried to impose on the women, and was empowering in the face of the isolation and pressure they were facing. In comfort stations, the women maintained their Korean identity by stoking a sense of connectedness and cohesiveness against colonial endeavours to dislocate and deculturise them. At the same time, the women fuelled expressions of anger, and this anger acted as an instrument of empowerment for those of low status in an organisation in breaking their subdued silence.

The national identity of the military 'comfort women' was developed and reinforced in opposition and resistance to the colonial endeavours to destroy or redefine their identity as inferiors. Their sense of Korean identity was strengthened in response to the pressure to be 'less Korean'.

This counter-identity, unsurprisingly, contained a highly anti-Japanese sentiment. This, therefore, can be called a 'reactive' national identity emanating from the colonial encounter, but one founded upon a prior sense of being a distinct 'people'. The 'comfort women's' own identification was profoundly affected by their experiences of colonisation and sexual oppression.

Resistance and agency are limited in conditions of forced sexual exploitation, and this results in particular forms of coping, survival and accommodation. Women have been actors in shaping their own definition of need. The practices of everyday life have offered spaces for women to plot out their own lives, albeit very limited in scope. Not only do different women make different decisions but the same woman makes different ones in the context of what is possible in particular situations.

Finally, based on the experiences of the comfort women, I would like to suggest that the definition of resistance needs to be broadened to recognise actions which may be read as 'collusion' or 'negotiation', also interpretable as forms of resistance. In this broadened definition of resistance, survival strategies which appear to be 'collusive' as well as active contestation can be considered as forms of resistance, especially in highly oppressive circumstances. Survival itself can be seen as a form of resistance, with various forms of survival strategies and the reaffirmation of subjecthood included in the broadened definition. This redefinition could be useful in overcoming representations of women as nothing more than defenceless victims of male and colonial violence. In this way we can begin to view women, not as silenced beings shamed by sexual atrocity, but as actors demonstrating their resilience within the limited space they had for agency.

'Damaged' Bodies: The Aftermath of War

This section delineates the construction and interconnection of body, subjectivity and society in the post-war life of the victims/survivors. There could be no simple return to pre-war life for 'comfort women' who had survived the war and returned to Korea. As the end of the war approached and the reality of Japan's impending defeat became clear, many had to follow units in the process of movement or withdrawal.

According to a Japanese Prisoner of War Interrogation Report, even in these circumstances, the system of sexual servitude was sometimes continued: 'they [comfort women] spent most of their last days in foxholes. One or two even carried on working there' (United States Office of War Information, 1944: 5). In the course of the troops' withdrawal, women suffered from injury, disease and starvation. Women too wounded to keep up were abandoned or sometimes even shot (Bang, 1997: 237). Pae Ponggi (1917–1991) recalled the suffering of starvation as exceeding even the fear of war: 'A common experience among the women in Okinawa at the end of the war was serious malnutrition from starvation. Some suffered nervous breakdowns in the end' (Kawata, 1992: 107–108).

Most of the women were not informed that the war had even ended. Following the Japanese surrender, the army had three common approaches to handling the 'comfort women'. The simplest was to abandon them. Women in comfort stations were left behind by fleeing Japanese soldiers without knowing what had happened when the war ended, or they were left to perish in the jungles, or to succumb to starvation and disease. Hwang Kŭmju described the day of being deserted:

> One evening, nobody called us for supper. Nobody came in and there seemed to be nobody around, and it was strangely silent. I quietly opened the door and went out, but there wasn't a single horse and there were no cars. I crept quietly to the dining room and found the place completely untidy without a single man to be seen (Han'guk chŏngsindae, 1993: 103).

Another approach was to disguise the women as military nurses in order to conceal the existence of the comfort station system from the Allies (Jûgun ianfu hyakutôban, 1992: 30; Han'guk chŏngsindae, 1997: 79). Miyamoto, a high-ranking officer veteran, asserted that the reason for this was to 'protect' the women from the Allied Forces:

> When the war finished, comfort stations were to be closed. And all of the Japanese and Korean 'comfort women' were

> allocated to hospitals as nurses, to keep the women from being raped by the Allied Forces. Thanks to our protection of them, no Korean women were raped by the Forces (Miyamoto, personal interview, 1996).

Those who were found by the Allies and transferred to their camps had to wait for a long time, in some cases almost a year, to return to Korea (Han'guk chŏngsindae, 1999: 271). The final approach—also intended to cover up the existence of the 'comfort women' system, or for security reasons—was to kill the women (Zainihon chôsen, 1992: 44). Some were killed after being put into underground shelters or caves which were then demolished with explosives by the retreating Japanese military forces (Choi, 1992: 103). The treatment of the 'comfort women' at the end of the war confirms that the army viewed them as disposable.

The stigma and the masculine phraseology, common to colonisers and to Korean men, that defined the women's bodies as damaged, contaminated, unacceptable and unwelcome in their homeland led some of them (like Ha Kunja) to give up the wish to return home 'with a dirtied body' after the war (Han'guk chŏngsindae, 1995: 75). Chungmoo Choi (1992), a USA-based Korean Studies scholar, draws attention to the fact that many former 'comfort women' committed suicide upon returning to Korea, fearing allegations of 'promiscuity' and contempt for not having safeguarded the nation's Confucian ideals of female virtue. There seemed to be no place for them to return, despite their strong attachment to their nation. Substantial numbers of the women remained where they were abandoned after the war (Senkyûhyakunanajûni, 1992: 277). For example, after many days of agonised indecision, waiting in a Thai refugee camp to be repatriated, No Subok decided not to go back home to Korea. She ran away from the camp and lived out the rest of her life in Thailand rather than returning home (Asian Women, 1996: 8).

Their post-war lives, whether they remained where they were during the war or returned to Korea, have been haunted by the same shame, guilt and stigma. Many of them could not take up the social identities and roles for which their gendered childhood socialisation had prepared them. In so far as the Korean 'comfort women' had internalised Confucian virtues, they experienced sexual exploitation within its terms, and to some extent interpreted their own sexual violation by the soldiers as 'shameful'. Kim Haksun spoke of her bitterness, saying that she did not feel herself to be like other 'ordinary' women and that she had missed out on a life free from shame (personal interview, 1992). This personal sense of self-doubt or failure that the women felt with regard to their ability to conform to Confucian norms and values concerning virtuous womanhood, particularly chastity, often kept them from repatriating or drove them to leave their families after returning home.

Yun Sunman expressed the view that she hated herself for not having been given the chance to be 'a good girl' (Dolgopol and Paranjape, 1994: 80). This self-shaming mechanism restrained some of the women from entering into marriage. Mun P'ilgi reported that she could not bear the thought of becoming someone's wife, not with her haunting past as a 'comfort woman' (personal interview, 1992). An Pŏpsun who was taken to Singapore during the war lamented: 'To get married to a man, that is what I wanted. But with my body spoiled like that… why on earth, for conscience's sake, would I dare to get married…' (Han'guk chŏngsindae, 2001a: 236).

In addition to chastity, another core Confucian value attributed to women's bodies is reproductive capacity. Womanhood in the patriarchal Confucian code is conceived of as being actualised by one's reproductive capacity, especially the ability to produce descendants within marriage, chiefly sons, to continue her husband's family line through her fertile body. Persistent sexual exploitation from an early age had left the majority unable to have children, and this reinforced their sense of themselves as an 'unworthy' woman, not entitled to marriage. Some had hysterectomies during or after the war (Hwang Kŭmju, personal interview, 1995). The women frequently experienced their inability to give birth 'with great regret' or 'resentment' (Han'guk chŏngsindae, 1993: 92, 180). Kim Poktong gave up on her marriage and left her husband because of her inability to conceive:

> I found another woman for my husband [when I got to know that I was not able to have a child]. It would be a great sin not to bear a child to him. So I went to Buddhist temple to

> ask a monk to look for one [woman for my husband] and
> he provided him with the woman. She was not so good
> looking. She gave birth in the following January (Han'guk
> chŏngsindae, 1993: 213).

Being physically unable to conceive induced in Kim a sense of disqualification, or guilt for 'ruining' her husband's life. Thus the women often judged their own existence as well as their experience at the comfort stations in terms of the patriarchal Confucian codes of chastity and motherhood. In some cases, where they have married, this sense of shame haunted them and kept them mute, obliging them to accept further injustice, like Ch'oe Myŏngsun: 'He [my husband] tormented me while he was young since he had affairs, but I was in no position to complain' (Han'guk chŏngsindae, 1993: 268). One alternative living arrangement that a substantial number of the women entered into was cohabitation without official marriage; a situation which helped the women to deal with feelings of being unable to become a 'virtuous' wife.

The socially induced disgrace, prejudice, shame and stigma the 'comfort women' suffered are voiced by Kim Sundŏk who says that survivors, including herself, have lived for the past half century keeping all the pain and suffering to themselves, not opening their hearts even to their own close families because of humiliation and self-loathing (Korean Council, 1995: 19).

The wartime ordeal has had a range of long-term consequences on the victims/survivors' psychological and physical health. Various kinds of trauma or illness have been reported, such as continuous gynaecological infections, venereal diseases, endometriosis, vaginitis, urethritis, prolapse of the uterus, high blood pressure, tuberculosis, stomach trouble, heart trouble, mental disorders, suicide attempts, insecurity, negative attitudes to men and sex, loss of self-respect, and alcohol or drug addiction (Han'guk chŏngsindae, 1993: 56, 219, 222, 1997: 246).

Some women like Pae Ponggi, who remained in Okinawa after the war, have been on tranquiliser drugs[25] and remain haunted by trauma. Pae had developed a near obsession with cleanliness—washing her hands five times within a 30-minute conversation.[26] This O.C.D. (Obsessive Compulsive Disorder) behaviour might reflect her desire to cleanse the body she viewed as damaged or unclean. The traumatic experiences of the generation of survivors were also transferred to their children. Yu Hŭijŏng (pseudonym), a daughter of a 'comfort women' survivor, confirms that her own life has been impacted by aspects of her mother's trauma:

> This has not ended with my mum's life, but has entangled us, her children. We [my brothers and I] all have been caught up in my mum's life and we have lived with so much hardship. I really don't want to pass down this pain of war from my mother to my daughter. For that I think I should work to engage with this [comfort women] issue. [Lack of] spare time and my health are problems... I have to work hard to earn a living.... (personal interview, 1996).

Yu clearly attempts to discontinue this transgenerational transmission of trauma and shame which her mother took to the grave: 'On the night she passed away, she was saying that she felt too resentful to die.... She wouldn't be able to close her eyes due to her bitterness' (personal interview, 1996).

Most research on the impact of sexual violence notes that 'it often has a profound impact on women's attitudes to sex and men' (Kelly, 1988: 187). Some of the women had a reluctance to marry because they developed repugnance towards men and sex in general as a result of the trauma of long-term sexual violence. Yun Turi says that she is even conscious of the smell of men when they are in the same room (personal interview, 1992). Many who entered sexual relations with men again, inside or outside marriage, experienced sex only as harassment. Such trauma was shared by Jan Ruff O'Herne, Dutch victim/survivor of wartime sexual violence by the Japanese military during the Japanese occupation of Dutch East Indies (present day Indonesia) between 1942 and 1945: 'The one thing that ties us together is that we can never enjoy the pleasure of sexual intercourse even with our husbands' (Dudden, 2001: 595).[27] Another Korean survivor even says that she felt thankful when her husband had an affair with another woman (Yi, S., 1997: 266).

A victim/survivor, Oh Omok, suggested self-isolation as a method for handling social stigma and disgrace: 'Okhŭi [another 'comfort woman' survivor] who returned together with me used to say that, since we couldn't have children or be married, we should live together on our own' (Han'guk chŏngsindae, 1993: 92). In this case they entered 'a chosen period of celibacy' as 'a self-protective response' as Liz Kelly explains in the context of rape survivors (Kelly, 1988: 187). Hwang Kŭmju expressed her distrust of men and the fact that, as a result, she kept no male friends (personal interview, 1995). Another victim/survivor, Song Sindo (1922–2017), who remained in Japan after the war, reveals negative feelings towards men: 'I am sick and tired of men, even just looking at them, as I lived as a comfort woman…' (Sŏultae in'gwŏnsentŏ, 2018: 241) In her study on coping with sexual violence, Kelly sees distrust of men and conflicts about heterosexuality not as dysfunctional reactions, but as part of the women's active and adaptive attempts to cope with the reality of sexual violence (Kelly, 1988: 216). I distinguish this practice of consciously *refusing* relationships or marriage from the view the women have of themselves as *unfit* for normal marriage for reasons ranging from the loss of chastity, to venereal disease, to uncertainty about the ability to have children.

This refusal meant a 'subversion of embodied norms through the agency of performing differently, deliberately transgressing expectations' (Price and Schildrick 1999: 414) of a woman's social belonging to a man. In the Confucian code, refusing to embark on marriage was a radical step indeed. The assumption that a woman belonged to a man was a social norm for most women, and a condition for a woman's acceptability in patriarchal Confucian society. A 'comfort woman' victim/survivor described a single woman as being like 'a dog without an owner' (Yi, S., 1997: 263); with nobody to belong to and no 'protector'. In post-war Korean society, there is a social prejudice attached to women who have remained single throughout their lives, or who cohabited without officially being married or having descendants. Despite the strong influence of the Confucian value of what constitutes a 'decent' woman, some victims/survivors questioned the basic premises of Confucian patriarchal ideology and courageously attempted to refuse the fundamental opposition between ideas of the 'good wife/wise mother' and the 'whore' which recurs in post-war Korean society, and which serves the patriarchy all too well.

Chapter 4 of this work has explored the masculine colonial power's shaping of Korean 'comfort women' through the comfort station system and its repercussions in post-war Korean society. Fertile, virgin bodies are essential to the ideological construction of 'decent' womanhood. Being a wise mother and a good wife was the only respectable existence recognised for women within the context of Korean social codes. However, the body of a 'comfort woman' was defined as sexualised and 'defiled' through routinised practices of prostitution and identity reconfiguration. In this process of redefinition, analyses of the women's traumatic encounters with the Japanese soldiers reveals the complexity of personal relationships between the two groups, which sometimes leads to the formation of a long-term relationship or even a 'shadow family'.

A sexual script of the 'fallen' woman was forced upon her, stripping an individual woman of her respectability. In this way, the concept of a 'damaged' body was created through daily practices, and this inscribed upon the woman a self-image that she had become 'the defiled other' due to her supposed impurity; viewed as unworthy even after the war in the eyes of her family and society. This communal concern over womanhood reveals the existence of relationships between body, subjectivity and the nation. The damaged body then became the basis of a woman's own embodied identity. The 'comfort women's' bodies have been used not only in the Japanese colonial war project, but in Korea's nationalist post-war decolonisation project, and also Confucian ideologies of womanhood, through everyday life in multiple ways. Here the women's bodies become contested terrain where competing powers exercise their nationalist projects. Masculine colonial powers were exercised on the sexualised and racialised bodies of a 'comfort woman', and the actual bodies of women themselves became the sites of national suffering and humiliation in post-war Korea. The women's reclamations of the constructed ideas of despised bodies and the retrieval of their dignity in the face of social stigma will be explored in the following chapter.

Notes

1 Approximately 110,000 Korean conscripts served as soldiers or as low-rank para-military personnel to carry out the lowest tasks, including the guarding of captives in the Japanese military, by the end of the war. Some of them were charged and convicted after the war for committing crimes against Allied prisoners (Sŏ, 1989: 18; Cook and Cook, 1992: 113). Details on Korean soldiers in the Japanese Imperial Army can be found in the book, *Fighting for the Enemy: From Korean Unification to Transnational Korea*, by Brandon Palmer, Berghahn Books, 2013.

2 For instance, accounts by Yoshioka and Nakano (personal interview in 1996), Kim Haksun, Yi Sunok, Yi Sangok, Yi Tŭngnam and Pae Ponggi (Han'guk chŏngsindae, 1993, 1995; Kawata, 1987: 85; Senda, 1992a: 102) among others.

3 Wianbu halmŏnidŭl 'ch'iyogŭi chŏnjaeng', *Han'gyŏre Shinmun*, 19 September 1995.

4 *Chôsenjin* is a derogatory term for Korean.

5 *Shireibu, Daini-gun jokyo gaiyo* (General Situation of the Second Army), 10 December 1938, cited in Chung, 1997: 229.

6 The comfort station system differed from spontaneous war rapes in terms of the routinised and systematically organised aspects of sexual coercion employed in its maintenance. The rapes in comfort stations were not single events, but occurred repeatedly as everyday routines until the end of WWII.

7 There is a controversy about whether the ideal of chastity applied only to royal and upper class women, or to the commoners as well, in Korean women's history. Kim Yŏngchŏng proposes that the influence of Confucianism on the commoners can only be assumed (Kim Yung-Chung, 1976), while Yi Okkyŏng highlights the practice of the ideology of chastity across the whole social hierarchy (Yi, 1985). Class might have been manifested in the splitting of sex and reproduction projected onto different classes of women—prostitutes and 'ladies'.

8 In 1485, a new law was introduced regulating those who remarried, their offspring were barred from government service (Ewha yŏjadaehakkyo, 1972: 122–123), excluding them from the higher reaches of society. Remarriage for widows was legalised in 1894 with the *Kabo* reform (Kim, 1976: 83–84, 213).

9 'Shina fujin no shogai(2)', *Fujin kyofukai zasshi*, No. 14, December 1894, 'Chôsen no fuzoku', *Fujin kyofukai*, No. 14, December 1894, *Fujin kyofukai zasshi*, No. 12, October 1894 cited in Fujime, 1997: 158–159.

10 *Donga Ilbo*, 10 November 1933.

11 Yi (1996) underlines the role of the Japanese language for assimilation as a core policy of Japanese colonialism.

12 This statement was given by Chin Kyŏngp'aeng and Kim Poktong (Han'guk chŏngsindae, 1997: 24, 93). Most of the women thought that if Japan lost the war, they would all be killed as well — this is according to Ch'oe Chŏngnye, a 'comfort woman' victim/survivor (*ibid.*, 1997: 221).

13 In bigger cities, there were separate comfort stations for officers and soldiers. When it was not possible to have two stations, there were different time allocations in a single

comfort station for the two groups (Kang, C., 1997: 221). In some cases, there was a separate entrance to the comfort station for the officers and the soldiers (Yoshimi, 1992: 92).

[14] Editorial in *Donga Ilbo*, 16 January 1992. Another article in the newspaper asserts: 'Nation's pride could at least be partly recovered when apology and reparation are achieved through cracking the arrogant attitude of the Japanese government' ("Wianbu munje Kwansim Ssodaya", *Hankyoreh Sinmun*, 1 September 1997).

[15] Hun halmŏni: Oeŏnnaeŏn, *Seoul Sinmun*, 17 June 1997.

[16] Kang Man'gil said this at a panel discussion session at a Korean and Japanese joint conference on the issue of 'comfort women', 18–19 December 1993.

[17] This chapter is primarily based on the recent publication, Ahn (2018).

[18] 'Wianbu ch'ulsin halmŏni ilbon'gun changgyowaŭi "yŏnghon kyŏrhonshik"', *Joongang Ilbo*, 27 August 1998, https://news.joins.com/article/3689266.

[19] A 'comfort woman' Kang Sanghŭi tried three times to kill herself by drinking creosote (Yi, S., 1997: 293).

[20] *Sati* is a traditional Indian Hindu practice in which a widow throws herself onto her husband's funeral pyre.

[21] Dai 11 gun shireikan Anami Korechika, 'Tokubetsu hôkoku teishutsu no ken', entry for 30 March 1942, *Rikushifu dainikki* 9 (1942). Bôeichô bôei kenkyûjo toshokan cited in Yoshimi, 1995b: 148.

[22] References 42 (1938) and 44 (1939) in Yoshimi, 1992: 197–199, 200–201.

[23] Some feminist research has criticised the focus on the victimisation of women, especially research on sexual violence. As Carol Vance points out, women who stress sexuality as a form of social control have also been criticised for neglecting its pleasure (Vance, 1984). I am aware that there is an aspect of pleasure in women's sexuality, but in the context of 'comfort women', this point is of little relevance.

[24] See note 4.

[25] '"Chamae wianbu" mi p'oro suyongso kirok chŏŭm konggae', *Donga Ilbo*, 22 August 1998.

[26] Chŏngshindae halmŏniŭi chugŭm, iguksŏ pigŭkchŏk sam…'yuhaerado koguk ttange', *Donga Ilbo*, 25 October 1991.

[27] See also Ruff-O'Herne, *Fifty Years of Silence: Comfort Woman in Indonesia*. London: Thomas Beeler, 1998.

Chapter 5

Current 'Comfort Women' Issues: Breaking the Silence and Global Solidarity

T his final chapter explores current 'comfort women' issues such as the eventual breaking of the 'comfort women' survivors' silence and the negotiation of their memories and commemoration. In the wider context of global movements for gender justice, solidarity with other victims/survivors of wartime sexual violence will be reviewed. This chapter will conclude with the assertion that the 'comfort women' issue remains unresolved and therefore continues to be significant, not only domestically in Korea and Japan but also on the international stage.

Silence

Silence surrounding the 'comfort women' system endured for half a century. How did silence last such a long period of time? In addition to the silence of the Western Allies during the war crime trials (such as the Tokyo War Crimes Trials, 1946–1948) and the Japanese government's position of denial as noted in the introductory chapter of this book, neither Korea nor any of the other nations whose citizens had been subjected to such harsh treatment made any attempt to bring this issue to the fore in the early post-war years. The politics of 'collective amnesia' were active in South Korea after the war and Japanese colonial history—including the 'comfort women' issue—is often deemed 'a matter of the past', implying that it is neither relevant nor constructive to bring these issues to light again in the future-oriented present. The politics of 'forgetting' this particular episode of the past and the 'collective amnesia' in which the state participated are important points of investigation that help to explain how it was possible to maintain silence for so long, even within South Korea itself.

In the hegemonic, masculinist narratives of resistance by 'national heroes' which dominate Korea's nationalist literature, the 'comfort women' issue has been both embarrassing and emasculating for Korean men, and shameful for the women and their families. The 'comfort women's' exclusion from reckonings with the colonial past thus brings up questions of representation and voice linked to the unequal social power of the sexes (Choi, 1992: 98). This situation helps to explain why, among the many issues discussed in post-war Korea, those of casualties and forced labourers[1] emerged as matters of public concern much earlier than that of the women involved in the comfort station system.

Familial, communal and internalised pressures for silence kept the women's 'shameful' pasts hidden. In her powerful statement, Kim Haksun (1924–1997), a victim/survivor who first made her wartime past public in 1990, indicated possible family pressure to refrain from speaking out: 'I have neither husband nor son, nothing to lose. That's why it should be me coming out first rather than anybody else. Who else could come out first if not me.'[2] In her case, having no surviving close family members freed her from the unspoken obligation to remain mute in order to preserve their reputation.

Indeed, salvaging the family's honour was often an issue when the victims/survivors attempted to break their silences, as Kim Tŏkchin experienced:

> I went to visit and told one of my nephews, whom I supported in his studies, about my past and asked if I should register at the Council [Korean Council for the Women Drafted for Military Sexual Slavery by Japan]. He said 'your children will be shocked.' He discouraged me from registering. I discussed the matter with another nephew. He wept as he listened to my story and advised me not to register. He said

'It will break your son's heart. What will your son [stepson] in America say when he hears all this?' But I felt uneasy and couldn't sleep at all …. I told my son about the whole thing, and he wept uncontrollably, saying 'Mother, you have lived so courageously even with such a rough past …. I am proud of you'. But the wife of my youngest son became despondent, and even my son is now disheartened. I feel very sad and guilty when I see them (Han'guk chŏngsindae, 1993: 56–57).

The social trope of shame and impurity associated with the women's pasts is therefore not only an individual matter, but one concerning the family and community they belong to. For those women who have come forward like Kim, the outcome has been to trigger feelings of guilt within the family.

The conceptualisation of 'chastity' and 'virtuous' female sexuality in relation to national 'purity' permitted the silencing of the women for 50 years after the end of war. The sense of shame that many of the victims/survivors felt and ideas of Korean national pride combined to collude with the interests of the Japanese in denying what had taken place, in silencing the women into a state of 'collective amnesia'.

After the war, the victims/survivors initially attempted to purge their wartime memories, and to suppress the feelings evoked by recalling their experiences as 'comfort women'. Yet these women could only suppress their memories to an extent. Certain visual stimuli might trigger memories of their ordeals, such as representations of Japan or of any form of violence: for example, the Japanese national flag, men in military uniform, or watching violent scenes on TV. These types of flashbacks made it possible for the women to retrieve memories buried deep within their subconscious. Yi Okpun says that in order to obliterate the memory of her time in the comfort station, she cut off the part of a photo showing her with Japanese soldiers (Han'guk chŏngsindae, 1993: 143).

The women's memories of their past as 'comfort women' are inscribed in their bodies. As Elaine Scarry puts it, 'what is remembered in the body is well remembered' (Scarry, 1985: 109). Their embodied scars from the days at the comfort station seem too deep to be cured: 'I will not be able to forget what happened even after I die' (Yun Turi, personal interview in 1992). There is a complex interplay between processes of forgetting and remembering.

Most of the women's memories of the war crystallised around anti-Japanese resentments. Expression of 'ineradicable anger and resentment' (Han'guk chŏngsindae, 1993: 49) towards Japan is very common in their narratives. Yun Turi stated that 'even when I see the Japanese national flag, my anger against Japan still pours out' (personal interview, 1993). The Japanese flag is still regarded as a symbol of Japanese colonial power at the hands of which they consider their lives to have been ruined. Another victim/survivor, Chang Ch'unwŏl, who has remained in China, commented that 'only if there had been no Japanese colonialists, or no war, would I not have ended up in China' (Han'guk chŏngsindae, 1995: 121).

In post-war Korean society, silence and forgetting have been a way of avoiding social blame and stigma, and these tactics have even allowed certain victims/survivors to cling to a modicum of resilience. Liz Kelly convincingly describes the motivation to forget in the context of victims of sexual violence, 'if one fears being blamed, there is a strong incentive to forget rather than risk this response' (Kelly, 1988: 195). Such analysis partially explains why certain military 'comfort women' victims/survivors like Kim Punsŏn opted to participate in their own silence and the politics of forgetting: 'I don't want to remember the dirty episode. It is too painful to remind myself of. It is wise to forget it. If I keep remembering this, it might drive me to my death….' (Han'guk chŏngshindae, 1997: 116).

Therefore, repression of memory cannot be interpreted as mere denial, but should be seen as an active coping strategy in order to avoid the traumatic reliving of distressing experiences and to facilitate rebuilding one's life in the aftermath of the war. Remaining silent might be considered a form of conscious choice or an exercise of autonomy for women who remained vulnerable in these circumstances. Homi Bhabha's (1998: 11) concept of employing negotiation instead of negation is relevant in interpreting the women's choice of silence as a positive effort to rearticulate themselves post-war, rather than as an attempt to negate antagonistic social responses by speaking out.

Dubravka Zarkov points out that rigid concepts of agency, emancipation and empowerment may not be the best framework for studying women's diverse positioning within violent conflicts (Zarkov, 2007: 225). Building on this point, I argue that these concepts need not be discarded, but could be redefined to embrace women's nuanced and complex decision-making processes in very precarious circumstances, which are often interpreted as failures in exercising agency or power. A foundational principle of second-wave feminist thought, that 'the personal is political', should be reflected in this reconceptualisation as personal choice is itself a site of politics. The challenges confronted by 'comfort women' in the face of both masculine colonialism and Korean nationalism were met with resistance or coping strategies ranging from vague or nuanced expression to direct action, demonstrating that the women have lived as both victims and survivors. The women exercised different degrees of embodied agency. Their responses varied over time and space, ranging from vulnerable victims exploited in their relationships, to engaged agents actively managing their relationships with the military men as seen in Chapter 4. This reality poses a challenge to the simple, dichotomous approach to women's experiences as either victims or agents—a rigid binary which does not accommodate the complexity in constant negotiation of self-subject positioning that takes place within the context of daily life under a patriarchal colonial regime. In reality, there are variations and shifts in the self-positioning of the 'comfort women' victims/survivors between conscious agency and passive subjectivity. Exploring these multiple subject-positionings allows unitary concepts of identity which represent subjectivity as monolithic, fixed and non-contradictory to be challenged.

Breaking the Silence

Though their voices were muted, the women had not been completely silenced. In the period marking the end of the Cold War and the onset of Korean democratisation, the previously suppressed voices of South Korea's past during WWII and the Korean War (1950–1953) began to emerge. Concerns over 'coming to terms with the past' were taking a central role within the civilian administration in the process of replacing South Korea's last military government (1963–1993). The silence surrounding the 'comfort women' issue was finally broken and brought to the attention of the public for the first time in 1990 by an advocacy group, the Korean Council for the Women Drafted for Military Sexual Slavery by Japan, which launched a 'comfort women' redress campaign. Starting with the late Kim Haksun (1924–1997), victims/survivors gradually began to come forward and share their traumatic wartime experiences.

Ever since the repressed issue came to light, the South Korean public and policymakers have struggled to negotiate the disruption of the state's 'collective amnesia' towards the 'comfort women' issue, and to come to terms with these silenced horrors; voices long unheard in the reported history of WWII. This issue has ignited a host of other concerns, including the state's reluctance to deal with its own standing in the global arena, and questions related to national identity and understandings of the past. South Korea was coming to terms with the mirror of modernity, and this involved revisiting long-forgotten ghosts. The conversations I was fortunate enough to participate in with the Korean victims/survivors and their Japanese soldier counterparts seemed long overdue. Furthermore, while the world saw them as living history, tucked away in some remote corner of social consciousness, this past was deeply embedded in contemporary questions. Where to go from here? How to reconcile the colonial past? Social norms were being unsettled, and at the centre of this disruptive process stood the issue of the 'comfort women'.

In the late 1970s, the issue of sex tourism carried out by Japanese men in Korea was raised by the women's movements in both South Korea and Japan.[3] It was out of this initial campaign that the 'comfort women' issue later emerged, with the realisation that sex tourism had a more sinister historical antecedent in the context of Japan's colonial relationship with Korea. In the 1980s, before survivors started coming forward, Yun Chŏngok, a former professor and contemporary of the victims/survivors, started conducting pioneering work on this ignored history. Yun made investigative trips to the sites of WWII comfort stations in Japan, Thailand, Papua New Guinea and China and exposed the issue by making presentations at public forums (personal interview, 1996).

In August 1991, Kim Haksun's courageous decision to be the first 'comfort woman' victim/survivor in South Korea to make her past public was a statement that counteracted the Japanese government's denial of the very existence of comfort stations, and provided a direct challenge to the politics of forgetting this part of colonial history:

> I felt outraged about Japan. How can the Japanese government deny what they did [with the comfort station system], even though here I am as a living witness! I have lived so far by burying my horrible past in the depths of my heart, but I can no longer bear the fact that Koreans forget the past (personal interview, 1992).

The rupture of silence is situated in temporality. Most of the women, like Kim, only broke their silence in the later stages of their lives. Their advanced age may have been a major factor influencing their decision to share their pasts, as there may have been a sense of personal urgency in releasing long-repressed pain and agony before it was too late. With limited access to support and only a remote possibility of achieving justice, many other women chose to take their pasts with them to their graves. Kim's powerful testimony provided other victims/survivors with the courage to break their long silence as well. As the 'comfort women' campaign gained momentum and provided a collective and supportive forum for the victims/survivors, more and more of those either directly affected or witnesses to the events began to share their testimonies and experiences of what had happened in comfort stations. The women's 'collaborative silence' (Pettman, 1996: 191) had been broken and the search for social recognition of the wartime injustices the women had endured had begun.

On the one hand, rupturing one's long silence to give testimony concerning appalling suffering could be a deeply painful process, since it involves the traumatic re-enactment of suffering, and a re-experiencing of bitterness, anger, pain and humiliation. On the other hand, the women's testimonial narratives were finally given a platform. The practice of giving testimonial narratives developed as a form of contestation and became the basis of demands for an apology and reparations from the Japanese government. Some of the victims/survivors testified in court to pursue judicial action by filing lawsuits against the Japanese government. The first lawsuit filed by a Korean 'comfort woman' survivor, Kim Haksun, claiming damages and compensation was launched in the Tokyo District Court in 1991. Another survivor, Song Sindo (1922–2017), also filed a lawsuit against the Japanese government which dragged on for 10 years (1993–2003).[4] These women's testimonies were actively engaging with redressing both a wider unresolved colonial legacy issue and the harm inflicted on individuals by the state of Japan. However, the conservative Japanese government's stance has been to deny any legal responsibility and it has thus far failed to fully atone for this issue.

The 'comfort women' campaign led by women's groups in South Korea and Japan gained momentum in the early 1990s, due to the re-emerging civil movement for democratisation occurring in Korea[5] at the end of the Cold War. The development of Asian feminism and transnational advocacy links between Asian countries and the rest of the globe have promoted increased awareness of sexual violence and have been crucial in bringing issues of sexual enslavement to light. The 'comfort women' victims/survivors along with advocacy groups in Asia, including some in Japan, brought heavy pressure on the Japanese government to address this issue directly. The impact of what had been kept quiet for so long was explosive, bursting forth initially in Korea, then Japan and eventually across the world.

Domestic, regional and global shifts alongside the civic-initiated 'comfort women' campaign which began in 1990 in South Korea have also played important roles in bringing the long hidden issue of Japan's military 'comfort women' system to the forefront in both the domestic and international communities. At the same time, other cases of sexual violence in conflict zones, such as those of the former Yugoslavia and African regions such as Rwanda, the Democratic Republic of the Congo (DRC), Uganda and Sierra Leone among others, have been brought before bodies such as the International Criminal Court (ICC). This publicity created global momentum for addressing sexual violence in the context of armed conflict, which contributed to the quest to obtain redress for the long-silenced issue of the 'comfort women' system.

What is quite remarkable in this new period of contestation is that, during this time, the former 'comfort women' have had to fight against their own Korean society, not just against their foreign Japanese tormentors. Survivors and advocacy groups such as the Korean Council for the Women Drafted for Military Sexual Slavery by Japan (Han'guk Chŏngshindae Hyŏbŭihoe) denounced both the South Korean and the Japanese governments for their negligence and irresponsibility in dealing with the gravity of the Japanese military 'comfort women' issue.[6] In breaking their own silence, the women broke the silence not only of the colonial oppressors, but that of the male Korean nationalists and of the Korean government as well. Kang Tŏkkyŏng (1929–1997) drew attention to the fact that the women's sexual oppression was seen as 'a shame of the nation, Korea': 'There are still some who say that what we did is shameful [a shame to our nation], but they are indeed ignorant people' (Han'guk Chŏngshindae, 1993: 184). Refusal to be silenced was hence a form of resistance against social stigmatisation and the concept of 'national dishonour'. The act of speaking about their experiences was a means of reclaiming dignity and self-respect while simultaneously seeking justice and recognition.

The victims/survivors made another important challenge to the nation's memory and their exclusion from the ranks of those who had been war victims, in their request to be buried in *Manghyan-ŭi tongsan* (The Hill of National Commemoration) the national burial ground and monument for those Koreans who have passed away abroad, such as forced labourers during the Japanese colonial period. In a gesture that holds great significance in challenging the stigma of national dishonour, and transforming perceptions of the women from 'defiled prostitutes' to war victims on par with the forced labourers, more than 40 former 'comfort women' who have died since the 1990s have now been buried at this national cemetery, providing state recognition of the harm the women endured under colonial rule. Another societal effect of the victims/survivors' public emergence is that their narratives have provided a potential basis for reconstructing new feminine, anti-colonial identities. Indeed, the very act of speaking out itself creates challenges to patriarchal concepts of femininity.

Figure 1. Kim Seokyung and Kim Eunsung, *P'yŏnghwaŭi sonyŏsang* (Peace Girl Statue) was erected in 2011 to mark the 1,000th Wednesday Demonstration, a weekly rally which has taken place since January 1992. Bronze sculpture, studio view. (Photo courtesy of the artists)

Remembering and Commemorating

The 'comfort women's' testimonies transformed the collective amnesia surrounding gendered harm rooted in colonial history into a collective national memory. Survivors' testimonies have mobilised domestic support, with the younger post-war generation becoming active in participating in the associated campaigns. Rallies called 'Wednesday Demonstrations' have been held on a weekly basis by the surviving 'comfort women' and their supporters in front of the Japanese embassy in Seoul, Korea since January 1992, and call on the government to address Japan's responsibility for its wartime wrongdoings.[7] With the 1,386th demonstration taking place on 8 May 2019, this weekly demonstration represents the longest running protest rally in the world.

To mark the 1,000th Wednesday rally on 14 December 2011, a 'comfort women' monument called *P'yŏnghwaŭi sonyŏsang* (Peace Girl Statue), representing a young girl sitting on a wooden chair with her clenched fists resting on her lap, was erected in front of the

Japanese embassy in Seoul, South Korea (Fig. 1). The Korean Council for the Women Drafted for Military Sexual Slavery by Japan (*Han'guk Chŏngshindae Hyŏbŭihoe*), which is the leading Korean advocacy group focused on redressing the 'comfort women' issue, has been working on a project to erect similar statues nationwide in South Korea and across the globe. This initiative has led to diplomatic tensions between Japan and the countries where the memorials are being erected—including Korea. The Abe administration has demanded the removal of the monuments, both in Korea and other countries. The 'comfort women' monument erected in San Francisco in 2018 depicts three women—from China, Korea and the Philippines—who symbolise women and teenage girls forced to work at comfort stations from the early 1930s until Japan's defeat in 1945. Controversy surrounding this particular statue resulted in the termination of the sister-city relationship between Osaka and San Francisco on 2 October 2018, as the Japanese city protested against the public display of the 'comfort women' monument.[8]

Since gaining power in 2017, the Moon Jae-in administration in South Korea has paid attention to the issue of 'comfort women', and even dedicated 14 August (the date the first survivor, Kim Haksun, went public) as Comfort Women Memorial Day. This date was first recognised in 2013 via a civic initiative and the first official commemoration ceremony was organised by the Ministry of Women and Family of South Korea at *Manghyang-ŭi tongsan* (The Hill of the National Commemoration) in 2018.[9]

In addition to constructing 'comfort women' monuments, advocacy groups in Korea and Japan have helped in fundraising for the establishment of museums featuring artefacts associated with war and women's rights, such as the 'Women's Active Museum on War and Peace' in Tokyo, 2005 and the 'War and Women's Human Rights Museum (*Chŏnjaenggwa yŏsŏng pangmulgwan*)' in Seoul, 2012 (Ahn, 2015: 109–110). Establishing such museums and monuments serves as a commemoration of, and symbolic reparation for, the victims/survivors and has recently become a key objective of the campaign's agenda. Just as the campaign to redress this issue started from a civic initiative, rather than being state-sponsored, the museums and the 'comfort women' memorials represent cultural mnemonic devices funded from the ground up. The numerous 'comfort women' monuments, *P'yŏnghwaŭi sonyŏsang* (Peace Girl Statues), nationwide display the women's past in public spaces to seek the public recognition they deserve. The past is represented in the present in these physical sites of memory which also represent powerful sites of counter-narrative directed at Japan's current posture of denial. They are mnemonic platforms which function to stage the experiences and images of the victims/survivors.

The half-century of amnesia about the issue in post-war South Korea has turned into a 'memory boom' (Ahn, 2008b), and is now commemorated through various sites of memory including museums in Korea and Japan. Exhibitions and memorial services have been held in honour of the victims/survivors. The artefacts, exhibits, museum displays and Peace Girl Statues are shaped by memory politics associated with interpretations of the 'comfort women's' past emerging from the collective memory of post-war South Korean society. Within this remembering, a mainstream narrative has emerged which features a young, innocent 'virgin' who has been lured against her will or kidnapped into the comfort station system.

Though this master narrative is not without basis, one may raise questions as to how accurately the memorials or museum displays reflect the complicated, lived experiences of the 'comfort women'; in other words, how such complex experiences can be recognised and remembered through sites of memory. Unfortunately, the Peace Girl Statues do not appear to permit challenges to the patriarchal concepts of femininity which were embedded in the wartime 'comfort women' system. These post-war spatial representations of gender discourses surrounding the issue run the risk of reinforcing the very same patriarchal gender norms in question, based on a dichotomy of innocent and virtuous 'virgins' as opposed to guilty or 'virtue-less' women. In fact, it is this very framework that has haunted the 'comfort women' victims/survivors throughout their lives and imposed upon them a sense of shame. Questions arise as to what extent this memorial statue creates alternative ways of remembering and commemorating gender-based violence in war, transcending the patriarchal binary of womanhood: How is this particular past to be remembered and commemorated within the broader scope of gender justice? Does the commemoration of this part of Korea's past through monuments or museum displays go beyond the framework of ethnic nationalism in order to build alliances and solidarity across national boundaries?

As nationalist sentiments have been gaining momentum in East Asia since the early 2000s, memories and representations of Korea's colonial past have been essential to the building of a national future. Although the problem of contextualising the comfort station system during the war has become crucial to the formation of a collective memory of Japanese colonialism in South Korea, the past of the 'comfort women' themselves remains gendered and nationalised. The story of Korean collaborators in the programme, or the role of local Koreans operating as brokers in procuring women and running or managing the comfort stations, has yet to be adequately discussed in post-war South Korea, even though this collaboration is so central to nationalist issues. Japanese neo-nationalists who seek to mould a positive collective image of Japan's wartime past still actively engage in memory politics, especially during the current Abe administration in effect since 2012, making strenuous efforts to frame a bright future for Japan. As identified earlier, contested memories concerning the 'comfort women' issue have been actively presented in the nationalist narratives of both Korea and Japan.

Solidarity: A Global Phenomenon

In contrast to the contested and divided nationalist narratives, victims/survivors' testimonials and narratives have given rise to a sense of solidarity with countries in which there are other women who survived the comfort station system, as well as victims of other incidents of conflict-related sexual violence. When their stories were made public, individual survivors became members of a greater collective resistance. Women's groups working alongside them have undertaken joint global demonstrations on several occasions. For example, on 14 December 2011, rallies were held in 50 global cities to mark the 1,000th Wednesday Demonstration.

Since 2012, Korean 'comfort women' victims/survivors have been forming groups to support and empower each other, and these groups have now branched out to offer support to other victims/survivors across the globe. Unfortunately, armed conflict-related sexual violence is still widespread in Africa, Asia, Europe and Latin America. For this reason, the Korean Council for the Women Drafted for Military Sexual Slavery by Japan founded the 'Butterfly Fund' (*Nabi Kigŭm*) in 2012 to support victims of gender-based violence in armed conflicts. This fund was established with the support of donations from the Korean public and two 'comfort women' survivors, Kim Poktong (1926–2019) and Kil Wŏnok. The Butterfly Fund sends regular monetary support to civil activist groups in the Democratic Republic of the Congo (DRC) working to rehabilitate Congolese victims/survivors of conflict-related sexual violence perpetrated by armed groups operating in the eastern part of the DRC. In a letter dated 18 April 2012, Kim and Kil expressed a sense of solidarity with Rebecca Masika Katsuva[10] (1966–2016), a Congolese activist who survived multiple rapes by armed groups. The letter reads: 'I lived with pain in my heart for 72 years. As there are still people in foreign countries who suffer the same pain as ours, if I receive any legal compensation from the Japanese government, I want to use it for them' (Yun, 2016: 266). In this letter, Kim and Kil share sympathy, pain and encouragement with other victims/survivors. Congolese survivors subsequently responded to the letter and have attended solidarity meetings in Korea. A Congolese survivor, Safi, shared her story in Korea on 16 November 2015:

> Today I want to thank the sisters of Korea. People from The Korean Council came to our village and gave us hope. We were told what the Koreans are doing and we are not the only ones who got through this. Thanks for giving us hope (Yun, 2016: 273).

The interactions between the Korean and Congolese victims/survivors through correspondence, visits and financial support have consolidated reciprocal trust and enabled mutual empowerment.

Since 2013, the scope of Korean victims/survivors' solidarity has also extended to sufferers in Vietnam. What is striking about the alliance with their Vietnamese counterparts is that war atrocities here, including sexual violence and massacre, were committed between 1964 and 1973 by South Korean military forces during the Vietnam War (1955–1975). Since 2015, Korean activists, 'comfort women' survivors and their supporters in the post-war young generation have actively investigated the wartime harm inflicted on Vietnamese women by visiting them in person, and have worked to redress this sensitive issue within South Korea in a reflective way. Unsurprisingly, efforts to publicise the Vietnamese survivors' testimonies have been met with resistance and even threats on the part of Korean veterans who fought in the Vietnam War. Their resistance asserts that raising the issue of sexual violence in wartime Vietnam is a case of defamation against servicemen who fought against communists in the cause of 'world peace'. However, Korean civic advocacy groups have continued campaigns to address these atrocities and support the Vietnamese victims/survivors, with the Butterfly Fund having sent them financial support since 2015.[11] A couple of surviving Korean 'comfort women' have also donated to another civic organisation, the Korea–Vietnam Peace Foundation (est. 2016), which seeks to raise awareness and gain redress for Korea's wrongdoings during the Vietnam War.[12]

The Korean Council for Women Drafted for Military Sexual Slavery by Japan also organises the annual Butterfly Peace Tour to Vietnam, which gives the South Korean public a chance to visit sites of wartime violence against civilians, and sites of memory like museums and memorials and to meet with victims and their families. The tour's purpose as stated in an advertisement for the 2019 tour from 17 to 23 January includes the following statement:

> In order not to forget our accountability and in order to build peace hand in hand, we undertake a Butterfly Peace Tour, heading for Vietnam, where the wounds of war have not yet been healed. Accumulated, our activities will become a bridge needed to recognise historical fact and the responsibility of the Korean government, and will lead to peace for our future generation. We are looking for fellow travellers.[13]

Addressing this unresolved issue from the Vietnam War makes possible the formation of bonds of solidarity amongst victims/survivors of wartime sexual violence across borders by transcending the very ethnic nationalism which has played such a significant role in the Korean 'comfort women' issue within the country itself.

Experiences of transnational/global solidarity are intertwined with global issues of wartime gendered harm and local issues concerning the 'comfort women' campaign which is posited within the framework of colonial legacy which Korea still has to come to terms with. Transnational interactions sometimes reveal existing tensions between the nationalising aspects of the 'comfort women' campaign (which takes an ethnic nationalist stance) and the denationalising aspects of transnational solidarity with other survivors. As noted in Chapter 4, the 'comfort women' are often seen as a symbol of Korean victimisation. Collective Korean victimhood is juxtaposed with the collective guilt of the Japanese—a campaign which has created a source of Korean unity against Japan and has also served as a source of reconciliation between the two Koreas since North and South Korean actors began cooperating on the issue (Ahn, 2015: 99). A sense of shared experience as a victim of wartime sexual violence which transcends nationalist affiliations has functioned as a catalyst for the foundations of solidarity (Ahn, 2015: 105) such as physical harm, emotional trauma, stigma, social ostracism and inability to experience sexual pleasure. Therefore, maintaining a nationalist approach or hierarchy of victimhood may act as an impediment against transnational/global solidarity amongst survivors.

The South Korean survivors' links to others have continued to expand to include women who took refuge in Germany. Survivor Kil Wŏnok visited Berlin in 2017 to meet and support African refugees who have lived through conflict-related sexual violence in their countries of origin.[14] South Korean survivors were also involved in the 2018 establishment of two peace prizes, the Kim Poktong Peace Prize and the Kil Wŏnok Peace Prize, which are awarded to activists who contribute to eradicating wartime violence and to promoting women's rights. Acan Sylvia Obal, a wartime sexual violence survivor and women's rights activist in Uganda, won the first

Kim Poktong Peace Prize in 2018.[15] This effort expands the global network of solidarity and further publicises issues of sexual violence in armed conflicts globally.

These efforts and experiences in forming and diffusing interactive transnational/global solidarity networks have allowed for the emergence of reflective reviews on the nationalist narratives about 'comfort women' and an increased awareness of the adverse gender hierarchy and paradigm, which has been persistent in Korean nationalist narratives. Consequently, this awareness has brought about a gradual shifting and strengthening of transnational gender perspectives in the 'comfort women' campaign in Korea (Ahn, 2015: 107), through the search for transnational gender justice beyond the framework of ethnic nationalism. On a macro level, the solidarity stemming from the Korean survivors' movement has helped to influence local and global politics on sexual violence in armed conflicts, including combating a culture of impunity towards gender-based violence. On a micro level, the movement has brought attention to problems of multiple, overlapping and discrete oppressions, and to the need for rehabilitation for women caught up in such situations.

The subject of 'comfort women' has functioned as a transnational platform and has provided an impetus to address gender justice and gender-sensitive human rights, rather than adhering to the narrow and rigid boundaries of ethnic nationalism. In this process, the personal pain of Korean victims/survivors has been transformed into a shared experience within the broader context of gendered harm and gender justice. Some of the more confident survivors, like Kim and Kil, have been transformed into activists, enthusiastically engaging not only in the 'comfort women' campaign, but also in broader global issues of wartime sexual violence. They have preached peace and a world without war: 'No more war to be waged. No one needs a war' (Yun, 2016: 155). This single message is among the most sincere and powerful to emerge from the once silent, now audible voices of the 'comfort women' victims/survivors.

As noted at the beginning of this book, tensions between South Korea and Japan have recently escalated because of trade restrictions on exports of hi-tech materials to South Korea imposed by the Abe administration in July 2019. Although on the surface this diplomatic conflict stems from a trade dispute between two countries, the roots of the dispute lie in the underlying tensions between the two nations, including the unresolved issues of the 'comfort women' and forced labour during WWII. Recent events demonstrate the continued contemporary relevance of this aspect of the colonial legacy and its profound impact on Korea–Japan relations (on both an inter-governmental level and in terms of each nation's citizens' sentiments toward each other). Beyond the regional context, the issue arguably has significant global implications given the debate around sexual violence associated with current armed conflicts worldwide. On the basis of achieving gender justice, unless and until all the issues that have not yet been settled are dealt with to the satisfaction of those involved, it will not be possible for wounds to heal or for reconciliation to be achieved — at either an individual or a national level — as a precursor for peace and stability in East Asia. In order to secure some degree of 'closure' for dying or deceased victims/survivors and their families, allowing them to come to terms with this part of their past, priority must be given to resolving long-standing issues outlined in this volume. Both reconciliation and justice represent essential foundations for the process of individual healing and efforts to improve inter-governmental relations which will enable both citizens and nations to 'move on' from the troubled past towards a more harmonious future.

Notes

1 The issues of male casualties and former forced labourers were raised by members of the Korean Association for the Pacific War Victims (t'aep'yŏngnyang chŏnjaeng hisaengja yujok'oe) during the late 1980s and early 1990s.

2 'Suyo siwi 25nyŏnŭl marhada' iCOOP, http://m.blog.naver.com/icoopkorea/22064 8195646.

3 In the late 1960s and throughout the 1970s, many Japanese men went on sex tours to Taiwan and Korea. This sex tourism expanded to Southeast Asia, particularly the Philippines and Thailand. See Murata (1995) and Matsui (1987).

4 Naŭi maŭmŭn chiji anatta:,Chaeil Wianbu P'ihae Song Sinto Halmŏni Pyŏlse, *Hankyoreh Sinmun*, 19 December 2017, http://www.hani.co.kr/arti/international/international_general/824185.html.

5 The last military government in Korea was replaced by a civilian administration in 1993.

6 'The Korean Council for the Women Drafted for Military Sexual Slavery by Japan 99th Weekly News', 2–9 March 2008.

7 On the Wednesday Demonstration, see Yun, 2016.

8 Justin McCurry, "Osaka drops San Francisco as sister city over 'comfort women' statue", *The Guardian*, 4 October 2018. https://www.theguardian.com/world/2018/oct/04/osaka-drops-san-francisco-as-sister-city-over-comfort-women-statue

9 Another 'comfort women' memorial was erected at the national cemetery in 2018. See P'yŏnghwarŭl wihan kiŏk, Ilbon'gun wianbu p'ihaeja kirimŭi nal, Chŏt Chŏngbu Kinyŏmshik Kaech'oe, Yŏsŏnggajokpu (Ministry of Women and Family), 13 August 2018, http://www.mogef.go.kr/nw/enw/nw_enw_s001d.do?mid=mda700&bbtSn=706451.

10 Rebecca Masika Katsuva obituary, *The Guardian*, 9 February 2016, http://www.theguardian.com/world/2016/feb/09/rebccca-masika-katsuva-obituary.

11 'Nabigigŭm, Pet'ŭnam han'gukkun sŏngp'ongnyŏng p'ihae halmŏni-dŭlkke saenghwal chiwŏn'gŭm chŏndal', http://cafe.daum.net/hopenabi/5S8W/22. From September 1964 to March 1973 South Korea sent more than 300,000 troops to South Vietnam, https://en.wikipedia.org/wiki/South_Korea_in_the_Vietnam_War.

12 Information available on the homepage for the Korea–Vietnam Peace Foundation Homepage, http://www.kovietpeace.org/p/page09.

13 2019 nyŏn Pet'ŭnam Nabi P'yŏnghwa Kihaeng sinch'ŏng hagi, https://docs.google.com/forms/d/1e_YtfABrhRx3dkaDfUNaj4Ns57JBTEqvRkPTr5wQm_s/viewform?edit_requested=true.

14 'Berlin-sŏ nanmin yŏsŏng wirohan Kil Wŏnok halmŏni', *Hankyoreh Sinmun*, 3 December 2017, http://www.hani.co.kr/arti/society/rights/821839.html.

15 'Chelhoe Kim Poktong p'yŏnghwasange Yŏsŏng in'gwŏn undongga, Acan Sylvia Obal', *Yŏsŏng shinmun*, 6 June 2018, http://www.womennews.co.kr/news/142501.

Appendix: List of Former 'Comfort Women' and Japanese Veterans

List of former 'comfort women' and Japanese veterans interviewed in person or whose narratives were used for this book.

Interviewees: 'Comfort Women' Victims/Survivors

Name	Place taken to	Year of birth
1) Kim Haksun	China	1924
2) Mun Okchu	Burma, China	1924
3) Mun P'ilgi	China	1925
4) Chŏn Kŭmhwa	China	1924
5) Kim Ŭllye	Nanking, China	1926
6) Kang Tŏkkyŏng	Japan	1929
7) Yi Yongsu	Taiwan	1928
8) Hwang Kŭmju	China	1922
9) Yun Turi	Korea	1928
10) Ch'oe Myŏngsun	Japan	1926
11) Yu Hŭijŏng (daughter)		

(1) Kim Haksun (1924–1997) was at a comfort station in China during WWII and the first in South Korea to testify in public that she had been taken as a 'comfort woman' by the Japanese military, in 1991. She filed a lawsuit against Japan in the Tokyo District Court, for damages and other compensation in 1991. She died on 16 December 1997 at the age of 73.

(2) Mun Okchu (1924–1996) was a 'comfort woman' initially in Burma and then in China during the war. Her Japanese name at the comfort stations was Fumihara Yoshiko. Her biography was published in Japan in 1996 (Mun Okchu. 1996. *Mun Oku-chu: Biruma Sensen Tateshidan no 'Ianfu' Datta Watashi*. As told to Morikawa Machiko. Tokyo: Nashinokisha). She was very talented at playing *Changgu*, a Korean traditional percussion instrument, and singing. When she sang Arirang, one of the songs the 'comfort women' secretly sang in comfort stations, all her regret, anger and pain poured out through her voice.

(3) Mun P'ilgi (1925–2008) left home in the hope of studying and earning some money in 1943, as one of her neighbours who collaborated with the Japanese police had promised. She was sent to a comfort station in Manchuria, China. She was an active participant in the 'comfort women' campaign.

(4) Chŏn Kŭmhwa (1923–1994) was held at a comfort station in China during the war. After returning to Korea, she had three children and died on 12 March 1994 as a result of cardiac failure. Her Japanese name was Sumiko.

(5) Kim Ŭllye (1926–2008) was born in 1926, but in her official registration papers it was stated that she was born 10 years later. She was in Nanking, China during the war.

(6) Kang Tŏkkyŏng (1929–1997) was initially sent to Japan with the first group of the *Yŏjajŏngsindae* (the Women's Volunteer Labour Corps) to the Fujikoshi aeroplane plant in Toyama-ken, Japan in 1944, and was later taken to a comfort station. She died on 2 February 1997, and left some paintings in which she depicted her life there.

(7) Yi Yongsu still remembered the Japanese military songs she learned at the comfort stations in Taiwan at the time I met her and spoke fluent Japanese. She mainly had to 'serve' a commando unit in Taiwan.

(8) Hwang Kŭmju (1922–2013) was a 'comfort woman' in China during the war and had been internationally active to give her testimony and to publicise the issue of 'comfort women' since the campaign launched in the 1990s.

(9) Yun Turi (1928–2009) was taken to a comfort station in Busan, South Korea.

(10) Ch'oe Myŏngsun used a pseudonym. She was taken to a comfort station in Japan. She married and had children after returning to South Korea.

(11) Yu Hŭijŏng is the daughter of one of my respondents.

Interviewees: Japanese Veterans

Name	Place Stationed
1) Yoshioka Tadao	Taiwan
2) Nakano Takashi	China
3) Miyamoto Shizuo	Indonesia
4) Dokoda Masanori	China, Thailand, Malaysia, Singapore, Burma
5) Yuasa Ken	China
6) Ebado	China
7) Mita Kazo	China
8) Goyama	China
9) Miki	China
10) Iwasaki*	China
11) Ogawara Goichi	China
12) Wada	China
13) Suzuki Yoshio	China
14) Itô*	China
15) Satô*	China
16) Hara*	China
17) Matsumoto*	China
18) Hayakawa*	China

For some of the veterans who did not provide given names, only family names are provided in the list above. Names marked with an asterisk are pseudonyms.

(1) Yoshioka Tadao was a former Japanese military officer drafted from the University of Tokyo. He served in the southern part of China during WWII and used to be a newspaper reporter in Japan. He later became a lecturer at a university in Korea. He died in 1997. I conducted three interviews with him.

(2) Nakano Takashi was a former Japanese military officer drafted from the University of Tokyo who served in China during WWII. He became a professor in Anthropology after he returned to Japan after the war. He wrote his autobiography.

(3) Miyamoto Shizuo was one of the highest-ranking officers in Indonesia during the war. He dealt with military affairs in Indonesia after Japan lost the war.

(4) Dokoda Masanori was a former Japanese military officer in China and the Pacific Islands during WWII. He was held in Russia as a war criminal after the war, and then returned to Japan.

(5)–(18) Yuasa Ken, Ebado, Mita Kazo, Goyama, Miki, Iwasaki, Ogawara Goichi, Wada, Suzuki Yoshio, Itô, Satô, Hara, Matsumoto, and Hayakawa are/were all members of the *Chûgoku kikansha renrakukai* (The Association of Returnees from China), a group of veterans held in China as prisoners of war after the WWII. All of them went through a 'rehabilitation' programme organised by the Chinese Communist Party while being held in China, and had returned to Japan in the 1960s. Since then they have spoken out in public about their war crimes.

List of 'Comfort Women' Whose Narratives are Already Released and Have Appeared in the Current Volume

(1) An Pŏpsun was born in 1925 and taken to Singapore during the war.

(2) Chang Ch'unwŏl was born in 1919 and was a 'comfort woman' in Wuchang and Guangshui, China between 1936 and 1945. She has remained and lived in China since the end of WWII. The desire of the 'comfort women' victims/survivors who remained in China to return to Korea is as strong as the desire to get the issue of 'comfort women' resolved.

(3) Chin Kyŏngp'aeng was born in 1923, and was taken to a comfort station in Taiwan in 1939.

(4) Ch'oe Chŏngnye was born in 1928, and was a 'comfort woman' in Hunchun, China from 1942 until 1945.

(5) Ch'oe Illye was taken to a comfort station in Manchuria, China in 1932, at an early stage when the comfort station programme was not yet systematically installed.

(6) Chŏng Soŭn was born in 1924 was taken to a comfort station in Jakarta.

(7) Ha Kunja was taken to a comfort station in Hankou, China in 1944 and remained in China.

(8) Hong Aejin was born in 1928, and was held in comfort stations in Shanghai, Harubin, and Hankou in China (1942–1945). She has stayed in China since.

(9) Han Oksŏn (1919–2009) was lured with the prospect of a good job and went to China.

(10) Hwang Suni (1922–2007) was at comfort stations in Hong Kong and Singapore during the war.

(11) Im Kŭma was born in 1923 and taken to a comfort station for the Japanese Navy in Hankou, China in 1939. She remained in China.

(12) Kang Muja is a pseudonym. She was born in 1928, and was in comfort stations in Palau and Saipan between 1941 and 1945.

(13) Kil Wŏnok was born in Pyongyang, North Korea in 1928 and was deceived into becoming a 'comfort woman'. After the war she settled in South Korea and adopted a son at the age of 31. She has been actively engaged in the 'comfort women' campaign on a global platform.

(14) Kim Sanghŭi was born in 1922, and was a 'comfort woman' in Sozu, Nanking and Singapore.

(15) Kim Poktong (1926–2019) was in comfort stations in Guangdong, Hong Kong, Singapore, Indonesia and Malaysia from 1941 till 1945. She had been active in giving her testimonies globally.

(16) Kim Punsŏn was born in 1922, and was a 'comfort woman' in Taiwan and Manila between 1937 and 1945.

(17) Kim Sundŏk (1921–2004) was taken to a comfort station in Shanghai in 1937. She left several paintings in which she expressed her experiences as a 'comfort woman'.

(18) Kim Tŏkchin is a pseudonym. She was born in 1921 and was in a comfort station in Shanghai between 1937 and 1940. She returned to Korea in 1940 with the help of a Japanese officer.

(19) Kim Ŭnjin is a pseudonym. She was born in 1932, and was selected for the Women's Volunteer Labour Corps (*Yŏjajŏngsindae*) out of her classmates and sent to the Fujikoshi aeroplane plant in Toyama-ken, Japan in 1944. Later she was taken to comfort stations in Aomori-ken and Shizuoka-ken, Japan.

(20) Kim Yŏngja was taken to Manchuria, China at the age of 16 and returned in 1946.

(21) No Subok (1921–2011) was taken to a comfort station in Singapore in 1942. After the war, she gave up returning home and ended up in Thailand.

(22) Oh Omok (1921–1999) was a 'comfort woman' in Manchuria, China in 1937.

(23) Maria Rosa Henson (1927–1997) was a Filipino 'comfort woman'. She was born in 1927, and was involved in an anti-Japanese guerrilla organisation. In January 1944, she was held captive as a 'comfort woman' for nine months in a Japanese garrison.

(24) Pae Chokkan (1922–2004) was in a comfort station in Hangzhou, China from 1938 to 1945.

(25) Pae Ponggi (1914–1991) was a 'comfort woman' in Okinawa in Japan, and continued to live there. She was found dead on 18 October 1991 in her home.

(26) Pak Turi (1924–2006) was taken to Taiwan in 1940.

(27) Pak Yŏni is a pseudonym. She was born in 1921 and taken to a comfort station in Guandong, China in 1938.

(28) Sin Kyŏngnan (1921–2005) thought she was going to work as a nurse but ended up at a comfort station in China.

(29) Son P'anim was born in 1924, and was in comfort stations in Rabaul, New Guinea and Borneo between 1941 and 1945.

(30) Song Sindo (1922–2017) was taken to Wuchang, China in 1938 and lived in Japan after the war.

(31) Yi Okpun was born in 1926, and was in a comfort station in Taiwan from 1937 until 1945.

(32) Yi Ponghwa believes she was born in 1920, but her identification card issued by the Chinese government shows her year of birth in 1922. She was in comfort stations in Fengtian and Hankou, China between 1933 and 1945. She remained in China after the war, and lives there.

(33) Yi Sunok was born in 1921 and was in comfort stations in Guangdong, China and Singapore between 1938 and 1945.

(34) Yi Tŭngnam was born 1918, and was in Hankou, China from 1939 to 1945.

(35) Yi Yŏngsuk was born in 1922, and was in a comfort station in Guangdong (1939–1945).

(36) Yun Sunman was initially taken to a textile factory in Japan and then taken to a comfort station in Osaka, Japan.

Bibliography

Ahn, Yonson. 2008a. 'Japan's "Comfort Women" and Historical Memory: The Neonationalist Counterattack.' In *The Power of Memory in Modern Japan*, edited by Sven Saaler and Wolfgang Schwentker, 32–53. London: Global Oriental.

Ahn, Yonson. 2008b. 'Wianbu munje kiŏk hagi: manggakesŏ kiŏkŭibumŭro.' *Suheng inmunhak* 38, No. 1 (May): 61–85.

Ahn, Yonson. 2010. 'Taming Soldiers: The Gender Politics of Japanese Soldiers in Total War.' In *Gender Politics and Mass Dictatorship*, edited by Jie-Hyun Lim and Karen Petrone, 213–234. London: Palgrave Macmillan.

Ahn, Yonson. 2015. 'Together and Apart: Transnational Women's Activism and Solidarity in the Comfort Women Redress Campaign in South Korea and Japan.' *Comparative Korean Studies* 23 (1): 93–116.

Ahn, Yonson. 2018. 'Yearning for Affection: Traumatic Bonding between Korean "Comfort Women" and Japanese Soldiers During World War II.' *European Journal of Women's Studies*. Online First: https://doi.org/10.1177/13505 06818796039.

Ajia Taihen chiikino sensô giseisha ni omoi wo hase kokoroni kizamu shukai gikkouiinkai. 1997. *Watashiwa ianfu dewanai; Nihon no shiryaku to seidorei*. Osaka: Toho shuppan.

Alison, Miranda. 2007. 'Wartime Sexual Violence: Women's Human Rights and Questions of Masculinity.' *Review of International Studies* 33, No. 1 (January): 75–90. http://www.jstor.org/stable/20097951.

Allied Translator and Interpreter Section, Supreme Commander for the Allied Powers. 1945. 'Amenities in the Japanese Armed Forces.' Research Report No. 120. 15 November 1945.

Anderson, Kathryn, and Jack Dana. 1991. 'Learning to Listen: Interview Techniques and Analysis.' In *Women's Words: The Feminist Practice of Oral History*, edited by Gluck, S.B. and D. Patai. New York, London: Routledge.

Ankomah, Augustine. 1992. 'Premarital Sexual Relationships in Ghana in the Era of AIDS.' *Health Policy and Planning* 7 (2): 135–143.

Asian Women's Resource Centre for Culture and Theology, ed. 1996. *In God's Image* 15 (2) (Summer).

Asô, Tetsuo. 1939. 'Karyûbyô no sekkyoku-teki yobohô.' In *Gun ikan no senjo hokoku ikensho*, edited by Ryuji Takasaki. Tokyo: Fuji shippan, reprinted in 1990.

Asô, Tetsuo. 1993. *Shanhai yori Shanhai e*. Fukuoka: Sekifûsha.

Bang, Son-ju. 1997. 'Ilbon'gun wianbuŭi kwihwan: Chungganbogo.' In *Ilbon'gun 'wianbu' munjeŭi chinsang*, edited by Han'guk chŏngsindae munje taech'aek hyŏbŭihoe. Seoul: Yŏksabip'yŏngsa.

Beasley, W. G. 1963. *The Modern History of Japan*. London: Weidenfeld and Nicolson.

Beasley, W. G. 1987. *Japanese Imperialism 1894–1945*. Oxford: Clarendon Press.

Benedict, Ruth. 1946. *The Chrysanthemum and the Sword*. New York: Houghton Mifflin.

Bhabha, Homi K. 1998. *The Location of Culture*. London: Routledge.

Blaunt, James M. 1987. *The National Question: Decolonising the Theory of Nationalism*. London: Zed Press.

Brownmiller, Susan. 1975. *Against Our Will: Men, Women and Rape*. New York: Simon and Achuster.

Caldwell, J.C., P. Caldwell, and P. Quiggin. 1989. 'The Social Context of AIDS in Sub-Saharan Africa.' *Population and Development Review* 15 (2): 185–234.

Caplan, Pat. 1993. 'Introduction 2: The Volume.' In *Gendered Fields: Women, Men & Ethnography*, edited by Diane Bell, Pat Caplan, and Wazir Jahan Karim, 19–27. London and New York: Routledge.

Carroll, Berenice, and Barbara Welling Hall. 1993. 'Feminist Perspectives on Women and the Use of Force.' In *Women and the Use of Military Force*, edited by Ruth H. Howes and Michael R. Stevenson, 11–22. Boulder and London: Lynne Rienner.

Ch'oe, Chaesŏk. 1983. *Han'guk kajok chedosa yŏn'gu*. Seoul: Iljisa.

Chai, Alice Yun. 1993. 'Asian-Pacific Feminist Coalition Politics: The Chongsindae/Jûgunianfu ("Comfort Women") Movement.' *Korean Studies*, No. 17: 67–91.

Chapman, Rowena, and Jonathan Rutherford. 1988. *Male Order: Unwrapping Masculinity*. London: Lawrence and Wishart.

Chesler, Phyllis. 1972. *Women and Madness*. New York: Doubleday.

Choi, Chungmoo. 1992. 'Korean Women in a Culture of Inequality.' In *Korea Briefing, 1992*, edited by Donald N. Clark, 97–116. Boulder: Westview Press.

Chŏng, Yŏnghwan. 2016. *Nugurŭl Wihan 'Hwahae'In'ga?: Cheguk Wianbuŭi Panyŏksasŏng*. Seoul: P'urŭn yŏksa.

Chonggun wianbu mit t'aep'yangyang chŏnjaeng p'ihaeja posang taech'aek wiwŏnhoe. 1995. *Chitpalp'in insaengŭi wech'im: Chonggun wianbu.* P'yŏngyang: Oegungmun chonghap ch'ulp'ansa.

Chung, Chin Sung. 1993. 'Hesol: Kunwianbuŭi silsang.' In *Kangjero kkŭllyŏgan chosŏnin kunwianbudŭl*, Vol. 1, edited by Han'guk chŏngsindae yŏn'guhoe. Seoul: Hanul.

Chung, Chin Sung. 1994. 'Ilbon kunwianbu jongchaekŭi bonjil.' *Hanmal iljehaŭi sahoesasanggwa sahoeundong*, No. 42: 172–201.

Chung, Chin Sung. 1997. 'The Origin and Development of the Military Sexual Slavery Problem in Imperial Japan.' *Positions* 5 (1): 219–255.

Cleary, Thomas. 1992. *The Japanese Art of War: Understanding the Culture of Strategy.* Boston & London: Shambhala.

Cockburn, Cynthia. 2004. *The Line: Women, Partition and the Gender Order in Cyprus.* London: Zed Press.

Connell, Raewyn W. 1987. *Gender and Power: Society, the Person and Sexual Politics.* Stanford, California: Stanford University Press.

Connell, Raewyn W. 1992. 'Masculinity, Violence and War.' In *Men's Lives*, edited by Michael S. Kimmell and Michael A. Messner, New York: Macmillan (2nd ed.).

Connell, Raewyn W. 2005. *Masculinities.* Berkeley: University of California Press.

Cook, Haruko Taya, and Theodore F. Cook. 1992. *Japan at War: An Oral History.* New York: The New Press.

Costello, John. 1985. *Love, Sex and War: Changing Values 1939-45.* London: Collins.

Coulter, C. 2009. *Bush Wives and Girl Soldiers: Women's Lives Through War and Peace in Sierra Leone.* Ithaca, NY, and London: Cornell University Press.

Dawson, G. 1994. *Soldier Heroes: British Adventure, Empire and the Imaging of Masculinities.* London: Routledge.

De Bary, William T., Donald Keene, and Ryûsako Tsunoda, eds. 1958. *Sources of Japanese Tradition*, Vol. 2. New York: Columbia University Press.

Demetriou, Demetrakis Z. 2001. 'Connell's Concept of Hegemonic Masculinity: A Critique.' *Theory and Society* 30, No. 3 (June): 337–361.

Dolgopol, Ustinia, and Snehal Paranjape. 1994. *Comfort Women: An Unfinished Ordeal.* Geneva: International Commission of Jurists.

Donaldson, Laura E. 1992. *Decolonizing Feminisms: Race, Gender and Empire-Building.* London: Routledge.

Douglas, Mary. 1966. *Purity and Danger: An Analysis of the Concepts of Pollution and Taboo.* London: Routledge.

Dower, John. 1986. *War Without Mercy: Race and Power in the Pacific War.* New York: Pantheon Press.

Dudden, Alexis. 2001. 'We Came to Tell the Truth: Reflections on the Tokyo Women's Tribunal.' *Critical Asian Studies* 33 (4): 591–602.

Duus, Peter. 1976. *The Rise of Modern Japan.* Boston: Houghton Mifflin Company.

Elshtain, Jean Bethke. 1987. *Women and War.* New York: Basic Books.

Enloe, Cynthia. 1987. 'Feminists Thinking About War, Militarism, and Peace.' In *Analyzing Gender: A Handbook of Social Science Research*, edited by Beth Hess, 527–547. London: Sage.

Enloe, Cynthia. 1988. *Does Khaki Become You? The Militarization of Women's Lives.* London: Pandora.

Ewha yŏjadaehakkyo han'guk yŏsŏngsa p'yŏnch'an wiwŏnhoe. 1972. *Han'guk yŏsŏngsa* II. Seoul: Ewha Women's University Press.

Folnegovic-Smalc, Vera. 1994. 'Psychiatric Aspects of the Rapes in the War against the Republics of Croat and Bosnia-Herzegovina.' In *Mass Rape: The War Against Women in Bosnia-Herzegovina*, edited by Alexandra Stiglmayer, 174–179. Lincoln: University of Nebraska Press.

Foucault, Michael. 2007. *Security, Territory, Population: Lectures at the Collège de France 1977–78.* Translated by Graham Burchell. New York: Palgrave Macmillan.

Foucault, Michel. 1991. 'Ethics of Care for the Self as a Practice of Freedom: An Interview with Michel Foucault on January 20, 1984.' In *The Final Foucault*, edited by James Bernauer and David Rasmussen, Massachusetts: MIT Press.

Freud, Sigmund. 1920. *Beyond the Pleasure Principle.* Harmondsworth: Penguin.

Fujime, Yuki. 1997. 'The Licensed Prostitution System and the Prostitution Abolition Movement in Modern Japan.' *Positions* 5, No. 1 (Spring): 135–170.

Fujioka, Nobukatsu. 1996. *Ojokuno kingendaishi.* Tokyo: Tokuma shoten.

Fujiwara, Akira. 1961. *Gunjinshi: Nihon gundaishi taikei.* Tokyo: Toyokeizai.

Fujiwara, Akira. 1977. *Tennôsei to guntai.* Tokyo: Aokishoten.

Gagnon, John H., and William Simon. 1973. *Sexual Conduct: The Social Sources of Human Sexuality.* Chicago: Aldine Publishing Company.

Gluck, Carol. 1985. *Japan's Modern Myths: Ideology in the Late Meiji Period.* Princeton: Princeton University Press.

Grenz, Sabine. 2005. 'Intersections of Sex and Power in Research on Prostitution: A Female Researcher Interviewing Male Heterosexual Clients.' *Signs* 30 (4): 2091–113.

Han, Myŏngsuk. 1986. 'Chosŏnsidae yugyojŏk yŏsŏnggwanŭi wŏllijŏk koch'al.' MA dissertation, Ewha Women's University Seoul (unpublished).

Han, Yŏngwu. 1983. *Chosŏn sigi sahoesasang yon'gu.* Seoul: Jisiksanopsa.

Han'guk chŏngsindae munje taech'aek hyŏbŭihoe 2000 nyŏn ilbon'gun sŏngnoye jŏnbŏm yŏsŏng gukche bŏpchŏng han'guk wiwŏnhoe chŭngŏnt'im, ed. 2001a. *Kangjero kkŭllyŏgan chosŏnin kunwianbudŭl: Kiŏgŭro tasi ssŭnŭn yŏksa*. Vol. 4. Seoul: P'ulbit.

Han'guk chŏngsindae munje taech'aek hyŏbŭihoe, and Han'guk chŏngsindae yŏn'guhoe, eds. 1993. *Kangjero kkŭllyŏgan chosŏnin kunwianbudŭl*. Vol. 1. Seoul: Hanul.

Han'guk chŏngsindae munje taech'aek hyŏbŭihoe, and Han'guk chŏngsindae yŏn'guhoe, eds. 1997. *Chunggugŭro kkŭllyŏgan chosŏnin kunwianbudŭl*. Vol. 2. Seoul: Hanul.

Han'guk chŏngsindae munje taech'aek hyŏpuihoe, and Han'guk chŏngsindae yŏn'guhoe, eds. 1995. *Chunggukŭro kkŭllyŏgan chŏsonin kunwianbudŭl*. Vol. 1. Seoul: Hanul.

Han'guk chŏngsindae munje taech'aek hyŏpuihoe, and Han'guk chŏngsindae yŏn'guhoe, eds. 1999. *Kangjero kkŭllyŏgan chŏsonin kunwianbudŭl*. Vol. 3. Seoul: Hanul.

Han'guk chŏngsindae munje taech'aek hyŏbŭihoe, and Han'guk chŏngsindae yŏn'guhoe eds. 2001b. *Kangjero kkŭllyŏgan chosŏnin kunwianbudŭl*. Vol. 5. Seoul: P'ulbit.

Hane, Mikiso. 1982. *Peasants, Rebels and Outcasts: The Underside of Modern Japan*. New York: Pantheon Books.

Hata, Ikuhiko. 1993. *Showashi no nazo o ou*. Vol. 2. Tokyo: Bungei shunjû.

Hata, Ikuhiko. 1996a. 'Waegoktoen naŭi nonji.' *Ilbon Forum* 29 (Summer).

Hata, Ikuhiko. 1996b. 'Ianfu mino uebanashi wo tetei kenshou suru.' *Shokun* (December): 54–69.

Hata, Ikuhiko. 1997. 'Jûgun ianfu mondai de kuni no hoteki sekinin wa toenai.' *Sekai* (May): 322–325.

Hayakawa, Noriko. 1996. 'Feminism and Nationalism in Japan, 1868–1945.' *Ferris Studies* 31 (March): 99–117.

Henson, Maria Rosa. 1996. *Comfort Woman: Slave of Destiny*. Manila: Philippine Center for Investigative Journalism.

Herman, Judith Lewis. 1997. *Trauma and Recovery*. New York: Basic Books.

Hicks, George. 1995. *The Comfort Women: Sex Slaves of the Japanese Imperial Forces*. London: Souvenir Press.

Hochschild, Arlie. 1983. *The Managed Heart: Commercialization of Human Feeling*. Oakland: University of California Press.

Hollway, Wendy. 1984. 'Gender Difference and the Production of Subjectivity.' In *Changing the Subject: Psychology, Social Regulation, and Subjectivity*, edited by Julian Henriques *et al.*, 227–263. London: Methuen.

Hosaka, Masayasu. 1996. 'Jûgun ianfu mondai o gojûnen atoni danzai suru na.' *Shokun* (November): 64–72.

Humphreys, Leonard A. 1995. *The Way of The Heavenly Sword: The Japanese Army in the 1920's*. Stanford: Stanford University Press.

Hunter, Mark. 2002. 'The Materiality of Everyday Sex: Thinking Beyond Prostitution.' *African Studies* 61 (1): 99–120.

Hunter, Mark. 2005. 'Cultural Politics and Masculinities: Multiple-partners in Historical Perspective in KwaZulu-Natal.' *Culture, Health and Sexuality* 7 (3): 209–233.

Iizuka, Kôji. 1950. *Nihon no guntai*. Tokyo: Todai kyodo-kumiai shuppanbu.

Jansen, Marius B. 1984. 'Japanese Imperialism: Late Meiji Perspectives.' In *The Japanese Colonial Empire 1895–1945*, edited by Ramon H. Myers and Mark R. Peattie, 61–79. Princeton, New Jersey: Princeton University Press.

Johnson-Hanks, Jennifer. 2006. *Uncertain Honor: Modern Motherhood in an African Crisis*. Chicago: University of Chicago Press.

Jûgun ianfu hyakutôban henshû iinkai, ed. 1992. *Jûgun ianfu hyakutôban*. Tokyo: Akashi shoten.

Kandiyoti, Deniz. 1993. 'Identity and its Discontents: Women and the Nation.' In *Colonial Discourse and Post-Colonial Theory*, edited by P. Williams and L. Chrisman, 376–391. London: Harvester.

Kang, Chŏngsuk. 1997. 'Ilbon'gun wiansoŭi chiyŏkchŏk punp'owa kŭ t'ŭkching.' In *Ilbon'gun 'wianbu' munjeŭi chinsang*, edited by Han'guk chŏngsindae munje taechek hyŏpuihoe. Seoul: Yŏksabip'yŏngsa.

Kang, Man'gil. 1997. 'Ilbon'gun wianbuŭi kaenyŏmgwa hoch'ingmunje.' In *Ilbon'gun 'wianbu' munjeŭi chinsang*, edited by Han'guk chŏngsindae munje taechek hyŏpuihoe. Seoul: Yŏksabip'yŏngsa.

Kaufman, Carol E., and S.E. Stavrou. 2004. ' "Bus Fare Please": The Economics of Sex and Gifts Among Young People in Urban South Africa.' *Culture, Health and Sexuality* 6 (5): 377–391.

Kawata, Fumiko. 1987. *Akagawara no ie: Chosen kara kita jûgun ianfu*. Tokyo: Chikuma shobô.

Kawata, Fumiko. 1992. *Ppalgan kiwajip chosŏnesŏ on chonggun wianbu iyagi*. Trans. Han Uchŏng. Seoul: Maeilgyŏngje shinmunsa.

Kawata, Fumiko. 1993. *Kôgun ianjo no onnatachi*. Tokyo: Chikuma shobô.

Kawata, Fumiko. 1995. *Sensô to sei: Kindai koushouseido ianfu seido wo megutte*. Tokyo: Akashi shoten.

Kelly, Liz. 1988. *Surviving Sexual Violence*. Minneapolis: University of Minnesota Press.

Kim-Gibson, Dai Sil. 1997. 'They Are Our Grandmas.' *Positions* 5 (1): 255–274.

Kim, Hyun Sook. 1997. 'History and Memory: The "Comfort Women" Controversy.' *Positions* 5 (1): 73–105.

Kim, Ilmyŏn. 1976. *Tennô no guntai to chôsenjin ianfu*. Tokyo: San'ichi shobô.

Kim, Puja. 2001. 'Global Civil Society Remakes History: The Women's International War Crimes Tribunal 2000.' *Positions: East Asia Cultures Critique* 9 (3): 611–620.

Kim, Unťe. 1986. *Ilbon chegukchuŭi han'guk t'ongch'ik*. Seoul: Pakyongsa.

Kim, Yung-Chung. 1976. *Women of Korea—History from Ancient Times to 1945*. Seoul: Ewha Women's University Press.

Kimura, Maki. 2016. *Unfolding the 'Comfort Women' Debates: Modernity, Violence and Women's Voices*. Basingstoke: Palgrave Macmillan.

Kobayashi, Yoshinori. 1998. *Sensôron*. Tokyo: Gentosha.

Korean Council for the Women Drafted for Military Sexual Slavery by Japan. 1995. 'Why the Issue of Military Sexual Slavery by Japan Has Remained Unresolved for 50 Years?; The Report of the 3rd Asian Women's Solidarity Forum on Military Sexual Slavery by Japan.' (unpublished).

Kurahashi, Masanao. 1994. *Jûgun Ianfu Mondai no Rekishiteki Kenkyû: Baishunfugata to Seitekidoreigata*. Tokyo: Kyôei shobô.

Kusaka, Kimihito. 1996. 'Chonggun wianbu munjeŭi pulgasaŭi.' *Ilbon Forum* 29 (Summer).

Lim, Jie-Hyun. 2010. 'Series Introduction: Mapping Mass Dictatorship: Towards a Transnational History of Twentieth-Century Dictatorship.' In *Gender Politics and Mass Dictatorship*, edited by Jie-Hyun Lim and Karen Petrone, 1–22. London: Palgrave MacMillan.

Lovett, Margot, 1989. 'Gender Relations, Class Formation, and the Colonial State in Africa.' In *Women and the State in Africa*, edited by Jane L. Parpart and Kathleen A. Staudt, 23–46. Boulder & London: Lynne Rienner Publishers.

MacKinnon, Catharine A. 1987. *Feminism Unmodified*. Cambridge: Harvard University Press.

Marcus, Sharon. 1992. 'Fighting Bodies, Fighting Words: A Theory and Politics of Rape Prevention.' In *Feminists Theorize the Political*, edited by Judith Butler and Joan W. Scott, 385–403. New York, London: Routledge.

Mark, Ethan. 1999. 'Greater East Asia Revisited.' In *Representing the Japanese Occupation of Indonesia: Personal Testimonies and Public Images in Indonesia, Japan and the Netherlands*, edited by Remco Raben, 141–143. Zwolle: Waanders Publishers and Netherlands Institute for War Documentation.

Matsui, Yayori. 1987. *Women's Asia*. London: Zed Press.

Matsumura, Janice. 2004. 'State Propaganda and Mental Disorders: The Issue of Psychiatric Casualties among Japanese Soldiers during the Asia-Pacific War.' *Bulletin of the History of Medicine* 78 (4): 804–835.

Matsunaga, Shigeo, and Tatsuki Matsunaga. 1968. *Sensô, bungaku, ai: Gakutohei kyôdai no ikô*, edited by Izumi Aki. Tokyo: Sanseidô.

McClintock, Anne. 1995. *Imperial Leather; Race, Gender and Sexuality and the Colonial Conquest*. London: Routledge.

McGregor, Katharine. 2016. 'Transnational and Japanese Activism on Behalf of Indonesian and Dutch Victims of Enforced Military Prostitution During World War II.' *The Asia-Pacific Journal: Japan Focus* 14 (16). http://hdl.handle.net/11343/118387.

McIntosh, Mary. 1978. 'The State and the Oppression of Women.' In *Feminism and Materialism: Women and Modes of Production*, edited by Annette Kuhn and AnnMarie Wolpe, 254–289. London: Routledge and Kegan Paul.

Millett, Kate. 1969. *Sexual Politics*. London: Virago.

Mills, Ros. 1995. 'The Confession as a "Practice of Freedom": Feminism, Foucault and "elsewhere" Truths.' *Law/Text/Culture*, no. 2: 100–117.

Mills, Sara. 1994. 'Knowledge, Gender and Empire.' In *Writing Women and Space: Colonial and Postcolonial Geographies*, edited by Alison Bunt and Gillian Rose, 29–50. New York, London: The Guilford Press.

Min, Hyŏnku. 1987. 'Kwŏnmunsejokkwa sinhŭngsadaebu.' In *Han'guksa yŏn'gu immun*, edited by Han'guksahoesa yŏn'guhoe. Seoul: Chisiksanŏpsa.

Ministry of Foreign Affairs of Japan. 1993. 'Statement by the Chief Cabinet Secretary Yohei Kôno on the Result of the Study on the Issue of "Comfort Women".' August 4 1993. https://www.mofa.go.jp/policy/women/fund/state9308.html.

Mitchell, Richard H. 1967. *The Korean Minority in Japan*. Berkeley and Los Angeles: University of California Press.

Miyake, Yoshiko. 1991. 'Doubling Expectations: Motherhood and Women's Factory Work Under State Management in Japan in the 1930s and 1940s.' In *Recreating Japanese Women, 1600–1945*, edited by Gail Lee Bernstein, 267–295. Berkeley, Los Angeles and Oxford: University of California Press.

Morgan, David Hopcraft John. 1992. *Discovering Men*. London: Routledge.

Moser, Caroline O.N., and Fiona Clark, eds. 2001. *Victims, Perpetrators or Actors? Gender, Armed Conflict and Political Violence*. London: Zed Books.

Mosse, George L. 1985. *Nationalism and Sexuality; Middle-Class Morality and Sexual Norms in Modern Europe*. Madison: The University of Wisconsin Press.

Mun, Okchu. 1996. *Mun Okchu: Biruma sensen tateshidan no 'ianfu' datta watashi*. As told to Morikawa Machiko. Tokyo: Nashinokisha.

Murata, Noriko. 1995. 'The Trafficking of Women.' *AMPO-Japan Asia Quarterly Review*, no. 26: 63–65.

Muta, Kazue. 2016. 'The "Comfort Women" Issue and the Embedded Culture of Sexual Violence in Contemporary Japan.' *Current Sociology* 64 (4): 620–636.

Nakamura, Akira. 1996. 'Kentei: Pasushita rekishi no ôso.' *Seiron* (November): 62–73.

Nanbara, Yukio. 1983. *Haruka naru futsuin*. Yokohara: Privately published.

Nishino, Rumiko. 1992. *Moto heishitachi no shôgen; Jûgun ianfu*. Tokyo: Akashi shoten.

Norma, Caroline. 2017. 'Abolitionism in the History of the Transnational "Justice for Comfort Women" Movement in Japan and South Korea.' In *Remembering the Second World War*, edited by Patrick Finney, 115–139. London: Routledge.

Oguma, Eiji. 2018. 'The Oral History of a Japanese Soldier in Manchuria.' *The Asia-Pacific Journal*, vol. 16, issue 8, no. 2 (1 October 2018). https://apjjf. org/2018/19/Oguma.html.

Ohnuki-Tierney, Emiko. 2006. *Kamikaze Diaries: Reflections of Japanese Student Soldiers*. Chicago: University of Chicago Press.

Okigbo, Chinelo. C., D.R. McCarraher, M. Chen, and A. Pack. 2014. 'Risk Factors for Transactional Sex Among Young Females in Post-conflict Liberia.' *African Journal of Reproductive Health/La Revue Africaine de la Santé Reproductive* 18 (3): 133–141.

Pak, Kyŏngsik. 1986. *Ilbon chegukchuŭiŭi chosŏnjibae*. Inchon: Hengji.

Pak, Yongok. 1985. 'Yukyojŏk yŏsŏngkwanŭi chejomyŏng.' *Hanguk yŏsonghak*, no. 1: 7–43.

Palmer, Brandon. 2013. *Fighting for the Enemy: Koreans in Japan's War, 1937–45*. Seattle, Washington and London: University of Washington Press.

Park, Yu-ha. 2013. *Chegugŭi wianbu: Shingminji chibaewa kiŏgŭi t'ujaeng*. Seoul: P'ulppuriwa ip'ari.

Park, Yu-ha. 2015. *Hwahaerŭl wihayŏ: Kyogwasŏ wianbu yasŭk'uni tokto*, 2nd Edition. Seoul: P'ulppuriwa ip'ari.

Park, Yu-ha. 2018. *Chegugŭi wianbu: Chishiginŭl marhanda*. P'ulppuriwa ip'ari.

Park, You-me. 1995. 'From "Comfort Women" to Women Warriors: Domesticity, Motherhood, and Women's Labour in the Discourse of Imperialism.' PhD dissertation, The George Washington University (unpublished).

Parker, Andrew, Mary Russo, Doris Sommer, and Patricia Yaeger. 1992. 'Introduction.' In *Nationalism and Sexualities*, edited by Andrew Parker *et al.*, 1–20. New York and London and New York: Routledge.

Pettman, Jan Jindy. 1996. 'Boundary Politics: Women, Nationalism, and Danger.' In *New Frontiers in Women's Studies; Knowledge, Identity and Nationalism*, edited by Mary Maynard and June Purvis, 187–202. London: Taylor & Francis.

Plummer, Ken. 1995. *Telling Sexual Stories: Power, Change, and Social Worlds*. London: Routledge.

Poulin, M.J. 2006. 'The Sexual and Social Relations of Youth in Rural Malawi: Strategies for AIDS Prevention.' PhD dissertation, Boston University (unpublished).

Price, Janet, and Margrit Schildrick. 1999. *Feminist Theory and the Body: A Reader*. Edinburgh: Edinburgh University Press.

Robinson, J., and E. Yeh. 2011. 'Transactional Sex as a Response to Risk in Western Kenya.' *American Economic Journal: Applied Economics* 3 (1): 35–64.

Ropers, Erik. 2014. 'Life on the Front Lines: Testimonies By Two Japanese "Comfort Women".' In *Writing the War in Asia—A Documentary History*, edited by Mark R. Frost, Daniel Schumacher. http://www.uniRkonstanz.de/warRinRasia/ropers.

Ruff-O'Herne, Jan. 1998. *Fifty Years of Silence: Comfort Women in Indonesia*. London: Thomas Beeler.

Ryang, Sonia. 1988. 'Love and Colonialism in Takamure Itsue's Feminism: A Postcolonial Critique.' *Feminist Review*, No. 60 (Autumn): 1–32.

Sakamoto, Takao. 1998. *Rekishi kyôiku o kangaeru*. Tokyo: PHP Kenkyûjo.

Scarry, Elaine. 1985. *The Body in Pain: The Making and Unmaking of the World*. New York, Oxford: Oxford University Press.

Schütze, Fritz. 1987. *Das narrative Interview in Interaktionsfeldstudien*. Hagen: Fernuniversität-Gesamthochschule, Fachbereich Erziehungs-, Sozial- und Geisteswissenschaften.

Scully, Diane. 1993. 'Understanding Sexual Violence.' In *Women's Studies: A Reader*, edited by Stevi Jackson, 234–235. New York, London: Harvester Wheatsheaf.

SEATIC (Southeast Asia Translation and Interrogation Center) *Air Bulletin*, No. 131, 28 April 1945.

Segal, Lynne. 1987. *Is the Future Female?* London: Virago.

Segal, Lynne. 1990. *Slow Motion: Changing Masculinities*. London: Virago.

Segal, Lynne. 2008. 'War and Militarism: Making and Questioning the Links.' *Feminist Review*, No. 88: 21–35.

Seidler, Victor J. 1989. *Rediscovering Masculinity: Reason, Language and Sexuality*. London: Routledge.

Seidler, Victor J. 1992. *Men, Sex and Relationships: Writing from Achilles Heel*. London: Routledge.

Seidler, Victor J. 1997. *Men Enough: Embodying Masculinities*. London: Sage.

Seifert, Ruth. 1994. 'War and Rape: A Preliminary Analysis.' In *Mass Rape: The War Against Women in Bosnia-Herzegovina*, edited by Alexandra Stiglmayer, 54–72. Lincoln: University of Nebraska Press.

Senda, Kakô. 1978. *Jûgun ianfu*. Tokyo: San'ichi shobô.

Senda, Kakô. 1992a. *Chŭngŏn: Yŏja chŏngshindae 8manmyŏng-ŭi kobal*. Seoul: Tamul.

Senda, Kakô. 1992b. *Jûgun ianfu to Tennô*. Kyoto: Kamogawa shuppan.

Senkyûhyakunanajûni Kyoto oshietakutasai ianfu jyoho denwa hokokushu henshû iinkai, ed. 1992. *Sei to shinryaku: Guntai ianjyo hachijuyon kasho motonihonheirano shogen*. Kyoto: Shakai hyoronsha.

Sin, Hyesu. 1997. 'Ilbon'gun wianbu munje haegyŏrŭl wihan kukchehwaldongŭi sŏnggwawa kwaje.' In *Ilbon'gun wianbu munjeŭi chinsang*, edited by Han'guk chŏngsindae munje taechek hyŏpuihoe, 359–389. Seoul: Yŏksabip'yŏngsa.

Sinha, Mrinalini. 1995. *Colonial Masculinity: The 'Manly Englishman' and the 'Effeminate Bengali' in the Late Nineteenth Century*. Manchester: Manchester University Press.

Suh, Kyungsik. 1989. *Kôminka seisaku kara shimon natsuin made: Zainichi chôsenjin no shôwashi*. Tokyo: Iwanami Booklet.

Soh, C. Sarah. 2008. *The Comfort Women: Sexual Violence and Postcolonial Memory in Korea and Japan*. Chicago and London: University of Chicago Press.

Son, Chongŏp *et al.*, 2016. *Cheguk-ui Pyŏnhoin Pak Yuha-ege Mutta*. Seoul: Tosŏch'ulp'an mal.

Song, Youn-ok. 1997. 'Japanese Colonial Rule and State-Managed Prostitution: Korea's Licensed Prostitutes.' *Positions* 5 (1): 171–217.

Sŏultae in'gwŏnsent'ŏ chŏngjinsŏng yŏn'gut'im. 2018. *Kkŭllyŏ kada, pŏryŏjida, uri ap'e sŏda*. Vol. 1. Seoul: P'urŭn yŏksa.

Stacey, Judith. 1991. 'Can There be a Feminist Ethnography?' In *Women's Words: The Feminist Practice of Oral History*, edited by Sherna Berger Gluck and Daphne Patai, 111–120. New York and London: Routledge.

Steedman, Carolyn. 1988. *The Radical Soldier's Tale: John Pearman, 1819–1908*. London and New York: Routledge.

Stoebenau, Kirsten, L. Heise, J. Wamoyi and N. Bobrova. 2016. 'Revisiting the Understanding of "Transactional Sex" in Sub-Saharan Africa: A Review and Synthesis of the Literature.' *Social Science and Medicine*, No. 168: 186–197.

Strobel, Margaret. 1991. *European Women and the Second British Empire*. Bloomington: Indiana University Press.

Suzuki, Yûko. 1992. *Jûgun ianfu naisen kekkon*. Tokyo: Miraisa.

Suzuki, Yûko. 1993. *Jûgun ianfu mondai to seibôryoku*. Tokyo: Miraisa.

Swidler, Ann, and S.C. Watkins. 2007. 'Ties of Dependence: AIDS and Transactional Sex in Rural Malawi.' *Studies in Family Planning* 38 (3): 147–162.

Tadashi, Dukutake. 1989. *The Japanese Social Structure: Its Evolution in the Modern Century*. Tokyo: University of Tokyo Press (2nd ed.).

Takahashi, S. 1988. *Senki mono wo yomu*. Tokyo: Akademia shuppankai.

Takaki, Kenichi. 1992. *Jûgun ianfu to sengo hoshô*. Tokyo: Sanichi shobô.

Takeda, Seiji, Kobayashi Yoshinori and Hashizume Daizaburô. 1997. *Seigi, sensô, kokkaron*. Tokyo: Keishobô.

Tamai, Noriko. 1984. *Hinomaru o koshi ni maite*. Tokyo: Gendaishi shuppankai.

Tanaka, Yuki. 2005. 'Japan's Kamikaze Pilots and Contemporary Suicide Bombers: War and Terror.' *The Asia Pacific Journal: Japan Focus* 3, no. 4 (6 July 2005). https://apjjf.org/-Yuki-Tanaka/1606/article.html.

The Korean Council for the Women Drafted for Military Sexual Slavery by Japan. 2016. 'Report submitted to Committee on the Elimination of Discrimination Against Women (CEDAW), 63rd Session.' 2016. https://tbinternet.ohchr.org/Treaties/CEDAW/Shared%20Documents/JPN/INT_CEDAW_NGO_ JPN_22816_E.docx.

Thompson, Janna. 1991. 'Women and War.' *Women's Studies International Forum* 14 (1/2): 63–75.

Tojo, Hideki. 1941. *Senjinkun* (Field Service Regulations). Tokyo: The Army Ministry, reprinted by Boei mondai kenkyukai, Tokyo, no. 4, 1972.

Tosh, John. 2004. 'Hegemonic Masculinity and the History of Gender.' In *Masculinities in Politics and War: Gendering Modern History*, edited by Stefan Dudink, Karen Hagemann and John Tosh, 41–58. Manchester: Manchester University Press.

Tsurumi, Kazuko. 1970. *Social Change and the Individual: Japan Before and After Defeat in World War II*. Princeton and New Jersey: Princeton University Press.

Tylee, Claire M. 1988. 'Maleness Run Riot—the Great War and Women's Resistance Militarism.' *Women's Studies International Forum* 11 (3): 199–210.

Ueyama, Shunpei. 1964. *Dai tôa sensô no imi*. Tokyo: Chûôkôronsha.

UN Commission on Human Rights. 1996a. 'Report of the Special Rapporteur on violence against women, its causes and consequences/submitted by Radhika Coomaraswamy, submitted in accordance with Commission on Human Rights resolution,' by Radhika Coomaraswamy, 5 Feburary 1996a/ E/CN.4/1996/53. Geneva: UN Commission on Human Rights. http://www.awf.or.jp/pdf/h0003.pdf.

UN Commission on Human Rights. 1996b. 'Report on the mission to the Democratic People's Republic of Korea, the Republic of Korea and Japan on the issue of military sexual slavery in wartime,' submitted by Radhika Coomaraswamy, 4 January 1996b, E/CN.4/1996/53/Add.1. Geneva: UN Commission on Human Rights. http://www.awf.or.jp/pdf/h0004.pdf.

UN Sub-Commission on the Promotion and Protection of Human Rights. 1998. 'Systematic rape, sexual slavery and slavery-like practices during armed conflict,' submitted by Gay J. McDougall, E/CN.4/Sub.2/1998/13.

United States Office of War Information, Psychological Warfare Team Attached to U.S. Army Forces India–Burma Theater. 1944. 'Japanese Prisoner of War Interrogation Report' No. 49.

Uno, Kathleen S. 1993. 'The Death of "Good Wife, Wise Mother"?' In *Postwar Japan as History*, edited by Andrew Gordon, 293–324. Berkeley and Oxford: University of California Press.

Ussher, Jane M. 1991. *Women's Madness: Misogyny or Mental Illness?*. New York: Harvester Wheatsheaf.

Vance, Carole S. 1984. *Pleasure and Danger: Exploring Female Sexuality*. London: Routledge and Kegan Paul.

Weeks, Judith R. 1985. *Sexuality and Its Discontents: Meaning, Myths and Modern Sexualities*. London: Routledge.

Weiner, Michael. 1994. *Race and Migration in Imperial Japan*. London: Routledge.

Weiner, Michael. 1995. 'Discourses of Race, Nation and Empire in Pre-1945 Japan.' *Ethnic and Racial Studies* 18 (3): 433–456.

Wyrod, Robert, K. Fritz, G. Woelk, S. Jain, T. Kellogg, A. Chirowodza, and W. McFarland. 2001. 'Beyond Sugar Daddies: Intergenerational Sex and AIDS in Urban Zimbabwe.' *AIDS and Behavior* 15 (6): 1275–1282.

Yamashita, Youngae. 2012. N*aesyŏnŏllijŭmŭi t'ŭmsaeesŏ*. Seoul: Hanul.

Yang, Hyunah. 1997. 'Revisiting the Issue of Korean Military Comfort Women: The Question of Truth and Positionality.' *Positions* 5 (1): 51–71.

Yang, Hyunah. 1998. 'Re-membering the Korean Military Comfort Women: Nationalism, Sexuality, and Silencing.' In *Dangerous Women: Gender and Korean Nationalism*, edited by Elaine H. Kim and Chungmoo Choi, 123–140. New York and London: Routledge.

Yang, Jingja. 1995. 'Zainichi kankokujin Song Sindo san no nanajûnen.' In *Motto Shiritai 'Ianfu' Mondai; Sei to Minzoku no Shiten kara*, edited by Kim Puja and Yang Jingja. Tokyo: Akashi shoten.

Yi, Hochŏl. 1987. 'Iljeŭi singminji chŏngch'aek.' In *Han'guksa yŏn'gu immun*, edited by Han'guksahoesayŏn'guhoe. Seoul: Chisiksanŏpsa.

Yi, Manyŏl. 1997. 'Ilbon'gun wianbu chŏngch'aek hyŏngsŏngŭi chosŏnch'ŭk yŏksajŏk paegyŏng.' In *Ilbon'gun wianbu munjeŭi chinsang*, edited by Han'guk chŏngsindae munje taechek hyŏpuihoe. Seoul: Yŏksabip'yŏngsa.

Yi, Okkyŏng. 1985. 'Chosŏnsidae chŏngjŏl ideollogi hyŏngsŏng kiban'gwa chŏngch'ak pangsige kwanhan yŏn'gu.' MA dissertation, Ewha Women's University, Seoul (unpublished).

Yi, Sangwha. 1997. 'Ilbonin wianbuŭi kwiguk hu salmŭi kyŏnghŏm.' In *Ilbon'gun wianbu munjeŭi chinsang*, edited by Han'guk chŏngsindae munje taechek hyŏpuihoe. Seoul: Yŏksabip'yŏngsa.

Yi, Yŏnsuk. 1996. *Kokugo toiu shisô: Kindai nihono gengo ninshiki*. Tokyo: Iwanami.

Yoshimi, Yoshiaki and Hayashi Hirofumi, eds. 1995. *Kyodŏ kenkyû Nihongûnianfu*. Tokyo: Otsuki shoten.

Yoshimi, Yoshiaki. 1992. *Jûgun ianfu shiryôshû*. Tokyo: Ôtsuki shoten.

Yoshimi, Yoshiaki. 1995a. *Jûgunianfu*. Tokyo: Iwanami shoten.

Yoshimi, Yoshiaki. 1995b. *Comfort Women: Sexual Slavery in the Japanese Military During World War II*. Translated by Suzanne O'Brien. New York: Columbia University Press.

Yun, Chŏngok 1991. 'Chŏngsindae muŏsi munjein'ga.' In *Chŏngsindae munje charyojip*, Vol. 1, edited by Han'guk chŏngsindae munje taechek hyŏpuihoe. Seoul: Han'guk chŏngsindae munje taechek hyŏpuihoe.

Yun, Chŏngok. 1997. 'Chosŏn singminjŏngch'aek'ŭi irhwanŭrosŏ ilbon'gun wianbu.' In *Ilbon'gun wianbu munjeŭi chinsang*, edited by Han'guk chŏngsindae munje taechek hyŏpuihoe, 277–310. Seoul: Yŏksabip'yŏngsa.

Yun, Mihyang. 2016. *25nyŏn'ganŭi Suyoil*. Seoul: Saihaengsŏng.

Yuval-Davis, Nira, and Floya Anthias, eds. 1989. *Woman-Nation-State*. Basingstoke: Macmillan.

Zainihon chôsen minshu josei dômei. 1992. *Chôsenjin ianfu: Chôsen minshushugi jinmin kyôwa koku karano shiûgen*. Tokyo: Zainihon chôsen minshu josei dômei chûô jônin iinkai.

Zarkov, Dubravka. 1997. 'War Rapes in Bosnia: On Masculinity, Femininity and Power of the Rape Victim Identity.' *Tijdschrift voor Criminologie* 39 (2): 140–151.

Zarkov, Dubravka. 2007. *The Body of War: Media, Ethnicity, and Gender in the Break-up of Yugoslavia*. Durham, NC and London: Duke University Press.

Lightning Source UK Ltd.
Milton Keynes UK
UKHW040820171019

351739UK00002B/55/P